"The physioneuro[sis] [induced by?] terror can apparentl[y be reversed?] through the use of words. (Herman ..., ...)

"Because fragmentation creates a profoundly disturbing sense of self, victims go to great lengths to resist it. Consequently, the attempt to create or maintain a sense of agency and order and reject fragmentation is a common strategy of the [_Trauma and Survival in Contemporary Fiction_] narrator/protagonists of trauma fiction." p. 24

- Clarissa Dalloway – why she marries Richard Dalloway instead of
- Rachel Vinrace whom she really loved.
- Lily Briscoe – why she becomes an artist – the artist has the power and agency to create order and reject fragmentation

"How do [trauma survivor] authors engage readers narratively and stylistically? They employ means that aid readers to more readily identify with individual characters' struggles with being and telling. Readers are engaged to help reconstruct experience and retelling as trauma writers expose them to a variety of voices, subject positionings, and symbolizing that highlight the chaotic and disorienting aspects as well as representational possibilities or approximations." p. 27

TRAUMA AND SURVIVAL IN CONTEMPORARY FICTION

Shifts in time, memory and consciousness

LAURIE VICKROY

UNIVERSITY OF VIRGINIA PRESS

Charlottesville and London

The University of Virginia Press
©2002 by the Rector and Visitors of the University of Virginia
All rights reserved
Printed in the United States of America on acid-free paper
First published 2002

9 8 7 6 5 4 3 2 1

Library of Congress Cataloging-in-Publication Data
Vickroy, Laurie, 1954–
  Trauma and survival in contemporary fiction / Laurie Vickroy.
    p. cm.
Includes bibliographical references and index.
  ISBN 0-8139-2127-9 (alk. paper) — ISBN 0-8139-2128-7 (pbk. : alk. paper)
  1. American fiction—Women authors—History and criticism. 2. Women and
literature—West Indies—History—20th century. 3. Women and literature—
United States—History—20th century. 4. Psychological fiction—Women
authors—History and criticism. 5. Duras, Marguerite—Knowledge—Psychology.
6. African American women in literature. 7. West Indian Americans in literature.
8. Psychic trauma in literature. 9. Abused women in literature. I. Title.
  PS374.P7 V53 2002
  813′ .509353—dc21

2002005398

FOR TONY

CONTENTS

PREFACE

This book explores how contemporary fiction narratives represent trauma, defined as a response to events so overwhelmingly intense that they impair normal emotional or cognitive responses and bring lasting psychological disruption. Why consider a topic that is not only discomforting but might futilely immerse us in a quagmire of victimization? This becomes a compelling and potentially far-reaching topic, however, if we consider how trauma literature poses a number of thought-provoking questions and dilemmas for writers and readers, ranging from the potentially ethical function of literature, to reconsidering our cultural assumptions about identity, relationality, and intentionality, to what contingencies determine how or if individuals survive the devastations causing trauma. This study identifies these questions and assumptions by investigating the complex interrelationship between the sociocultural demands and intimate personal relations portrayed in this type of fiction and how these portrayals direct difficult material to readers.

My previous studies on transferential relationships between mothers and daughters in the writings of Marguerite Duras and Toni Morrison led me to the larger and more complex question of trauma in their work. Because my study began with these two writers, the concerns I absorbed from them suggested to me the great import of considering trauma, how it can be represented, and its relationship to social and cultural life. The works of these two authors have been concerned with how trauma helps to reveal the constitution of identity, the dynamics of power, and how intimate bonds are affected by the social environment and its guiding ideologies. My emphasis on Morrison and Duras throughout this study reflects their eminence as writers, their large bodies of work, and the groundbreaking variety of traumatic elements and narrative techniques in their texts as they take on forces of social oppression and demystify the complex role of mothering in adversity. I discovered that many other contemporary writers shared Duras's and Morrison's concerns and also felt the need to write about the revenant quality of past traumas—whether those of war veterans or incest survivors, or the racial trauma of slavery. These issues remain personally and culturally alive years, even decades later. All of these writers are committed to bringing social, historical, and psychological awareness to readers.

In order to help me understand the many complexities of traumatic situations in these works, I have adopted an interpretive method that combines literary, cultural, and psychological approaches. Accessing postcolonial, trauma, and object relations theories has illuminated the cultural aspects of traumatic experience that shape relationships, identity formation, and the possibilities for articulating such experience, helping me to better discern the issues suggested by this fiction. Trauma narratives, I contend, are personalized responses to this century's emerging awareness of the catastrophic effects of wars, poverty, colonization, and domestic abuse on the individual psyche. They highlight postcolonial concerns with rearticulating the lives and voices of marginal people, rejecting Western conceptions of the autonomous subject and describing the complex negotiations of multicultural social relations. The writers and theorists discussed in this study see trauma as an indicator of social injustice or oppression, as the ultimate cost of destructive sociocultural institutions.

My approach also attempts to make readers sensitive to the ways trauma can be manifested in narrative; contemporary writers' development of formal techniques has been crucial for conveying characters' traumatic experience. Duras and Morrison have most remarkably incorporated dissociative symptoms and fragmented identity and memory into their narrative voices. After listening to Larry Heinemann read from *Paco's Story*, I was immediately struck with the innovative uses of narrative he employed to convey the ways that the past haunts his protagonist. Further reading made me realize that such innovations have characterized fictionalizing trauma in this century. Precursors like Virginia Woolf and Jerzy Kosinski employed modernist techniques such as interior monologues and surrealism, and the fragmentation of narrative and identity common to the postmodern period gave more contemporary writers other means to express traumatic experience. These stylistic innovations have reflected our understanding of consciousness as well as our capacity to imagine the human psyche in all its facets, and have proved effective in approximating for readers the psychic defenses that pose obstacles to narrating and recovering from trauma. Also examined here is how writers respond to the difficult challenge of translating traumatic experience to readers while not losing connection with the fearful and painful aspects of this experience. Thus they try to invoke in readers what Dominick LaCapra terms "empathic unsettlement," or empathy without overidentification with victims, which can enable readers to work through problems or mourn rather than merely to sentimentalize victims (*Writing* 40–41).

My choice of writers besides Morrison and Duras was based on those who best exemplify the concerns outlined above and who have also developed fictional techniques to express those concerns; they include Edwidge Danticat, Jamaica Kincaid, Dorothy Allison, Larry Heinemann, and Pat Barker. Though Duras's career spans from the 1940s through the 1990s, her narrative innovations in *The Lover,* a text from the 1980s, mark a new shift in her work and link her with the contemporary period. Except for Morrison, Duras, and Allison, most of these writers have received little or no attention from the perspective of narrativizing trauma. I have narrowed this study to a particular time period to acknowledge a general cultural knowledge of trauma familiar to readers, and for practical considerations of reasonable length and focus, and to avoid overlap with other studies. Though I acknowledge the testimonial and therapeutic value of other literary texts covering trauma, I am more concerned with the problematic nature of reconstructions. I leave out worthy and important works (such as Maya Angelou's *I Know Why the Caged Bird Sings*) that do not yet emphasize formal innovations, testimonial influences, or the symptoms and defenses common to conflicted traumatic memory. Similarly, I have not focused on the huge area of Holocaust literature, with its own unique complexities, which has already been the focus of numerous studies. Nevertheless, scholarship and fiction about the Holocaust have been essential to theorizing about trauma and its effects. Lawrence Langer's *Holocaust Testimonies*, camp survivor Charlotte Delbo's *Auschwitz and After*, and Claude Lanzmann's documentary film *Shoah* have been invaluable for me in considering how to represent the effects of posttraumatic memory, identity, and relationships as well as the impact of survivors' oral testimonies on the trauma narratives, which help to convey the fragmentation of identity and thought. Likewise, recent assessments of the conditions and aftermath of slavery help to elucidate the contingencies and methods of survival and resistance engaged in by slaves and former slaves. Orlando Patterson's study *Slavery and Social Death* chronicles the personal and collective destructions wrought by slavery as well as the sociocultural and psychological use of authority (1–14).

John Beverley's and Doris Sommer's examinations of testimonio (testimonial narrative) also inform my discussion of the impact of testimony on trauma narratives. The characteristics Beverley attaches to testimonio are also characteristic of the narrative approaches of many trauma narratives: "a literary simulacrum of oral narrative" that seeks to create a truth effect, a feeling of lived experience, and expresses a "problematic collective social situation" through a representative individual (94–95). Sommer's notion of resistant testimonial texts has bearing on trauma narratives in its assertion that textual contexts and meaning can elude readers and make them realize there may be gaps in interpretation and understanding. This is especially true of trauma narratives, where readers are drawn into the perspectives of characters who are not in touch with the traumatic pasts that drive their behavior. The purpose of such an approach in trauma literature involves the additional consideration that the author wants readers to understand the difficulty of living with traumatic memories.

I have focused more on the cultural, sociopolitical, and psychological causes and contexts of trauma because I believe that trauma narratives primarily focus on these aspects. The psychoanalytical literature, including Freud's theories on the originary nature of trauma, traumatic responses, its belatedness, the defenses it initiates, and so on, were important bases for conceptualizing trauma. But because Freud's and subsequent psychoanalytic studies have not focused on the psychocultural aspects of trauma, I have turned to more psychological, humanistic, and cultural/sociohistorical theorists of trauma as more relevant to my interpretations since the literary texts themselves do not focus on primary/originary traumas as much as on socially induced and perpetuated ones. Much as Kalí Tal argues in *Worlds of Hurt: Reading the Literatures of Trauma*, I value literatures of trauma that challenge cultural myths about traumatic experience. I believe the trauma narratives I discuss do this by uncovering suppressed personal histories and consequences to traumatic events. Whereas Tal focuses solely on literary and other narratives related by actual survivors of trauma, not all of the writers in my study have experienced extreme trauma, or if they have, they significantly fictionalize it. Kirby Farrell's *Post-Traumatic Culture: Injury and Interpretation in the Nineties* raises important questions about the value of cultural representations of trauma and if they provide simplistic solutions or easy consolations. Truthful trauma narratives avoid this by often critiquing oppressive forces and questioning the effectiveness and costs of the survival tactics victims employ, which often diminish their lives significantly.

After establishing the history and theoretical approaches to trauma and the ways of narrating it in the first chapter, I have divided the remaining chapters according to topics based upon the primary concerns of the trauma literature, particularly the different social and personal aspects that help to create and allow survival of trauma. Preeminent among these concerns are the impact of trauma within family relations, especially between mothers and children, as this relation defines subjectivity and carrying on behaviors (chapter 2); the extent that trauma can devastate individuals and preclude their own and others' futures (chapter 3); the resourceful if contingent and restricting survival responses to trauma (chapter 4); and the historical-cultural origins of trauma, how representative characters exemplify social conflicts and wounds, and how the individual body becomes a historical marker to unspeakable experience but also a marker for potential change if healed (chapter 5). The question of legacy pertains throughout: What does one generation pass on to another? Do they pass on oppression, constrictive coping mechanisms, or methods of resistance? What is the consequence of a destructive past to both individuals and the culture at large if historical traumas are not sufficiently acknowledged or submitted to a working-through or critical reevaluation process? Or is there even a possibility of legacy if families are damaged or destroyed by unrelenting oppression or dispossession?

This study begins by examining the history and theorizing on trauma in the past 140 years in order to provide readers a context within which to understand my approach to the narratives and the issues at stake with regard to trauma. Trauma is defined as a psychological and sociocultural phenomena, and culture wields a significant influence on the contexts, severity, and reception of traumatic experience. The psychocultural investigations are important references for understanding how trauma narratives critique culturally dominant views of identity and marginality and resist suppression of traumatic events. These references also help locate where traumatic processes are approximated in narrative elements. Trauma narratives, I contend, go beyond presenting trauma as subject matter or in characterization; they also incorporate the rhythms, processes, and uncertainties of trauma within the consciousness and structures of these works. I then outline the aspects of traumatic response prominent in the narratives and the narrative strategies used to approximate these responses. This section forms the basis for my textual analysis in succeeding chapters.

In chapter 2, traumatizing contexts and their psychological impact are examined through writers' focus on mothers and daughters facing obstacles of poverty, sexual exploitation, class, and race prejudice. I investigate how these fictional depictions make explicit the subjective and relational complexities of postcolonial theorists' formulations of the psychological effects of colonization (e.g., Frantz Fanon, Ashis Nandy, Homi Bhabha, and Stuart Hall). Morrison's *Beloved* (1987) and *Sula* (1973), Duras's *The Sea Wall* (1950), and Danticat's *Breath, Eyes, Memory* (1994) illustrate how the mother/child bond provides a crucial affective locus for readers to understand the impact of social forces on consciousness and the interactions necessary for individual development, as argued by object relations and feminist theorists such as Jessica Benjamin, Nancy Chodorow, Patricia Hill Collins, and D. W. Winnicott.

Chapter 3 focuses on how trauma texts demonstrate key issues in the aftermath of traumatic experience; that is, the losses attending severe trauma and the costs of denying trauma, both to the individual and to the community. I consider how these texts struggle to give voice to those silenced by oppression and how they represent the traumatic effects of subjugation in the way their protagonists carry both personal and collective histories within them. Traumatized children become poignant metaphors and individualized examples of the neglect, exploitation, disempowerment, and disavowal of communities, or even entire cultures. Morrison's *The Bluest Eye* (1970) and *Jazz* (1992), and Duras's *The Vice-Consul* (1965) and *The Ravishing of Lol V. Stein* (1964) portray characters' struggles to survive despite being impaired by isolation and by static and repetitive actions and memories. Trauma narratives also recognize the significant role of defenses in determining responses to abuse or neglect that can aid self-creation in the absence of adequate nurturance.

Chapter 4 examines how Kincaid's *The Autobiography of My Mother* (1996), Duras's *The Lover* (1984), and Allison's *Bastard out of Carolina* (1992) present more elaborated and functional ways of surviving. The protagonist narrators generate a constructive narcissism that helps them replace the mother's nurturing gaze with their own, and they compensate for their isolation with emotional substitutions of sexual activity or fantasy at times. These protagonists are created as storytellers who use narratives in attempting to overcome abuse, but their impaired symbolization processes indicate how traumatic repetitions and emotional stasis distort their creative and relational capacities.

Chapter 5 analyzes works by three writers that embody significant traumatic historical events through individuals living the personal consequences of this history. Wider cultural traumas are contained in the psychological and physical experiences of a few characters. In Pat Barker's *Regeneration* (1991–95) trilogy, British cultural crises around class, homosexuality, and war are embodied in the experiences of a World War I soldier named Prior. In Toni Morrison's *Beloved*, the title character coalesces many traumatic aspects of slavery: ancestors' experience of the Middle Passage, traumatic memory, emotional and physical suffering, lost family connections, and so forth. Similarly, Larry Heinemann's *Paco's Story* (1986) expresses the collective traumatic legacies of the Vietnam War through the thoughts and experiences of his shattered protagonist. These narratives do not posit full reconstruction, but rather they elaborate the dynamic relationship between individual and collective memory and attempt to redefine and personalize readers' consciousness of traumatic historical events.

Can trauma fiction make overwhelming psychosocial dilemmas available to individual readers by personalizing them? They attempt this, I argue, by using narrative to try to make readers experience emotional intimacy and immediacy, individual voices and memories, and the sensory responses of the characters. Do they succeed? This investigation aims to position these works as examples of ethical fiction that try to absorb readers into personal and historical trauma. It also attempts to explain why this fiction is an important contribution to a necessary public understanding of complex psychosocial quandaries that continue to haunt us all in more or less disguised forms.

ACKNOWLEDGMENTS

I am grateful to the scholars and writers who helped pave the way for my own explorations of trauma, whose work I hope I have sufficiently paid homage throughout this study. I am also indebted to the readers of my manuscript, whose knowledgeable suggestions helped to make this study more complete and informed. Portions of chapter 3 appeared in *Mosaic, a journal for the interdisciplinary study of literature,* volume 29, number 2 (1996). Many thanks for the editorial guidance of Evelyn Hinz, which helped enormously in focusing that article publication as well as this book. Portions of chapter 5 appeared in *The Comparatist,* volume 32 (May 1998). The 1999 NEH Summer Seminar on Object Relations Theory with Mary Jacobus gave me the means to elaborate my interpretations of identity and language in chapter 4. I also want to thank my colleagues at Bradley University for their support and assistance with the many permutations of this project. I am especially thankful for the camaraderie and encouragement of my friend and editor extraordinaire, Christine Blouch. Many thanks to Kevin Stein for his suggestions on structure and presentation, his assistance in navigating the difficulties of academe and publishing, and for his creative and scholarly example. Thanks also to Tim Conley for helping with the title and keeping the intellectual flame alive. I dedicate this work to my husband, Tony Trawitzki, who inspires me in so many ways and who is always at the center of my heart and mind.

Trauma and Survival
in Contemporary Fiction

ONE

REPRESENTING TRAUMA

Issues, Contexts, Narrative Tools

True history or true fiction has always required an extraordinary act of the sympathetic imagination: an identification with experiences or stories not our own. GEOFFREY HARTMAN

The dilemma of remembering a painful past has been crucial in the last two hundred years: periods of unprecedented social, economic, and political changes; genocide; and disappearing cultures.[1] Testifying to the past has been an urgent task for many fiction writers as they attempt to preserve personal and collective memories from assimilation, repression, or misrepresentation. Their work reflects a growing awareness of the effects of catastrophe and oppression on the individual psyche, a perspective that has emerged with examinations of the psychological consequences of wars, the Holocaust, poverty, colonization, and domestic abuse.[2] Discoveries about the nature of traumatic experience as overwhelming, alien, amnesiac, and often incomprehensible have necessitated new historiographic, testimonial, and representational approaches to help interpret and reconfigure the enigmatic traces of evidence and memory.[3] Trauma narratives—fictional narratives that help readers to access traumatic experience—have taken an important place among diverse artistic, scholarly, and testimonial representations in illuminating the personal and public aspects of trauma and in elucidating our relationship to memory and forgetting within the complex interweavings of social and psychological relationships.[4] These texts also raise important questions and responsibilities associated with the writing and reading of trauma as they position their readers in ethical dilemmas analogous to those of trauma survivors.

Writing and reading about trauma presents painful dilemmas for writers and readers alike. Why would we want to read about an event in an individual's life so overwhelming that it is "defined by its intensity, by the subject's incapacity to respond adequately to it, and by the up-heaval and long-lasting effects that it brings about in the psychical or-ganization" (Laplanche and Pontalis 465)? What are the concerns here for readers who do not share such extreme experience? In the last twenty years, an array of fictional works on traumatic experience and its representation have appeared. The narrative approaches in many of these works are informed by theorizing and testimony of the Holocaust, Vietnam, and incest, as well as postcolonial analyses of the psychic costs of colonization and racism. Contemporary writers in this mode include Toni Morrison, Marguerite Duras, Larry Heinemann, Jamaica Kincaid, Pat Barker, Dorothy Allison, and Edwidge Danticat, among others.

These trauma narratives engage readers in a number of important social and psychological issues. First, these works attest to the fre-quency of trauma and its importance as a multicontextual social issue, as it is a consequence of political ideologies, colonization, war, domes-tic violence, poverty, and so forth. Second, trauma narratives raise ques-tions about how we define subjectivity as they explore the limits of the Western myth of the highly individuated subject and our ability to deal with loss and fragmentation in our lives. Third, the dilemmas experi-enced by characters in such narratives confront us with many of our own fears—of death, of dissolution, of loss, of loss of control—and pro-vide a potential space within which to consider these fears. Lastly, trauma writers elucidate the dilemma of the public's relationship to the traumatized, made problematic by victims' painful experiences and psychic defenses that can alienate others, and by the public's resistance. All these phenomena can isolate survivors and exacerbate the effects of trauma. This chapter's epigraph from Geoffrey Hartman suggests the trauma writer's task: to help readers discover their own sympathetic imaginings of humanity in extremis.

Narratives about trauma flourished particularly in the 1980s and 1990s with increased public awareness of trauma and trauma theory.[5] However, these narrative approaches have varied in their depth and pur-poses. Although popular culture has at times offered some insight into the psychology of fear, it has more often exploited such anxieties with tales of terror, suspense, or prurience.[6] Trauma narratives go beyond presenting trauma as subject matter or character study. They internalize the rhythms, processes, and uncertainties of traumatic experience within their underlying sensibilities and structures. They reveal many obstacles to communicating such experience: silence, simultaneous knowledge and denial, dissociation, resistance, and repression, among others. Some writers (Duras, Allison, Barker, and Heinemann) have drawn upon their personal observations of trauma, revisiting specific traumatic contexts armed with a new knowledge of their effects and consequently new ways of expressing them. But these writers and others also deal with trauma as a collective experience, an instrument of oppression, or as a means to explore and understand gender identity formation, memory, and creativity.[7]

Trauma narrativists endeavor to expand their audiences' awareness of trauma by engaging them with personalized, experientially oriented means of narration that highlight the painful ambivalence that characterizes traumatic memory and warn us that trauma reproduces itself if left unattended. Walter B. Michaels suggests such approaches to narrative should powerfully effect readers because "[i]t is only when the events of the past can be imagined not only to have consequences for the present but to live on in the present that they can become part of our experience and can testify to who we are" (7). Further, they immerse readers in characters' attempts to remember, filtering survivors' experiences through the lens of individual consciousness, with variable levels of awareness such that memory is explored through affective and unconscious associations rather than through conscious memories or structured plots. Thus the reader is guided through the narrative via the disorientations and conflicts of traumatic memory. For traumatic memory to lose its power as a fragment and symptom and for it to be integrated into memory, a form of narrative reconstruction or reexternalization has to occur (Felman and Laub 69). This is what trauma narratives do; they enact the directing outward of an inward, silent process to other witnesses, both within and outside the texts. Such reconstruction is also directed toward readers, engaging them in a meditation on individual distress, collective responsibilities, and communal healing in relation to trauma. These writers engage in a delicate balancing act by trying to lure readers into uncomfortable or alien material, sharing victims' pain with readers, shifting between what can and cannot be revealed, or appealing to readers through popular forms of writing (memoir and fiction).

Trauma narratives are often concerned with human-made traumatic situations and are implicit critiques of the ways social, economic, and political structures can create and perpetuate trauma. They offer us alternatives to often depersonalized or institutionalized historiographies. One method of doing this is characterizing dispossessed individuals and examining what their internalization of their personal and collective histories reveals about the effects of living under subjugation. Trauma can be a powerful indicator of oppressive cultural institutions and practices. In Pat Barker's World War I trilogy, soldiers' severe psychological conflicts illustrate the social contexts and causes that reinforce trauma. Rendered helpless and terrified in war, soldiers' recovery is problematized when therapeutic expression of their fears and feelings contradicts their upbringing as men and the attendant duties authorities demand of them. In Morrison's *The Bluest Eye* and Duras's *The Vice-Consul*, traumatized children exemplify the disempowerment and disavowal of communities and even entire cultures, such as African American and Third World citizens. Wandering, displaced characters in Duras, Morrison, and Heinemann's *Paco's Story* are haunting reminders of dead memories or bleak realities (Third World poverty, unremitting loss, the failed Vietnam War) that they unconsciously and repetitively relive. But their suffering is excessive and frightening for the other characters, who isolate the protagonists, forcing them to carry what should be a collective burden. Thus the texts expose readers to the dilemma of facing a traumatic past, whether remembered or repressed. Collective repression and suppression may bring temporary comfort but carry their own destructive costs: further victimization, lost human connections, and unresolved anguish.

The frequent focus on mother/child relations in these texts, particularly with daughters deeply identified with their mothers, provides a locus for considering many sociocultural aspects of trauma. These intimate relationships bear the effects of social, cultural, and economic mediations more powerfully because of traumatic circumstances. As their identities are formed in these circumstances, daughters feel a conflicted protective fearfulness toward their mothers and a dread of reliving their mothers' traumas. Homi Bhabha suggests that such feminization of colonized situations provides a model from which to explore other forms of "social affiliation" and to reformulate a "political rearticulation of private values and public virtues" (*Location* 65). Individualized relational situations reflect the impact of more generalized social situations but also have the potential to reconfigure them. This focus is representationally significant because women and children are more frequent exemplars of subjugation worldwide in that they are the most vulnerable to poverty and abuse.[8] Mothers and children also provide a sympathetic focus for readers (particularly women), but not an idealized one, as many of the writers (Morrison, Allison, Danticat, and Kincaid) lay out the fissures and conflicts that develop in these relationships under extreme stress.

Another significant aim of trauma narratives is to reshape cultural memory through personal contexts, adopting testimonial traits to prevent and bear witness against such repetitive horrors. Testimony and testimonial literature have had a huge impact on twentieth-century culture in preserving personal recollections of collective catastrophes and have been valuable venues for politically or socially marginalized witnesses. "Testimonio" or testimony narratives do not just concern individuals but also the individual as representative of a social class or group assuming relationship and responsibility to others beyond personal interests (Beverley 95; Felman and Laub 204). Some commentators value direct testimony over narrative or literary representations, whose distortions and intentions they find suspect. Written accounts, even survivor memoirs, argues Lawrence Langer, retain intrusive literary conventions such as chronology, characterization, dialogue, and a directive narrative voice. "This voice seeks to impose on apparently chaotic episodes a perceived sequence, *whether or not that sequence was perceived in an identical way* during the period that is being rescued from oblivion by memory and language" (*Testimonies* 41, italics in original). Written testimonies can also rationalize or reinterpret after the fact, philosophizing about death or universalizing personal experience (58). Survivors' experience resists normal chronological narration or normal modes of artistic representation. For example, because they live in durational rather than chronological time, they continue to experience the horrors of the past through internal shifts back in time and space rather than experiencing the past as differentiated from the present (14–15). Moreover, witnesses do not feel the sense of agency characteristic of being in control of a narrative. Rather, their oral testimonies seem more faithful to what they endure than do written or official accounts, Langer indicates, because survivors' voices and body language produce the uncertain reconstructions and emotional reenactments common to traumatic reactions. In *Worlds of Hurt*, Kalí Tal similarly advocates accounts told or written by actual trauma survivors, noting that nonsurvivors often have other agendas in representing traumatic experience (7).

Much of the testimonial trauma literature deals with extremely disturbing subjects such as incest and other sexual violence, breaking the silence on previously taboo topics. As Suzette Henke's study demonstrates, these are common events in many women's twentieth-century autobiographies. Deborah Horvitz observes that many contemporary writers "deconstruct the relationship between political power and sexual violence" toward women. Horvitz feels such analysis and testimony are needed to resist cultural repression and to bear witness to oppression (2, 18). Narratives by and about female sexual abuse survivors have borne witness to systematic violence against women, broken silence around incest and rape, and challenged "laws and social conditions that protected sexually abusive men" (Tal 156). Breaking silence for these women is of primary importance, as incest and rape often go unwitnessed or denied (Meiselman 1; Freyd 4). According to psychiatrist Alice Miller, the girls and women who are most damaged are those who are unable or prevented from voicing their anger and pain (cited in Tal 215). This points to the healing and educational value of testimony, which has been a successfully used therapeutic method, provided there is an empathic listener (Herman 182–83; Agger and Jensen 116, 118; Felman and Laub 58).

Kalí Tal, as well as Kirby Farrell in *Post-Traumatic Culture*, both discuss cultural influence and ways of coping with traumatic material particular to specific historical and social contexts. Tal's study examines how survivor accounts differ from mainstream cultural interpretations of the Holocaust, the Vietnam War, and incest survivors. She identifies three ways U.S. society constructs coping with trauma: mythologization, medicalization, and denial (6). She particularly critiques the self-interested ways American culture has redefined traumatic experience to suit mythical views of itself, drawing the focus away from its political implications and the fact that particular groups—especially racial minorities, women, children, and the poor—

are targets for abuse (6, 9). Farrell focuses on trauma as both a clinical syndrome and a trope, or symbolic means, for coping with death anxiety in the 1890s and 1990s and says that trauma has become "a strategic fiction that a complex, stressful society is using to account for a world that seems threateningly out of control" (2).

Tal and Farrell consider the ways culture "tames" traumatic material. Tal refers to the political purposes of this strategy; for example, the reconfiguring in the 1980s of Vietnam veterans as victims and the war in more positive terms, establishing a heroic tradition and a bridge toward more positive feelings about the next war, the Persian Gulf War (12–13). For Farrell, the violence presented on news programs and in other media offers the public mediated ways to deal with its horror and dread and to find meaning while keeping a safe distance from the disasters of the world (17).[9] Both scholars ask the important question of how culture is engaged in creating "consoling symbols," as Farrell describes it (19). This is an important consideration in evaluating writers of traumatic fiction as they approach readers with difficult material and translate complex behaviors. There are times when they do make the reader feel safe as they are entering into the story and create various ways of distancing from traumatic material (often as those who experience it do). However, the purpose of the writer's approach is significant here: Does it help bring the reader into the disturbing but weighty aspects of the material, or is it too comforting? An important indicator might be the kind of resolutions (if any) that are offered to traumatic circumstances and to what degree of optimism they are offered.

In my own approach to trauma narratives, I examine the way they employ elements of testimony, attempt to draw readers into the more complex and painful social and personal implications of trauma, and how these texts represent the targeted populations to whom Tal refers. I am looking at the self-reflective, uncertain, ambivalent aspects of these works and how they are often subversive in challenging oppressive practices and relations. Their structures and characterizations demonstrate how such experience resists the narrativizing, chronologizing, and moralizing to which Langer and Tal take exception. Narrative and symbolic approximations of testimony have been adopted to help access survivor voices for their immediacy and potential emotional impact on readers. Such approaches are necessary, Tal notes, because "survivors emerge from the traumatic environment with a new set of definitions" (16), definitions that can transform readers' perceptions of this experience, humbling our attempts at interpretive mastery. Tal believes nontraumatized writers and readers are not sensitive to the "signs that invoke traumatic memory" the way trauma survivors are (16), but I contend that serious trauma writers attempt to guide readers through a re-created process of traumatic memory in order that this experience be understood more widely, as in Morrison's *Beloved*.[10]

Cathy Caruth's, Shoshana Felman's, and Dori Laub's theorizing of trauma and its representation have directed my conceptions of literary trauma and the power of literature to suggest what is inaccessible, unbelievable, and elusive about traumatic experience. Caruth's contention that literature and psychoanalysis are particularly interested in the relationship between knowing and not knowing is significant to my studies of character, and her work guides my interpretations. However, my ideas about knowing and not knowing and how this is conveyed in character and narrative are also influenced by Dori Laub and Shoshana Felman, who have clearly formulated narrative manifestations of trauma. The shifts between knowledge and its repression or suppression structure in part some of the trauma narratives I discuss, from invasive thoughts to characters' defenses, which function to simulate control, to the splitting and recombining of narrators and protagonists. Caruth's demonstration of how "unclaimed" or unprocessed traumatic experience is enacted in the body is essential to my consideration of repetitive bodily movement and other forms of replaying trauma on the body that occurs to most of the characters discussed. Like other scholars of trauma and the Holocaust, Caruth also recognizes that faithfulness to the dead is a common burden of traumatized survivors, particularly evident in several trauma texts. Her observations on how trauma eludes comprehension suggests how narrative can simulate this for the audience and bring them closer to the victim's position of uncertainty (*Unclaimed* 1–9).

Although they focus on autobiographical writing, Suzette Henke's *Shattered Subjects* and Leigh Gilmore's *The Limits of Autobiography: Trauma and Testimony* are valuable studies for considering identity as well as the testimonial and healing properties of narrative. Henke's concept of scriptotherapy—that writing about trauma can lead toward individual and collective healing and alleviation of symptoms—supports my argument for the ethical and healing functions of trauma literature and aids in the examination of subject positions and narrative structures in conveying this experience. Her explorations of women's autobiographical writings clarify the ways a writer/victim can create, in Jennifer Freyd's words, an "episodic interpretation and integration of previously disjointed sensory and affective memories" (qtd. in Henke xii). Henke's contention that scriptotherapy offers the possibility of reinventing the self and reconstructing the subject ideologically and reassessing the past pertains well to many fictional narratives that focus on protagonists who attempt to survive by creating enabling stories and self-concepts, thereby recovering a sense of self and agency in the face of devastating losses. My study puts more emphasis on the problematic nature of such constructions. Gilmore addresses the difficult positioning of the individual within family and society, which reinforces my discussion of problematic Western notions of self in traumatizing contexts. Gilmore's choices of autobiographies reflect the recent increased inclusion of women and people of color in such narratives, and we both choose texts that challenge oppressive social contexts. Although our interpretations of Allison and Kincaid have different focuses, our work shares common perspectives on social forces that enable abuse and trauma and the role of memory and imagination in testifying to true-life events using fictional forms.

Studies on incest and child abuse highlight the significance of these cases and narratives to trauma narratives generally and elucidate my discussion of the significant role of this kind of trauma, the elaboration of symptoms, and ways sexual abuse produces trauma in a child. Jennifer Freyd's *Betrayal Trauma*, Karin Meiselman's *Resolving the Trauma of Incest*, and Judith Herman's *Father-Daughter Incest* provide a background for situating the positions and interpersonal dynamics of the central characters in *Bastard out of Carolina* and *The Bluest Eye*. Important considerations in their works are the loss of the mother, feelings of betrayal, and connections between abandonment and fear of death. Although long-term incest is present only in Allison's work, these considerations resonate with some of the other literary texts as well, where the mother is lost to the child, either physically or emotionally.

Deborah Horvitz's *Literary Trauma*, J. Brooks Bouson's *Quiet as It's Kept*, (on shame and trauma in Morrison's novels), and Christine Van Boheemen-Saaf's *Joyce, Derrida, Lacan and the Trauma of History*, all help to support my arguments about socially induced trauma—especially the relationship between postcoloniality and trauma—and how these scholars (like myself), as well as the authors of the literary texts, address and implicate readers. They all attempt to enlarge readers' sensitivity to the subtleties of how trauma can be communicated and try to persuade them of the need for social action. Horvitz takes a sociocultural and political approach, as I do, but she locates the public/private trauma relation particularly in sexual violence toward women and how the convergence of political and psychological sadomasochism marks the occurrence of trauma. Her approach is more psychoanalytical than mine, but she also locates in trauma and its symptoms (e.g., silence) signs of repressive sociopolitical ideologies. Her interpretation, though focused differently from mine, similarly suggests how a character's inner life, sexuality, and imagination are tainted by trauma. Bouson's work demonstrates how Morrison's African American characters endure various trauma-inducing institutions of their lives in America: slavery, racism, cultural standards of beauty, poverty, and so forth. She focuses thematically on elements of shame, which is one kind of response to trauma. In examining James Joyce as a postcolonial writer who demonstrates the traumatic loss of Irish culture and language in his prose, Van Boheemen-Saaf's study helps illustrate the various important links between postcolonial situations and those of the traumatized. There is a sense of a doubled self, needing to recover from a traumatic history, and attempts to acknowledge or reconstruct either a repressed culture or repressed experience. Her arguments about the paradoxical and simultaneous absence and presence of trauma—present in the body but not in memory—foregrounds the importance of the material body over mental or spiritual agency. These arguments support my emphasis on how the literary texts utilize the survivors' bodies to demonstrate trauma while challenging the mind/body split and other typical Western notions of identity.

Though there are commonalities with most of the scholars discussed above, my work can be distinguished from theirs in its focus on fictional techniques, how characters narrativize new identities, my proposal of a contemporary trauma genre, mother/daughter relations as an important locus of identity formation and perpetuation of traumatic legacies, how trauma is manifested in the body and sexuality, and how gender and class influence these manifestations. I examine how these narratives bring us into the visceral experience of traumatizing events and their aftermath. The texts I examine explore these elements and the construction of identity, its fracturings and attempts at reconstruction. I explore the truth value of fictionalizations, and, like LaCapra and Morrison, I see the potential value of fiction in conveying experiences of historical and social value that have either been suppressed, forgotten, or overlooked by traditional historical scholarship.

Of course, no reader can apprehend trauma completely through narrative. Trauma narratives acknowledge ambivalence and doubts about successful retelling, but they also attempt to provide possible ways for traumatic experience to be re-created. Although Langer and Tal legitimately question how many symbolic representations distort the nature of traumatic experience, it is also important to consider that an audience needs assistance in translating unfamiliar experience in order to empathize with it. Toni Morrison engages her audience with a third-person narrative voice that helps her achieve an "intimacy in which the reader is under the impression that he isn't really reading this; that he is participating in it as he goes along" ("Site of Memory" 100). Morrison, Duras, and Kincaid particularly try to accomplish this "intimacy" by positioning readers in the narrative in the midst of the characters' various, even agitated, levels of consciousness. Readers are often oriented and receive information via a character's/narrator's memory and consciousness, engaging readers to reconstruct the past, along with the often unwilling characters. Trauma narratives such as *Beloved* endeavor to provoke "the active interweaving of anticipation and retrospection" that Wolfgang Iser regards as integral to an involved reading experience (57). This type of reader engagement indicates a commitment to representations that may be symbolic and fictional, but not necessarily appropriative or false. The following discussion on trauma should help illuminate trauma writers' approaches to narrative and audience.

Trauma

Traumatic experience can produce a sometimes indelible effect on the human psyche that can change the nature of an individual's memory, self-recognition, and relational life. Despite the human capacity to survive and adapt, traumatic experiences can alter people's psychological, biological, and social equilibrium to such a degree that the memory of one particular event comes to taint all other experiences, spoiling appreciation of the present. This tyranny of the past interferes with the ability to pay attention to both new and familiar situations. When people come to concentrate selectively on reminders of their past, life tends to become colorless, and contemporary experience ceases to be a teacher (Van der Kolk and McFarlane 4).

Kai Erikson emphasizes that trauma can result "from a constellation of life's experiences as well as from a discrete event, from a prolonged exposure to danger as well as from a sudden flash of terror, from a continuing pattern of abuse as well as from a single assault, from a period of attenuation and wearing away as well as from a moment of shock" (457). Symptoms of trauma include "periods of nervous, restless activity—scanning the surrounding world for signs of danger, breaking into explosive rages, reacting with a start to everyday sights and sounds—against a numbed, gray background of depression, feelings of helplessness, a loss of various motor skills and a general closing off of the spirit as the mind tries to insulate itself from further harm" (457).[11]

Fundamental to traumatic experience is that the past lingers unresolved, not remembered in a conventional sense, because it is not processed like nontraumatic information, either cognitively or emotionally. Because stress can change physiology, traumatic experiences are processed differently by the central nervous system (Van der Kolk and Van der Hart 442). Traumatic "memories" appear in the repetitive, intrusive forms of visualizations of the trauma scene, nightmares, or associated affects (Caruth, *Unclaimed* 11). Because traumatic memories are not affected by subsequent experience, they are reexperienced without change (Van der Kolk and Van der Hart 441–42). There are a number of "triggers" or associative conditions that cause returns to traumatic events. Human and animal research indicates that stress causes "state dependent returns to earlier behavior patterns"—a stressful situation will bring current thoughts along the same pathways as a previous stressful or traumatic event. This could account for individuals' repetitive behavior and returns to situations of abuse (445). Consequently, unlike nontraumatic memories, which "are constantly combined with previous knowledge to form flexible mental schemas," traumatic memories are often frozen in time and remain overwhelming experiences not subject to previous contexts or to subsequent experience or reevaluation, and are therefore repressed from memory and only reexperienced in repetitive, unconscious patterns (441–42). Van der Kolk and C. R. Ducey affirm that "a sudden and passively endured trauma is relived repeatedly, until a person learns to remember simultaneously the affect and cognition associated with the trauma through access to language" (271).

Those who have written about human responses to trauma agree that "a feeling of helplessness, of physical or emotional paralysis, is fundamental to making an experience traumatic: the person was unable to take any action that could affect the outcome of events" (Van der Kolk and Van der Hart 446). A failure to make sense of these past events results in fixed ideas that motivate impotent attempts to re-create these events, and in dissociation, where the individual becomes "emotionally constricted and cannot experience a full range of affects" (432). It is not uncommon for victims to separate or dissociate themselves from physical and emotional self-awareness to avoid pain; splitting off from one's body or awareness can reduce the victim's immediate sense of violation and help them to endure and survive the situation (Herman 43, 101–2). Unfortunately, this capacity can create defensive self-restrictions, which can become ingrained, prolonging expectations of punishment or failure, instigating debilitating depression, and precluding relationships outside the captive situation (42–47).

Social and Cultural Dimensions of Trauma

The social environment influences the causes and outcomes of traumatic experience in a variety of ways. It forms the circumstances out of which trauma is created, but it can also provide, or decline, needed supports for healing. Although trauma damages the individual psyche, collective trauma has further destructive consequences in that it breaks the attachments of social life, degrades the sense of community and support from that community, and dominates the mood and interactions of the group (Erikson 460–61). Traumatic experience can inspire not only a loss of self-confidence, but also a loss of confidence in the social and cultural structures that are supposed to create order and safety (470; de Vries 407–8; Langer, *Testimonies* 59, 201, 204).

Some trauma theorists have insisted that we extend the boundaries of how we view traumatic experience, because among vulnerable populations PTSD (posttraumatic stress disorder) can be a widespread cultural phenomena that societies and even the therapeutic community have tried to ignore.[12] Laura S. Brown asserts that limited (i.e., white, middle-class) therapeutic parameters have tended to minimize the effects of the constant stress and humiliation associated with being a person of low socioeconomic status. She further contends there is a collective will to repress how aspects of our social life (violence, poverty, and abuse, for example) allow and even encourage the traumatization of women, people of color, and gays (127). Children are particularly vulnerable to abuse because it effects the way they develop, as well as their life coping skills and their future relationships.[13] Children's symptoms that resemble those of adults include feelings of helplessness, immobilization, thought/behavioral/physical dysfunctions, hypervigilance, and extremes of passivity or overactivity (Pynoos and Eth 39). Unlike adults, they can suffer regression, misperceptions of time, pessimism about the future, disrupted attachments, and impaired social skills and cognitive development (40; Waites 63, 66).

The social environment, the severity of the event, and the individual's characteristics and experience all determine how someone will cope with trauma. Social supports are essential to survivors' adjustment. Cultural attitudes and practices influence notions of expected behavior, responses, and even symptoms. Life roles and emotional management are "facilitated and ordered" within a culturally prescribed social and community structure where stress, illness, and grief are dealt with on personal and group levels (de Vries 401). Optimum circumstances for healing exist when a "society . . . organizes the process of suffering, rendering it a meaningful mode of action and identity within a larger social framework" (401–2). Rituals for death and loss, for example, can help organize one's sense of grief, provide structure for behavior, emotions, and a sense of fragmentation, and link the suffering individual to the social group (403, 405; Markus and Kitayama 122). In some cultures there is an acceptance that trauma cannot always be completely worked through, as when a Dinka refugee in Kenya said in 1994: "There is no solution to these problems. One must endure the hardship" (qtd. in de Vries 398). When cultures do not function this way, individuals feel unprotected and are forced to cope in isolation. For example, in the U.S., attitudes about gender, the Vietnam War, and individual responsibility impeded the recovery of many Vietnam veterans and rape victims. Suffering from posttraumatic stress, survivors of both groups often experienced resistance from medical and social communities that discouraged them from reporting their suffering and thereby reestablishing personal and social connections. Moreover, survivors can risk or provoke rejection if they make others uncomfortable by voicing or showing their suffering, and often have to choose between their own views and connection with others (Herman 67; McCann and Pearlman 113).[14] The meaning that a society ascribes to a particular traumatic event is significant in how it will be defined and resolved for the individual and the group.

Social judgments have a huge impact on the way trauma is experienced, viewed, and treated:

> [M]ost people have no knowledge or understanding of the psychological changes of captivity. Social judgment of chronically traumatized people therefore tends to be extremely harsh. The chronically abused person's apparent helplessness and passivity, her entrapment in the past, her intractable depression and somatic complaints, and her smoldering anger often frustrate the people closest to her. Moreover, if she has been coerced into betrayal of relationships, community loyalties, or moral values, she is frequently subjected to furious condemnation. (Herman 115)

Believing they themselves would have behaved better under duress, outside observers often look for character or moral flaws in the victim—the notion of the Jews' "passivity" in World War II, for example. Victims of captivity are considered "traitors" if they give in under torture, and sometimes such individuals have been treated more harshly for the same crimes as their captors, as when Patty Hearst received a longer prison sentence than her abductors for similar crimes (115).

Cultural ideologies and particular public and special interests have had a considerable impact even on the way traumatic stress has been studied in the last 140 years. The earliest diagnoses of psychological trauma emerged from studies of hysteria but brought discredit upon the work of Jean-Martin Charcot, Pierre Janet, Joseph Breuer, and Sigmund Freud, because hysterical symptoms were associated with women, who were considered constitutionally overemotional. Initially this diagnosis was not thought transferable to men despite the fact that these same symptoms appeared in severely stressed or "shell-shocked" World War I combat soldiers (Herman 17; Showalter 169–72). Further, public incredulity and denial about Freud's contention that hysterical symptoms were indicators of sexual trauma and incest forced him to repudiate his theory and set back trauma studies significantly (Herman 17).

The horrendous volume of psychic trauma in World War I (eighty thousand cases treated during the war and over one hundred thousand more over the following decade) eventually overcame ideologies of inherited superiority or degeneracy, and of masculine stoicism, which sustained the idea that psychological disorders were really cowardice, and enabled psychological theories and treatments to gain influence (Stone 246, 248; Healy 96; Leed 169). Practitioners like W. H. R. Rivers utilized Freud's analytic method successfully and discovered that soldiers' traumatic neuroses were indicative of internal conflicts between duty and survival, and more importantly, that the most significant cause of psychological devastation is helplessness, that is, being deprived of one's ability to act (Stone 255; Leed 176, 182). Military therapists faced conflicts between their obligations to soldiers and to the war effort; the emphasis was on sending men back into combat. Military authorities in World War II resumed efforts to discourage and suppress reports of war trauma, with no pensions given to soldiers discharged for war neurosis, as well as attempts by psychiatrists to blame poor parenting and emotional instability for those suffering war neurosis (Healy 96–97).

Issues of compensation—for train wreck victims in the nineteenth century, veterans of many twentieth-century wars, or for rape or incest victims seeking redress years later—have invited suspicions toward the victims (Young 250). There are still enormous financial interests at stake that encourage minimizing the frequency of sexual abuse despite U.S. Justice Department estimates that 250,000 children are sexually abused each year (Van der Kolk and McFarlane 38). "Unfortunately, the multifaceted interest in denying the reality of trauma is so powerful, the fear of being taken advantage of is so deep, and the human need to find specific individuals and organizations to blame for our ills is so pervasive that this debate is unlikely ever to be driven primarily by attention to the facts" (39). All these aspects, as well as concerns about the reliability of memory, have provoked recent controversies about recovered memories in the 1990s. Fears about compensation for abuses, false memories, and survivors sending innocent people to prison are usually refuted when details are examined more closely. First, incest and rape victims are *less* rather than more likely to report abuses or seek compensation (Van der Kolk and McFarlane 30; Herman and Harvey 4; Levis, "Debate" 73). Second, relatively few cases go to court, and even fewer abusers are jailed (Van der Kolk and McFarlane 37). Finally, while the unreliability of memory and incompetent therapists are complex and thorny issues, professionals who have studied trauma extensively find that false claims of abuse are rare and that victims are more likely to seek therapy for memories that intrude on *them*, than to have memories suggested by a therapist (Levis 73; Herman and Harvey 4–5).

The political climate of the 1970s encouraged veterans to voice their outrage about the severe emotional consequences of their horrific experiences in Vietnam, thus initiating more substantive attention to traumatic stress.[15] The nature of the Vietnam War and how it was carried out and received by civilians contributed to elevating stress in soldiers and other personnel in such a way that the aftermath could not be ignored. The *Report of Findings from the National Vietnam Veterans Readjustment Study* found that "over the course of their lives, more than half . . . of male theater veterans and nearly half . . . of female theater veterans have experienced clinically significant stress-reaction symptoms. This represents about 1.7 million veterans of the Vietnam War" (qtd. in Tal 272). Angry veterans groups successfully pressured the Veterans Administration (VA) for better psychological treatment programs.

From the VA-commissioned psychological studies of veterans came an official diagnosis of the syndrome—posttraumatic stress disorder—appearing in the profession's *Diagnostic and Statistical Manual III* in 1980 (Herman 26–27). Significantly, "this was the first time that a psychiatric diagnostic system recognized the possible existence of a wholly environmentally determined psychiatric disorder," and the first time since Freud that psychological problems were described with regard to the sufferers' experiences and emotions (Healy 105–6). In addition, "the development of PTSD as a diagnosis has created an organized framework for understanding how people's biology, conceptions of the world, and personalities are inextricably intertwined and shaped by experience" (Van der Kolk and McFarlane 4).

The sexual abuse of children had been rediscovered by professionals in the late 1950s and early 1960s (Healy 109), but, as with the political agitation of veterans, the women's movement in the 1970s helped greatly to expose the extent and severity of domestic abuse to the public, who became increasingly aware that large numbers of women and children were being terrorized, abused, and raped (Herman 28–29; Tal 155–56).[16] Not only were rape survivors unique in that their traumas could still continue—in other words, they could still be at risk—but also that such abuse contributed to or coincided with women's gendered socialization and subordination through physical terror (Tal 155, 166; Herman 69). Further, survivors' defensive avoidance behavior could become so ingrained and restricting that they could become isolated and depressed (Kilpatrick et al. 117, 119). These symptoms bore enough similarity to war trauma symptoms that researchers called this the "rape trauma syndrome." Only after 1980, when characteristics of trauma became more familiar, did the similarities between rape and domestic battery symptoms and those of combat survivors become obvious (Herman 32).

This comparison prompted 1980s and 1990s overviews of the literature on traumatic stress with the specific goal of developing a "unified theory of the psychosocial consequences of traumatic stress," whereas earlier research had focused on only single types of situations and victims (Figley 1; Lindy et al. 44–57).[17] The vast interdisciplinary work on trauma has begun to challenge what was once perceived by the medical establishment as individual pathology and has linked trauma to sociopolitical agendas and expectations. The unique situations of trauma are very important, but ascertaining the commonalities of such experience has several benefits. To reconsider trauma as a generalized and socialized phenomena, perhaps even a frequent experience in certain contexts, opens up possibilities of removing the stigmas or isolation attached to it, of changing attitudes, and initiating cooperative means of prevention.

Readers of Trauma Literature

Traumatic experience raises many uncomfortable issues for public and professionals alike with regard to believability, personal agency and responsibility, perpetrators of trauma in society, and whether the world is a just and safe place (Van der Kolk and McFarlane 24–42). Trauma is underresearched compared to other disorders and can have harmful effects on therapists as they experience countertransference (30; McCann and Pearlman, "Traumatization" 498–99).[18] It forces us to face difficult human issues: vulnerability and our capacity for evil, bearing "witness to horrible events," and taking sides between victims and perpetrators (Herman 7). We often take the perpetrator's side, because it is easier to forget or to preserve our deeply held views of normality than to share the victim's horribly alienating memories (7–8). Perpetrators promote forgetting and defend themselves through secrecy, silence, denial, rationalizing, and undermining the victim's accusations. In short, they try to define reality counter to victims' experience (8).[19] Complicating public credence are victims' own failures of recall and appearing to be drawn into complicity with their abusers, both of which uncomfortably challenge our notions of agency and responsibility. Also, victims can often act out in disturbing ways or withdraw emotionally from others, causing rifts with potential supporters (Van der Kolk and McFarlane 29).

Transference of traumatic responses can continue for generations. Family relationships and the children of survivors are deeply affected by their parents' experience, as manifested in depression, mistrust, and emotional constriction brought on by excessive parental suffering and attempts to control their children. Moreover, children inherit patterns of traumatic response (Kogan 26–28; Laub 507–9).

Ignorance about traumatic responses also leads to misinterpretation. For example, the submissive quasi-paralysis or "play dead" reaction that is a "prewired autonomic response to stress" can lead others to conclude acquiescence in a victim rather than a survival mechanism (Healy 107).

The social support of groups or movements that encourage bearing witness is essential for individual and group survival of trauma, because "repression, dissociation and denial are phenomena of social as well as individual consciousness" (Herman 9). Scholarship and literature on trauma is an important part of a group support process, attesting to diverse voices articulating extraordinary experience and uncovering what has been suppressed and hidden. They clarify for readers the significant personal and social costs of ignoring the problems trauma poses, indicating that a lack of public sympathy exacerbates these problems and prevents healing. Their approaches often demonstrate in narrative and characterization what trauma researchers have emphasized—that for healing to take place, survivors must find ways to tell their stories and to receive some social acknowledgment if not acceptance (Herman 182–83; Felman and Laub 58, 69; Caruth, *Trauma* 153–54). This "scriptotherapy—the process of writing out and writing through traumatic experience in the mode of therapeutic reenactment," as Henke formulates it—is common to survivor discourse and women's autobiography in the twentieth century (xii–xiii).[20] Though the act of writing is important to survivors' self-catharsis and in sharing pain, as Henke demonstrates, survivors also need public forums, the chance to connect with fellow survivors, to overcome shame and silence and to win the awareness if not empathy of readers.[21] Depending on the reader, this can be a very direct process. If a writer happens to speak to readers' specific experience, it could have disturbing or healing consequences depending upon the reader's emotional capacity for confronting their situation. For many writers of trauma fiction, their greatest reward is a sense that their work has helped heal or inform their readers.

The purposes of recent trauma studies—that is, to note commonalities, attack stigmas and isolation, and initiate understanding—also motivate the approaches trauma writers take with their readers. Another aspect of this is an informational approach that illustrates how the social and the psychological merge in traumatic experience. Furthermore, trauma narrativists enlist their readers to become witnesses to these kinds of stories through the unconventional narrative translations of traumatic experience and memory that give them a different kind of access to the past than conventional frameworks (Caruth, *Trauma* 154; Lanzmann, "Seminar" 91). For example, in his 1985 film *Shoah*, filmmaker Claude Lanzmann creates a "trauma narrative" in his positioning and questioning of a variety of Holocaust witnesses. In doing this he recognizes and utilizes the obstacles trauma poses for communication: silence, simultaneous knowledge and denial, dissociation, resistance and repression (Vickroy, "*Beloved* and *Shoah*" 123–25). He is aware that although traumatic memory may not bring comprehensive knowledge, it does allow, as Caruth suggests, "*history* to arise where *immediate understanding* may not" (*Unclaimed* 11, italics in original).

Lanzmann's testimonial narratives reveal the tensions, conflicts, and dialogism implicit in retelling and reexperiencing traumatic events, where victims try to maintain a "balance between the emotion recurrently breaking through the 'protective shield' and numbness that protects this shield" (Friedlander 51). Lanzmann's use of dialogism creates a narrative wherein many voices, emotions, and experiences intermingle to produce memory. Individual witnesses counteract collective denial and repression, traditional historical accounts, and perpetrator evasions. Similarly, historical information and other testimonies can correct or reinforce individual perspectives. Thus, he is able to probe collective and personal aspects of testimonies. By focusing on a broad range of survivors' viewpoints, eliciting detailed descriptions and individual sense memories (e.g., what they saw, heard, smelled, etc.), Lanzmann is able to re-create specific experiences and make *Shoah* a "physical film" for its viewers, where "it was necessary to feel the fear" of witnesses as they lived through these events ("Seminar" 91). Contemporary fictional trauma narratives use many of these same methods to also suggest bits of history and of lived experiences of the past that are not totally recoverable but are suggested by affective or sense-memory details (see discussions in chapter 5).

Authentic trauma fiction has a similar potential for historical truth in its ability to convey specific lived experience as well as some critical distance. Historian and theorist Dominick LaCapra argues that the roles of empathy and affect—for example, being able to read the responses of survivors—are important to historical understanding (*Writing* xiv). Literary texts can provide pathways for reader empathy. LaCapra accepts, as I do, that fiction can be truthful and reveal the emotional experience of historical phenomena such as slavery (13–14). He favors texts that take readers through a process of working through trauma and put readers into a critical as well as empathic mode.

> Historical trauma is specific, and not everyone is subject to it or entitled to the subject position associated with it. It is dubious to identify with the victim to the point of making oneself a surrogate victim who has a right to the victim's voice or subject position. The role of empathy and empathic unsettlement in the attentive secondary witness does not entail this identity; it involves a kind of virtual experience through which one puts oneself in the other's position while recognizing the difference of that position and hence not taking the other's place. Opening oneself to empathic unsettlement is, as I intimated, a desirable affective dimension of inquiry which complements and supplements empirical research and analysis. (78)

Even if their protagonists do not always emerge from repetition, trauma narrativists demand more than pity. Rather, such narratives provide narrators, characters, or consequences that point to breakages or losses demanding deliberation and social action.

Psychotherapists like Dori Laub and Judith Herman recognize that trauma cannot be faced alone and that recovery is possible only "within the context of relationships" (Herman 133; Felman and Laub 57–58). If a survivor is encouraged to narrate his or her experience and emotionally relive it in a safe context with an empathic listener, such as therapy, this "can actually produce a change in the abnormal processing of the traumatic memory. With this transformation of memory comes relief of many of the major symptoms of PTSD. The physioneurosis induced by terror can apparently be reversed through the use of words" (Herman 183). Listeners must connect with the victim's inner experience (memories, fears, etc.), be aware of their own defenses, and yet retain a separate perspective so that he or she can be "at the same time a witness to the trauma witness and a witness to himself" (Felman and Laub 58).

The listener—in Laub's case, the therapist—helps the witness to re-externalize traumatic events and narrate his or her story in order to escape merely repeating and reenacting the traumatizing experience or embracing a comfortable but ultimately defeating silence (69). This suggests the importance of sharing such experience in social contexts such as testifying and writing to empathic witnesses (Langer 19; Kirmayer 188–89; Henke xix). Through careful attention and absorption of testimony, listeners—and I would extend this to readers of trauma literature as well—can participate in the process of translating traumatic experience and can take part in a process of reevaluation that this experience demands. Knowledge of trauma offers the opportunity to unveil new perspectives concerning relationships of power and their effects, to analyze what we repress and why, and to examine our need for cultural and individual myths that block understanding. As cultural attitudes affect the ways trauma is dealt with, changing public opinion is a worthwhile endeavor. Trauma literature has these potentially persuasive effects since the basis for these narratives is historical and contemporary social realities.

Trauma and Questions of Identity and Autonomy

Representations of trauma inevitably involve explorations around the constitution of self and the relational and situational properties of iden-

[handwritten annotation in top margin: Compromises the individual's capacities for remembering, knowing, and feeling.]

tity. Trauma often involves a radical sense of disconnection and isolation as bonds are broken and relationships and personal safety are put into question. Survivors feel, often justifiably, abandoned or alienated because of their differences with others. Trauma, and its concurrent shame, doubt, or guilt, destroys important beliefs: in one's own safety or competence to act or live in the world, one's perception of the world as meaningful and orderly, and one's view of oneself as decent, strong, and autonomous (Janoff-Bulman 19–22). Traumatic reactions verify how circumstances can radically change our behavior and should make us question often-sacralized notions of human self-control and free will. Trauma texts' depictions of the devastating effects of isolation, the necessity for connection, and the cultural influences on private relations and behavior all serve to challenge cultural and often class-based attitudes that define the individual as essentially agential and self-determining (Allen 7–9, 23; Cheek and Hogan 253–56; Fivush and Buckner 176–77). Increased public awareness of situational-contingent behavior could mitigate public responses to helplessness and other discomforting adaptive or defensive psychic responses.

In *Holocaust Testimonies*, Lawrence Langer formulates from concentration camp survivor testimonies several kinds of memories that illustrate how the remaining self is diminished. For example, "humiliated" memories recall individuals' helplessness before extremes of deprivation and violence, and "tainted" memories recall past actions at odds with individuals' sense of morality and behavior in more normative circumstances. "Unheroic" memory taints the joy of liberation because so much that is essential to personal identity has been lost or compromised: loved ones, dignity, choice, and an integrated sense of self (84–96; 122, 170–77). Langer's formulations of memory and identity emphasize the costs of losing relational bonds and validation, social status, and moral orientations, all essential elements of the self.

A diminished, even shattered sense of self is common in cases of severe trauma of any sort but seems particularly prevalent in accounts of domestic tragedies and sexual abuse. In *Betrayal Trauma*, Jennifer Freyd discusses how incest victims are coerced by family or shame to repress ("forget") their abuse and betrayal; consequently, they employ defenses to feel less pain. However, these defenses also compromise the individual's capacities for remembering, knowing, and feeling (85–95, 106). Incest, which usually provokes acute psychic trauma, deeply

[handwritten annotation in bottom margin: "A# Diminished, even shattered, sense of self is common in cases of ... sexual abuse."]

wounds a child's development as it "shatters the central organizing fantasies of self in relation to . . . [others] that cannot fully be restored" and disturbs the victim's personality with, among others, symptoms of shame, guilt, sexual problems, numbing, self-loathing, and intrusive ruminations (Ulman and Brothers 65–67). Suzette Henke chronicles women autobiographers' struggles to formulate cohesive life narratives out of identities and thinking that have become fragmented and chaotic due to incest and losses of close family members (xvii–xix). Because fragmentation creates a profoundly disturbing sense of self, victims go to great lengths to resist it. Consequently, the attempt to create or maintain a sense of agency and order and reject fragmentation is a common strategy of the narrators/protagonists of trauma fiction.

Psychocultural, analytic, and philosophical meditations on what constitutes the self illuminate what traumatic experience reveals about the dynamic and multiple nature of identity. These theories help us interrogate concepts of identity that are put into question by trauma. They also demonstrate how relational, sociocultural, and symbolic functions impact identity in complex and sometimes contradictory ways.

Object relations theorists emphasize the formation of self in a relational matrix: "[The] embeddedness of the child with others is the overriding feature of early development, and the need for attachment, connection, integration with others is the preeminent motivational thrust of the human organism throughout life" (Greenberg and Mitchell 221). The ego strength that develops from positive relations promotes learning processes that help make us subjects within culture. Dynamic relationships—especially between mother and child—should provide both safety and independent recognition of the child, making it possible for him or her to create symbolically meaningful internal and external objects that eventually help the child to affect and respond to the environment and discover him- or herself within a cultural framework (Winnicott, *Playing and Reality* 95–103; Klein 116–45). For D. W. Winnicott, "the structure of the self and the organization of psychopathology derive from the fate of these early relational needs" (Greenberg and Mitchell 222–23).[22] He demonstrated the role of play in enabling children to practice the interrelations and separations between inner and outer reality through engagement in interplay: in intimacy and in the discovery of a reliable relationship with another. The mother's (or primary caregiver's) input in play is essential to encouraging the child's creative, interactive, and adaptive capacities (*Playing* 12; see discussion in chapter 2). Consequently, a devalued self often emerges from living a socially marginal status, where traumas from poverty, racism, violence, and exploitation are more likely to occur (Yamamoto, Silva et al. 36). The traumatization of mothers and missing recognition diminishes intersubjective nurturance and can create destructive generational legacies.

The most difficult aspect of traumatic situations for victims, no matter what the context, is feeling that one is powerless to affect his or her situation (Van der Kolk and Van der Hart 446; Herman 47). Feelings of helplessness can lead to breakdowns, and to avoid this, victims' defensive mechanisms allow them a sense of agency, even if illusory, to help retain a sense of self. For example, a provisional if ineffective sense of control is achieved through repetition, acting out, self-destructive behavior such as self-mutilation, provoking an abuser into action (even if it is only taking the time of the abuse out of the abuser's hands), or provoking rejection so as not to suffer helplessly (Herman 109; Van der Kolk and Van der Hart 432; Prior 68–70). These defensive mechanisms only approximate a sense of the integrated self integral to our self-conceptions and to survival. However, these methods do not ultimately facilitate healing, where support and a sense of connection are essential.

Moreover, our conceptions of self are determined and interpreted within cultural histories and contexts. For example, Americans' predominant cultural framework of identity is that of independence, with a model of self as a "unique configuration of internal attributes (e.g., traits, emotions, motives, values and rights) [where one] behaves as a consequence of these internal attributes," with the social goal of maintaining separation from others and avoiding undue influence (Markus and Kitayama 96). Conversely, for many non-Western societies and minority cultures in the U.S., concepts of emotion and self are oriented toward relations with others (G. White 230). A multidisciplinary array of philosophical and psychocultural studies have suggested how this Western notion of the individuated subject is culturally and ideologically constructed. In "Social Constructions of Self," Douglas Allen argues that the post-Enlightenment, modern conceptions of self (as "atomistic, separate, autonomous") that underlie Western political, economic, educational, and cultural systems are not shared by many who live in the modern West and are more likely embraced by those of higher socioeconomic status. Groups who have been oppressed or exploited (such as women, Native Americans, and African Americans) "resist viewing themselves as independent, separate, autonomous individuals and thus retain a social, relational view of self . . . [except for] the more privileged and 'Westernized' classes in India and other Asian societies, that incorporate features of modern Western concepts of self" (Allen 23, note 3). The self is "realized through participation in cultural practices" (Markus et al. Kitayama 13) and "the self concept is not a stable structure but a highly malleable reflection of the ongoing processes of social interaction" (Cheek and Hogan 253). As studies on the cultural attitudes affecting Vietnam veteran and rape victims demonstrate, the denial of relational influences on subjective well-being increases the isolation and marginalization of trauma survivors.

Trauma narratives question concepts of radical individualism through identification and subject-fragmenting conflicts in mother/daughter relationships and in the important role of extended family or community for the possibility of healing. Trauma portrayed within the context of mother/child symbiosis demonstrates the devastation of isolation and helplessness, particularly in early, formative, and intimate contexts. Radical individualism, whether embraced or enforced, is often punished or takes the form of isolated suffering in these texts, and communal or family support is depicted as necessary for healing. Another important connection between trauma and identity is that the self is bound up closely with awareness of mortality and the fear of breakdown or death. According to Winnicott, these fears, which often accompany trauma, threaten to return us to a state that we dread, that unintegrated state existing before the ego created defenses against it (*Psychoanalytic* 88–89). Kirby Farrell's contention that cultural representations of trauma allow the audience to experience their own fears vicariously seems like a compelling argument for the frequency of these representations in popular media. However, if these representations are too safe—that is, overly mediated—they lose their authenticity and deprive the audience of a contemplative or experiential link to trauma. To avoid such disconnection, representations of trauma should create what LaCapra calls "empathic unsettlement . . . [or] performative engagement with unsettling events" (Lecture). Trauma narratives do confront readers with difficult issues such as preoccupation with fears of death, evoked frequently in characters' obsessions, dreams, and imagery (see discussions of *Beloved, Jazz, The Autobiography of My Mother,* and *Breath, Eyes, Memory* in subsequent chapters). Yet there is also considerable focus in these texts on changes to the self after undergoing trauma and learning to survive, even if in a marginal way. The obsessions and defenses that help the traumatized survive can become relational liabilities but also resourceful coping mechanisms, or assets to creativity, as in *The Lover* and *Bastard out of Carolina.* A sense of ego integration, developed through relationships, however, is needed to overcome the devastating fragmentation often occurring in trauma.

Positioning Readers with Characters

How do authors engage readers narratively and stylistically? They employ means that aid readers to more readily identify with individual characters' struggles with being and telling. Readers are engaged to help reconstruct experience and retelling as trauma writers expose them to a variety of voices, subject positionings, and symbolizing that highlight the chaotic and disorienting aspects as well as representational possibilities or approximations. One authorial approach combines testimonial elements with multiple subject positionings to create a dialogical conception of witnessing. In the narratives of *Beloved* and *Paco's Story,* for example, many voices, emotions, and experiences intermingle to produce individual and collective memory and to counteract silence and forgetting. Both writers employ multiple narrators who give first-person testimony, bear witness for characters silenced by trauma, provoke the protagonist's resistant memory, or suggest collective suffering. These multiple accounts sometimes reinforce and sometimes challenge one another, illustrating both the potential for sharing and healing but also missed connections, as when traumatic reactions isolate individuals with similar experience from one another. *Mrs Dalloway*

The complexities of traumatic memory and a subject's difficult relation to the past are suggested by the use of multiple voices and positionings within characters or narrators as well as between them. In *Beloved,* multiple positionings expose the struggle between memory and forgetting, between differing viewpoints and responses to oppression, and between explanation and the inexplicable. When readers absorb these stories through the division of voice (i.e., identity and points of

To The Lighthouse

view), they experience something analogous to splitting. Splitting is a common defense mechanism accompanying trauma that illustrates the nonintegration of traumatic memory with normal memory, whereby survivors can occupy dual positions, both inside and outside their pasts, and reenact the past without recalling it. Traumatized individuals are "possessed by an image or event" that returns "against the will of the one it inhabits" (Caruth, "Psychoanalysis" 3), and their memories or flashbacks indicate "the force of an experience that is not yet fully owned" (Caruth, *Trauma* 151). The complex internal conflicts, the "bifocal visions" and movements from avoidance to fear to helplessness that characterize trauma also suggest a multiple view of self in reaction to extraordinary circumstances. Therefore, trauma writers position their readers in the similarly disoriented positions of the narrators and characters through shifts in time, memory, affect, and consciousness. Thus situated, readers may compare this with their own, perhaps less problematic memory processes. At the conclusion of *Beloved*, for instance, the title character signifies something different for each of the characters who knew her, provoking behavior in each of them that represents their own difficult relationships to the past.

Marguerite Duras explores changing subject/narrative positions through a dialogism of emotion and detachment. Dissociation and diminished affect are recurrent in Duras's self-portrait of her traumatic youth in Indochina in *The Lover*. Her family's psychological brutalization under colonialism and poverty foster both her lonely desires and a distrust in intimacy. She portrays herself as a precocious girl whose passionate sexuality with her Chinese lover is tempered by her detachment, both in the impersonality she adopts with him ("I'd like you to do as you usually do with women," 37) and by keeping some distance even in the same bed ("We can't stop loving each other. . . . I sleep with him. I don't want to sleep in his arms," 63). These shifts acknowledge pleasure and pain and yet keep them at arm's length. Her changing affect expresses her conflicts in loving a man who exploits those whom she and her family have come to resemble. Duras here seems to be capturing the distance with which trauma victims observe their own pain or learn to live split between being "I," or functioning subject, or "she," that is, victim.

By assuming multiple roles and positions as the subject, object, and witness to her past life, Duras's narrative provides a medium for re-

<!-- marginalia: Virginia Woolf / Ettinger / Kane / Crash / Joyce -->
<!-- marginalia: Clarissa Dalloway (subject) / Richard Dalloway (agent) / Septimus Smith (object) / V W as agent of order -->

creating the past, reshaping its significance, and playing out conflicting tendencies within Duras's narrator/protagonist. The narrator appears to be engaged and detached, a dual subject who alternately refers to herself as "I" and "she." These subject shifts are frequent and not always chronologically consistent, thus indicating more than merely looking back in time as she remembers her youth. Her subject position changes during the narrator's first sexual encounter, for example. Referring to herself as "she" in the initial context as she loses her virginity, she then switches to first person within a page as the couple become more intimate emotionally and she describes her family's desperation to him (38–40). The multiple positionings could be the consequence of a defensive dissociation from painful memories, but they also help Duras reformulate identity and desire in a disjunctive narrative, created out of hindsight and out of the emptiness of family life and her doomed affair. She makes readers aware of the difficulty of reconstructing a painful past and identity when only bits of memory remain and there is no clear path to meaning: "The story of my life doesn't exist. . . . There's never any center to it. No path, no line" (8).

The dilemma of traumatic experience has been described as "being caught between the compulsion to complete the process of knowing and the inability or fear of doing so" (Laub and Auerhahn 288). Trauma narratives reveal the tensions and conflicts implicit in retelling and re-experiencing traumatic events. Despite the struggles to forget, victims' knowledge can emerge in a wide range of forms, including decontextualized memory fragments; transference episodes (i.e., where current life experiences are influenced and distorted by earlier traumas); "overpowering" narratives, where one can describe past events but continue to feel buried in that original experience; and in a "witnessed narrative," wherein an observant distance and perspective is maintained in the narrative voice even when describing overpowering events (Laub and Auerhahn 295, 297–98). Trauma texts incorporate these different forms and levels of awareness. Writers have created a number of narrative strategies to represent a conflicted or incomplete relation to memory, including textual gaps (both in the page layout and content), repetition, breaks in linear time, shifting viewpoints, and a focus on visual images and affective states.

Producing these narratives is difficult because traumatic memory is often "wordless and static," and the survivor's "initial account . . . may

multiple subjects are the consequence of defensive dissociation from painful memories but help to reformulate identity and desire in a distinctive narrative

be repetitious, stereotyped and emotionless" (Herman 175). Accordingly, writers create such effects with repeated words, phrases, or motifs that are narratively dissociative but affectively overdetermined. Morrison, Kincaid, and Duras, for instance, employ repetitive sentence structures and re-create fixed ideas for their traumatized characters particularly when they lose connection with others. In a traumatic context repetition can be an attempt to attack one's own fears, as in Cholly's rape of Pecola in *The Bluest Eye*, but it can also be a sign of being caught in stasis, of not being able to move on and resolve the initial trauma (Vickroy, "Politics" 99–100). Pecola's compulsion to repeat begins after her rape, in conversations with her imaginary friend and with obsessive but ineffectual self-questioning about what happened with her father—"He just tried, see? He didn't do anything. You hear me?" (Morrison, *The Bluest Eye* 154). Her imaginary dialogue expresses a desperate need to be believed, to understand, and yet to forget and deny— a complex response common in trauma victims (Lifton, 1991 Interview 162–63). In *The Vice-Consul*, Duras's beggar acts in a similarly repetitive fashion; as she leaves each of her newborn children, she repeats her own abandonment. Moreover, she continually repeats the name of her village, "Battambang," signifying a desire to return home to her mother and to the past (46, 48–49). Thereby Duras demonstrates to readers how reenactment and repetition replace memory for the severely traumatized. Similarly, Kincaid's narrator frequently verbalizes the loss of her mother.

The ability to symbolize—to create metaphors, for example—involves a recognition of differentiation and is associated with the processes of separation and individuation a child goes through in the first months of life: "Symbols are created in the internal world as a means of . . . recapturing . . . the original object" but are not equated with this object (Segal, "Notes" 55). Sigmund Freud noted that symbolization brings at least the illusion of control and mastery after observing his grandson's "fort/da" spool game that represented his mother's comings and goings. Later, object relations theorists Melanie Klein and D. W. Winnicott established use of symbols as crucial to the formation of an individual's relation to the world and to the interchange between external reality and personal psychic reality—symbolism, fantasy, and imagining are all important to self-construction ("Importance of Symbol Formation" 97–98; *Playing and Reality* 96–97). Jacques Lacan points out the ambivalence of entering the symbolic realm, as culture and language can work at cross-purposes with the self. In a postcolonial context, for example, individuals face the unique problems of living within two or more cultures.

Disturbed symbolization processes emerge out of poor early object relations, trauma, or other psychic upheavals, where the individual never develops or loses the ability to distinguish between inner and outer reality. Such disturbances are indicated in individuals' use of symbolic equations, which indicate a defensive fusion between self and object, or object and symbol. "Symbolic equation is used to deny the separateness between the subject and object [while the true] symbol is used to overcome an accepted loss" (Segal, "On Symbolism" 316). "Representation depends on separation" says psychoanalyst Juliette Mitchell, and "traumatized or . . . hysterical thinking, which I will call 'literal thinking,' is a process of consubstantiation . . . it is as though the bread and wine are equated with the body and blood" ("Trauma" 129). This happens because exposure to trauma involves "speechless terror" due to the fact that it is not organized or coded on a linguistic level but rather on a "somato-sensory or iconic level: as somatic sensations, behavioral reenactments, nightmares and flashbacks" (Van der Kolk and Van der Hart 442–43). Therefore, this information "cannot be easily translated into the symbolic language necessary for linguistic retrieval" (443). Physiological arousal also causes trauma victims to "immediately access sights, sounds and smells related to earlier traumatic events" (445).

The capacity for metaphor (separation of signifier and object) is related to ego integrity and boundaries, which can be broken down in traumatic circumstances (Grubrich-Simitis 305–7). In addition, symptoms of cognitive and emotional stasis and an inability to integrate the traumatic event with other memories can cause regression to earlier modes of symbolization, disturbing the recognition of symbols as differentiated, or metaphorical. With the decreased ability to separate one association with another, random exposure to anything remotely associated with a trauma could return the victims to that experience; for example, fog may recall a fire (Garland 111). Victims become obsessed with any associations that can be linked to the trauma, even if they exist within different contexts. This recalls the omnipotent thinking common to early stages of life, where self and object are still so inseparable that particular elements (words, images) become overdetermined, as in dreams where one element can be traced to multiple psychic causes. "Traumatic language is a verbal version of the visual language of dreams . . . [expressing] feeling rather than of meaning" (Mitchell, "Trauma" 132). Fiction writers indicate these obsessions in relation to character identity situations. For example, blackness and death/birth are equated in Kincaid's *Autobiography of My Mother;* a daughter's face becomes her father's face (that is, her mother's rapist's face) in *Breath, Eyes, Memory;* and mother's milk is a multidimensional symbol of nurturing and traumatic violation in *Beloved.*

Survivors' painful connection to past trauma is also displayed and replayed through the body, even branded into their flesh. In Heinemann's *Paco's Story,* Paco's scars are described as appearing alive, seeming "to wiggle and curl . . . the way many a frightful thing in this world comes alive in the dimmest, whitest moonlight" (171). This description suggests that his scars express horrors that remain largely hidden and unspoken, such as his narrow escape from death in a horrific barrage of air strike bombs and artillery fire. As with Sethe's lash scars in *Beloved,* the full implications of Paco's scars, as traumatic memories, are not fully available to their owner, and it is essential that what they signify be interpreted and understood by others as part of a collective mourning and healing process these writers feel is urgently needed.

Characters' scars become both connecting points and obstacles to potentially intimate or sexual relations, drawing others' sympathy until the agony that underlies them becomes overwhelming. Paul D tries to comfort Sethe by kissing her "tree," in effect saying "I share your wounds." He "rubbed his cheek on her back and learned that way her sorrow, the roots of it; its wide trunk and intricate branches" (17). Eventually her suffering and desperate action (Beloved's murder) horrify and overwhelm him. In *Paco's Story,* a young woman, Cathy, imagines Paco taking off his scars and laying them on her. She senses that Paco wants to share what has wounded him, and she is terrified and repelled by the prospect. Like most of the civilians in the novel, she seems incapable of understanding Paco's torments or the war context. Heinemann wants to put his readers in connection with what he realizes is alien to most of us. This sharing of scars expresses a desire for collective acknowledgment and understanding in both texts. Trauma writers make the suffering body the small, focused universe of the tormented and a vehicle for rendering unimaginable experience tangible to readers.

Some trauma narratives work from traces of memory and history, not positing full reconstruction but rather elaborating the dynamic relationship between individual and collective memory. In creating *Beloved*, Morrison focused on what was undeveloped in the nineteenth-century slave narratives, that is, slavery's effects on the inner lives of survivors. Morrison's narrative is structured on traumatic experience through characters' fragmented memories, their sensory and bodily responses, and by foregrounding testimonial voices and emotional immediacy unavailable in historical analysis. Thus she engages in a struggle to bear witness, despite what she regards as a "national amnesia" about slavery, wanting readers to confront slavery "in the flesh" (qtd. in Darling) with the character Beloved, who seems to represent, among other things, Sethe's tragic relationship to the past and collective suffering under slavery. Through the links in Beloved's consciousness, Morrison expresses a distorted and disjunctive sense of time typical of traumatic response, and by association we are exposed to collective and ancestral trauma. Beloved's simple litany of facts and desires resonates with historical, collective, and personal reverberations that have to be reconstructed by readers. Although it is not a history she can possess, her fragmented account offers powerfully suggestive impressions from which readers can contemplate the immediate realities of suffering on slave ships.

Beloved demonstrates that rethinking history through trauma does not bring comprehensive knowledge, because although trauma is often experienced communally, it also fragments memory and identity, thereby alienating individuals from their own experience and from others. With Beloved's monologue, Morrison creates an unfinished, repetitious, and emotionally distant narrative, distinct from fully realized stories, which gives her audience another perspective from which to reconsider a traumatic past. The nature of these narratives encourages readers to become more aware, to adopt a new consciousness of history, even if it is one that is fragmented, ambivalent, and at times inconclusive.

These histories must be recognized because traumatic contexts are radically different from those in which we expect ethical standards and notions of choice. Victims are often blamed for being complicit or co-operating with their abusers. True complicity, however, is only valid in situations where choices are possible (Herman 116; Langer, *Testimonies* 124). Individuals' actions under extreme oppression, whether in a domestic or war situation, cannot be understood by applying normalized values or moral systems. Rather than leading us to judge these individuals, trauma narrativists immerse us in individual experiences of terror, arbitrary rules, and psychic breakdown so that we might begin to appreciate these situations. These writers explore the problematics of action in coercive circumstances that seem impossible or unbelievable to outsiders and demonstrate that the standards by which these events can be measured and judged have to extend beyond the fact-based logic of historical inquiry or the myths of humanism. Many of the characters portrayed struggle with experiences of dehumanization so raw that holding onto their humanity becomes a precarious and conflicted process, and inevitably an ambivalent sense of identity and conscience arise out of such traumatic contexts, where humans were daily reduced to animal or object status. Lawrence Langer asserts that living in these extreme situations means lying outside moral systems (*Testimonies* 125) as victims are only allowed "a choice between impossibilities" (*Admitting* 44). Emblematic of such impossible contexts, Sethe (like her historical counterpart Margaret Garner) is placed in a situation where she feels she must kill her children to maintain their human integrity.

As with testimony, trauma narratives serve an important function; they similarly appeal to a community of readers (Agger and Jensen 116; Felman and Laub 204). Public mourning and narrativizing of complex and difficult experience is necessary because of the victims' limitations in speaking and because of collective repression. As Tal, Herman, Horvitz, and others point out, social/political institutions and agendas inflict or exacerbate trauma, so public knowledge is essential to changing this situation. What Tal names the "literatures of trauma" re-create that experience to "make it real both to victims and to the community"; storytelling is a personal and collective "reconstitutive" act (21). Trauma writers urge readers to become empathic witnesses to testimony such that they can recognize and perhaps transmit information dulled by time and repression and thereby revise their own assumptions. These writers also acknowledge a responsibility to reveal the uncertainties, complexities, and paradoxes of telling and to recognize that traumatic experience is driven by alienating and terrifying aspects of it that resist speech, resolutions, and categories of analysis more common to normal contexts. Readers are challenged to enter into a multifaceted examination of the past that is a dynamic, uncertain, and always-unfinished process, one that recontextualizes traditional historical, psychological, and narrative boundaries. Chapter 2 brings this project into a more specific focus by examining these recontextualizations in colonized situations where trauma texts focus on mothers and daughters facing obstacles of poverty, sexual exploitation, and class and race prejudice.

SUBJUGATION, NURTURANCE, AND LEGACIES OF TRAUMA

S ituations of subjection and colonization have fostered many of the conditions for feelings of hopelessness and helplessness that create trauma. Investigating trauma in these specific contexts can be a valuable focus of inquiry, indicative of the sociocultural contexts or causes of trauma and of the interconnections between the social environment and intimate relationships. A psychology of oppression emerges from these dehumanizing and conflicted situations, wherein a process of internalizing oppression brings about social and psychic manifestations of trauma, such as emotional restriction, fragmented or split identity, dissociation, and problems with self-knowledge. Symptoms of trauma are common where overwhelming pressures to become subordinate or to assimilate compel cultures and interests to clash violently, often sacrificing the integrity of the individual and family to social expectations. Although cultural and economic contexts may differ, situations of subjugation manifest similarities in the structures, workings, and effects of domination as well as in the psychological effects on the individuals involved.

For postcolonial era theorists and fiction writers, post–World War II definitions of "the colonized" have "expanded considerably to include women, subjugated and oppressed classes, national minorities, and even marginalized or incorporated academic subspecialities" (Said 207). Another important conceptual expansion of colonialism involves situations where relations of domination and subordination still prevail, which is often the case in situations of trauma, and in particular focus here, domestic situations troubled by oppressive social circumstances (Moane 10–12). To what extent are domination and subordination absorbed into the dynamics of personal relationships? Is there reproduction of a social dominant in the family, one that seeks to impinge, define, silence? Does the mother take on this role when pressed to the limits of her endurance? Further, as the psychological consequences of oppression are passed on to children, legacies of trauma become occasions for repetitions of domination in postcolonial contexts.

A powerful context for examining the traumatic consequences of living in colonized situations is domestic space and the relations between mothers and children therein. If, as Homi Bhabha suggests, postcolonial domestic space can be a place of historical invasion—where home and world meet, conflict, and become confused (e.g., mother/child relations can be emblematic of public/private rifts [*Location* 9])—analysis of the dynamics within such spaces can provide a useful pathway into understanding the key role colonized families play in contemporary trauma narratives. One indicator of a mother's power is her relationship to home and what this place signifies about her relationships to herself, to her children, and to the social realm, as well as the traumatic consequences of her inability to provide or maintain a safe home.

In their complex and multifaceted portrayals of mothers' influence on the socialization and identity formation of children, Toni Morrison, Edwidge Danticat, and Marguerite Duras challenge idealizations of motherhood by emphasizing the social, cultural, and economic forces that mediate nurturing. A mother's role in nurturing and socializing her children is compromised when mechanisms of oppressive control such as violence, economic or sexual exploitation, and cultural/mythological representations of women all limit her options and rights (Moane 39–53). Institutions can appropriate or manipulate nurturing functions, both biological and emotional, as in slavery or in cultural privileging of motherhood over political involvement. These trauma texts enhance and reinforce cultural and social science research on the psychological effects of colonization, which examines how racial, gender, and economic oppression distort the formation of identity and relational bonds. The writers' focus on subjugated mothers illuminates the interdependence between culture and individual circumstances. Such a focus also provides these writers with a forum for reformulating the important and complex position of mothers in this context, demystifying their motivations and presenting them as full subjects deeply conflicted between the social demands of motherhood, their own needs, and their children's well-being. Before discussing the specifics of mothering, I will briefly establish what makes colonized situations traumatic.

The Situation of Colonization

Morrison's, Danticat's, and Duras's narratives create alternative cultural histories from the perspectives of individuals forgotten or silenced by force or repression. All three writers seek redress in giving voices to the colonized; from their own histories each seems to carry with them some personal stake in exposing a traumatic past. Their work exemplifies what many postcolonial theorists have concluded: that the colonized who face physical or psychic violence are also denied agency, control, and even identity within their own cultural spaces. Moreover, the daily stress of deprivation, neglect, and belittlement makes the colonial situation a traumatic one.[1] Morrison describes a colonized situation as living "a way of life dreamed up for us by some other people who are at the moment in power." She thus urges all black writers to be aware of "what the enemy forces are [behind this way of life] . . . and knowing the ways in which it can be subverted" (Davis interview 146). Morrison grew up in the segregated America of the 1930s and 1940s that devalued and endangered African American lives, history, and culture. Living in colonial Indochina her first eighteen years, Duras also developed a strong sense of subjugating forces and was keen throughout her career to bear witness to injustices experienced by her family and social and political outcasts of every sort who have been denied a voice. In *The North China Lover* (1991) she declares her lifelong need to "write . . . my mother's life. How they did her in" (88). Danticat writes of the consequences and legacies of women living under the brutal postcolonial regime of François (Papa Doc) Duvalier in Haiti, learning of this time from the stories passed among family members, told to alleviate their pain and in coded form to avoid political oppression (Wachtel interview 112–13).

Several elements mark the situation of colonization as a traumatic one; each of these can induce the feelings of powerlessness and hopelessness that incite traumatic reactions. First, if the identity of the colonized is devalued (racially, culturally, etc.), it can become split or conflicted, whereby they may adopt the colonizers' definitions of themselves or absorb colonizers' identities (Fanon, *Black Skin* 143–44; Memmi, *Dominated* 86; Nandy 19–21). Second, a similar devaluing of the culture of the conquered proceeds until it is virtually forgotten or replaced with that of the colonizer (Fanon, *Wretched* 170; Nandy 19–21). Third, the colonized are reified or generalized into a collectivity rather than recognized as individuals by the dominant group (Memmi, *Colonizer* 85), a recognition these fiction writers clearly emphasize by focusing on individual lives and feelings. Fourth, as colonizers claim all rights to subjective agency, they claim all positions of responsibility and usefulness in the infrastructures of the countries they inhabit (this can also be said of much of the history of African Americans in the United States). Thus they prevent the colonized from being significant actors in the social or political realm and consequently from the historical process (Juneja 1, 3). Fifth, colonizers deny the colonized social involvement by imposing on them strict rules of conduct, harsh treatment, employing violence and more severe application of the laws, minimizing their influence on their history or their communities (Memmi, *Colonizer* 91–92). In short, in order "to subdue and exploit, the colonizer pushed the colonized out of the historical, social, cultural and technical current" (114).

The psychological process of internalization makes possible the personal absorption of social directions and reinforces patterns of domination. Internalization, wherein one incorporates an aspect of another into oneself, is based upon maintaining a duality within the psyche wherein others' wishes are brought into the ego and are acted upon as self-generated but are actually coerced or assigned by others. These "directives" or workings of internalization occur largely within the family, from whom we receive our instructions through attribution: We are told what we are like and ordered to do what *they* want in a way that makes us think it is what *we* want. Such is the process by which our desires are often constructed. Moreover, we can be induced to "become" someone others need us to be (Laing 78). R. D. Laing also asserts that families do not acknowledge individual members on their own terms but give them a "range of distinctions, options, identities, definitions, rules, repertoires of operations, instructions, attributions, loci, scenarios, roles, parts to play . . ." (121). Laing theorizes here an important connection between internalization and domination evolving within family situations. The process is usually subtle; it is often the unspoken rules, assumptions, and expectations that have the strongest hold on us. Nancy Chodorow posits that the influence of the "outside" is mediated through intrapsychic processes such as fantasy, ambivalence, conflict, substitution, distortion, splitting, association, compromise, denial, and repression (47). Therefore, the forces regulating our beliefs and behavior may be distortions of reality, mediated desires, creations born out of conflict, subordination, trauma, or the desire to please another for fear of abandonment (47).

Interpreting Theodore Adorno's work on authoritarianism, Jessica Benjamin links internalization to the process of domination and subordination, recognizing that as part of the identification process we internalize the values of those who seek to dominate or teach us ("Internalization" 44). Internalization precludes the idea of intersubjectivity, which presupposes both separation and connection between interacting subjects, where one could absorb part of another to help his or her own functioning. Internalization has a more absolute and disconnective function: One is either absorbed and same, or different and other (Bonds 43–45). Internalization can be a devastatingly traumatizing process if one is not validated as a separate, acting individual. Internal learning processes and self-perceptions become so ingrained as to create permanently destructive self-definitions, self-divisions, and ways of interacting.

Morrison demonstrates how dominant interests are internalized within family relationships, particularly between mothers and daughters. She illustrates how mothers, deprived of their own identities, become agents of culture, ideology, and personal history, and subsequently pass these interests on to their daughters. In The Bluest Eye, African Americans internalize denigrating gender, class, and racial designations that endanger their own cultural identities and at times destroy their relations to one another. This process illustrates what John Brenkman calls the social mediation of the ego: As human interaction is reified in particular social systems, so also is the constitution of subjectivity (169). In Morrison's works, mothers must contend with their own appropriation or devaluation, creating a conflict for them between reacting to social expectations and constructively interacting with their children.

In *The Bluest Eye*, Pecola's mother, Pauline Breedlove, is the most prominent example of a life dominated by internalization and its consequences. She continually defines herself through others' attributions; viewed as an outsider in her family, she becomes dependent on her husband Cholly's desires to define her identity and even her desires. When he disappoints her she then turns to God and to the wishes of whites, who dominate her thoughts through popular culture and the social and economic empowerment she gains in their employ. She has no identity to offer Pecola other than her own feelings of unworthiness, which Pecola absorbs through her mother's neglect and rejections. Eventually Pecola splits from her own black identity and longs for a white identity (or rather the love and recognition she believes this would bring) much as her mother does.[2]

In *The Bluest Eye*, Morrison critiques both white cultural dominance and black complicity.[3] Abdellatif Khayati asserts that in this early text Morrison presents an unyielding "binary division between the dominant values of American consumer culture and the suppressed values of black Americans," whereas in a later text like *Beloved*, she finds some room to affirm racial identity despite oppressive circumstances (315). She portrays 1930s American white culture as colonizing black Americans to the extent that valuing black identity or black beauty was impossible, so blacks internalized an idealized white identity, becoming alienated from their own being and consciousness, much as Fanon describes among West Indian children. Even young black girls learned to hate their own reflections and to value popular images of white beauty and prosperity through dolls and escapist films celebrating class and racial hierarchies that portray blacks only as servants. Furthermore, these racial attitudes create a hierarchy within the black community; light skin is admired and dark despised. This message is absorbed by the protagonist, Pecola, in her wish for blue eyes. Moreover, identity also becomes distorted from identification with members of the dominant group.

Seeking identification with a powerful other creates "an image of identity and the transformation of the subject in assuming that image" (Bhabha, "Remembering Fanon" 117). Pauline acquires an improved self-image by acting from a powerful position in serving her white employers. Her individual and racial identity worn down (through familial neglect, an abusive marriage, and feelings of inferiority because of her lower social and racial status), Pauline's passionate embrace of domestic duties in her employers' house helps her adopt a more forceful if false identity. "Pauline kept this order, this beauty, for herself, a private world, and never introduced it into her storefront, or to her children. Them she bent toward respectability and in doing so taught them fear: fear of being clumsy, fear of being like their father, fear of not being loved by God . . . Into her son she beat a loud desire to run away, and into her daughter she beat a fear of growing up, fear of other people, fear of life" (101–2). Pauline tries to instill subordination in her children so they will take on similar defenses and false identities. She enacts the white/black, master/subordinate roles in her own family.

Like Nandy and Fanon, Morrison recognizes that resistance can only take effect when the colonized become aware of how their own identities and cultural legacies have been replaced with those of the dominant culture. Morrison denounces false desires alien to African Americans and makes readers aware of the processes of cultural coercion by speaking through her principal narrator, Claudia, a young girl who, before she becomes socialized, maintains a healthy narcissism. For example, Claudia resists white standards of beauty by hating the white doll her parents give her. Significantly, dolls are important transitional objects in children's development as well as ways culture is inculcated through the family. Claudia's resentment of this object, despite its valuation by adults, and her desire for loving attention and sensual experience on her birthday highlight the idea that such a false idol must be imposed. Claudia also later describes the socialization process by which she learns to assimilate and like Shirley Temple. Though a critical voice, Morrison does not offer adult paths of resistance through Claudia. This novel is Morrison's strongest critique of how African Americans were psychologically coerced to absorb standards that were personally and culturally oppressive and, worse, passed on to their children.

Ashis Nandy argues that in order to resist powerful systems like colonialism, one must recognize one's own complicity with these systems. Strong pressures exist to conform to the dominant culture, and the costs have been high both for cooperation (internalization of the dominant culture) and for refusal (repressive measures). Nandy rejects the notion of hopeless victims of colonialism, yet also recognizes a psychological state wherein shared codes and secondary gains are established from living under colonialism as the rulers set the psychological parameters for relations. Like Fanon, Nandy sees an identification with aggressors and even emulation of them (7).

In *The Bluest Eye* and *Song of Solomon* (1977), Morrison enacts struggles between co-opted and authentic characters that demonstrate Nandy's observations. Characters who embrace behavior consonant with racial and social hierarchies, materialist and superficial standards, all of which Morrison associates with white culture, are portrayed as unhappy, repressed, and inauthentic. Pauline, Geraldine, and other mothers embrace racial and class hierarchies that cause them to reject others in their community (e.g., viewing the dysfunctional and dark-skinned Breedloves as "trash") and to deny their own cultural identity for a comfortable place in the social pecking order. Conversely, Claudia, who feels empathy and pity for Pecola and does not reject her because she is expecting her father's child, says, "I felt a need for someone to want the black baby [Pecola's] to live—just to counteract the universal love of white baby dolls, Shirley Temples . . ." (148). In *Song of Solomon*, authenticity is measured in the difference between Macon Dead and his sister, Pilate. Macon embraces interests that alienate him from his people; he builds his fortune as a harsh landlord, evicting poor blacks when they cannot pay and ignoring their problems. His coldness extends to his home as well; he neglects his wife and daughters, solely preoccupied with money, social status, and passing his legacy on to his son. Pilate, however, not only helps Macon's son, Milkman, recover his family's history, his identity, and his humanity, but she lives freely and spontaneously, rejecting materialism, name-brand standards of beauty, and social conventions. A nurturing yet free individual, Pilate is a liberating departure from the circumscribed lives of the more assimilated characters.

Colonizers must also play a role in any movement toward liberation from colonization, because they are also caught up in a culture of oppression (Nandy 63). The oppressed often sacrifice their identity and culture, but colonizers also suffer under their own pathology and dehumanization. Morrison's portrayals of racists and slave owners reflects her concern with what oppressors lose while objectifying others: "[T]he trauma of racism is, for the racists and the victim, the severe fragmentation of the self, and has always seemed to me a cause (not a symptom) of psychosis—strangely of no interest to psychiatry" ("Unspeakable" 16).

Her portrait of the slave master, Schoolteacher, who embodies the "white supremacist capitalist patriarch" (Keizer 107) in *Beloved,* emphasizes his dissociation from his own inhuman behavior, apparent in his comparisons of his slaves to animals, measuring his ability to train and punish them as he would any useful farm animal. "Schoolteacher's divisive logic and pseudo-empirical scientism is an example of what Morrison considers to be the language of control and surveillance with his monopolistic learning, his ruthless will to mute the suffering of others, and his arrogant rationalism. Schoolteacher seeks to fix others into inferiority and helplessness, to use their bodies as a free labor force, in order to preserve his privilege" (Khayati 320). Morrison explores the rationalizations of someone who completely denies his own responsibility as she initially presents the scene of Sethe's attempt to murder her children from Schoolteacher's perspective, with no true understanding of what he sees, bearing false witness to what leads Sethe to such desperate action (i.e., preserving her children's humanity). "But now she'd gone wild, due to the mishandling of the nephew who'd overbeat her and made her cut and run. Schoolteacher had chastised that nephew, telling him to think—just think—what would his own horse do if you beat it beyond the point of education. . . . What she go and do that for?" (149–50)

To have such power over other human lives destroys the humanity of the powerful as well, distancing them from other humans and from their own feelings. Duras and Danticat also portray a similar distancing from the horrors that surround them. Duras's British and French colonials try to repress or deny the poverty and misery surrounding them in India but must absorb it as they suffer traumatic symptoms themselves. The Haitian Ton Ton Macoutes whom Danticat describes cope with the atrocities they are ordered to commit by objectifying others or in repression, but they also diminish their own capacity to think and to feel. The rapists "double" or dissociate, much as the victims do. "This was the only way they could murder and rape so many people and still go home to play with their children and make love to their wives" (*Breath* 156). Colonizers are "camouflaged victims, at an advanced stage of psychosocial decay," says Nandy (xv–xvi), a point illustrated often by trauma writers who reveal the detrimental effects to perpetrators as well as victims.[4]

Morrison also considers the mentality of powerful whites who adopt a stance of "benevolent" paternalism despite their emotional distance. In their positions of mastery, whites assume they have the right answers for their black underlings even in the most personal aspects of their lives. Paternalism was a key element in the rationalizations for slavery, which Morrison notes in her portrayal of Schoolteacher in *Beloved*, thinking of Sethe and her family as "people who needed every care and guidance in the world to keep them from the cannibal life they preferred" (151). Are these presumptions of ownership or parental license held by the powerful partially internalized by powerless mothers, as Mary Jane Suero Elliot and other critics have observed? Morrison speaks of the "outrageous claim" of a slave woman to think of her children as her own (Bragg interview), to act as if they were hers, and in her portrayal of Sethe, she will suggest a loving if destructive concept of ownership.

Another important component of the colonial mentality, a strong sense of privilege based on race or ethnicity, is examined in several of Duras's novels set in French Indochina, where she grew up in the 1920s and 1930s. In *The Sea Wall*, greed dominates the corrupt French officials, described as vampires, who control the sale of the land, cheating natives and even their fellow colonists. Duras more fully explores the colonial mind-set in her portrayals of her elder brother and the Chinese lover in *The Lover*, a later, much altered version of the story in *The Sea Wall*. The brother's pathology arises in part out of his thwarted sense of privilege; as a French colonial he does not deserve to be poor. Duras mirrors the evils of this sense of colonial superiority in her brother's deterioration and his lack of humanity; because he cannot enrich himself as a colonist, he feels entitled to exploit those around him, stealing from his family and their servants to support his opium habit, and hating and exploiting the Chinese man, his sister's lover, for being Asian. Duras here demonstrates how dominant assumptions can be absorbed within a family context. For instance, her brother's self-esteem is intertwined with his view of himself as a failed colonizer. His desperate embrace of a powerful role (and the mother's failure to place any limits on him) is an important element of Duras's critique of the connection between power in the sociocultural realm and in the family. The rest of the family, primarily the younger brother, become victims of his selfish tyranny.

Psychological assessments of the nature of dominion have been invaluable to understanding the complex interconnections between the actors involved. As Fanon has contended, psychological functioning is not simply innate or prewired, but a force that works dynamically in cultural, racial, economic, and political circumstances (*Black Skin* 85–86). Many social and psychological theorists who have considered the nature of power have pointed to the family, particularly the mother/child relationship, as the locus of the dynamics of social and personal life.[5] These dynamics are enacted through mothers' socializing influence on children, which is always mediated and structured by social forces. In the remainder of this chapter I discuss mothering, its optimal situations, and its distortions under colonization. Separate sections on Morrison, Danticat, and Duras examine how these writers depict the difficulties of nurturance in extreme circumstances, mothers' resistance, and the loving but conflicted relations between mothers and daughters that result.

Mothers, Sociocultural Influences, and Nurturing

Human development theories that emphasize the cultural influences on mothers and children are most helpful for understanding mothering in colonized contexts. Object relations theorists posit that the most productive model for motherly nurturing and development of a secure, well-adjusted child is one where early, strong relational bonds enable the child to form an identity within culture. A strong need for attachment is a primary human motivation, and the mother is often the object of early crucial attachments (Greenberg and Mitchell 221). She acts as a safe psychic container, helping the child to fantasize, imagine, remember, and in short, process his or her experience of the world before taking it on (Ingham 106).

Micro and macro analyses of children's individual and social development affirm the social construction of subjectivity from birth. Recent studies of infants by Daniel Stern, T. Berry Brazelton, Colwyn Trevarthen, and others indicate that intersubjectivity is always part of the parent/child interaction; infants are never totally undifferentiated from their mothers—the two are never completely symbiotic. The most

striking discovery made by Brazelton and his associates in observing relations between infants and mothers was that "no actor's behavior was
ever independent of the expectancy of interaction" (69). Even while
learning to be separate or independent, children must play off of the
(m)other. Jacques Lacan also recognized the immediacy of the social
influence on children. From birth, infants are affected by others' "actions, gestures, wishes and intentions that are already imbued with the
symbolic and that occur within the constraints of specific, historically
determined institutions" (152). Lacan described the subject as "radically dependent" on the other: for objects of satisfaction, for conceptions of one's identity, and for the language that makes one's communication with others possible. "The push toward pleasure and the
orientation toward outside reality are both mediated by the relation to
others and to the symbolic. This relation is constitutive of subjectivity
itself" (154).

As the child develops, interactions with others and the environment
continue to gain importance. Psychoanalyst D. W. Winnicott demonstrated the importance of play in such development—especially in interplay—in intimacy and in the discovery of a reliable relationship
with another. The mother's (or primary caregiver's) input is essential to
the development of play and interplay. First, she gives the illusion that
"there is an external reality that corresponds to the infant's own capacity to create" (12). Next, her role is to allow or encourage transitional
spaces for the child, in play and in letting the child achieve a growing
progression of adaptation to less care, greater interaction, and independence with available support. In Winnicott's formulation, the balance
between assertion and recognition in the nurturer/child relationship is
vital to the child's independent development because one's sense of self
depends on response from the other.

Such responses "[make] meaningful the feelings, intentions, and actions of the self," because to recognize can also mean to "affirm, validate, acknowledge, know, accept, understand, empathize, take in, tolerate, appreciate, see, identify with, find familiar . . . love" (Benjamin,
Bonds 12, 15–16). The necessity of all these forms of validation cannot
be overemphasized, according to Jessica Benjamin. The recognition of
our own assertions in a supportive social context is crucial to human
development. A child achieves differentiation in relation to the mother's own autonomy within a particular sociocultural context. Circum-

stances such as poverty, racism, and exploitation become traumatic by virtue of this missing recognition, and traumatization of mothers makes intersubjective nurturance virtually impossible.

Investigations into the nature of dominance evaluate its perpetuation as a product of Western ideologies based on notions of progress, reason, control, and above all, autonomy as the preferable goal of individuation.[6] These notions have created structural dichotomies of the world, such as the dyad of the public and private spheres. Herein, control and autonomy are associated with the public realm, thus promulgating the idea that an independent adult must reject the regressive influence of a powerful mother who represents the private sphere and whose essential care in childhood is no longer applicable to adult life in the public sphere (Chodorow 181; Benjamin, *Bonds* 158–59, 171; Everingham 6; Benhabib 86). The assumptions surrounding our Western notions of rational human agency "inhibit our ability to conceive of the mother as a rational being, a critical agent, while engaged in nurturing activity" (Everingham 7). The belief in the autonomous, independent subject also promotes a misrecognition of connection and constructs a mothering persona that denies mothers' identity and ourselves the knowledge of how our identities are formed in connection with (m)others.

Social as well as personal interests are furthered by maintaining notions of the autonomous individual. For example, postcolonial theorists have noted very similar fantasizing about the colonized and the idealizing of the powerful colonial "father" that Benjamin speaks of with regard to the idea of "omnipotent" mothers. Again, there is the heightened sense of difference, the disidentification with the other, and dichotomies of self and other. Those who need most to dominate others fear most the self-knowledge that includes dependency and connectedness. Worse, they inflict this disconnection on those they oppress by invalidating their subjectivity, acknowledging them only as instrumental to their own gratification or power (Benjamin, "Internalization" 57). Mothers denied power overcompensate with futile assertions of control that, for very different reasons but following patterned learned responses, deny their children's difference.

In colonizing situations mothers are caught within the interconnections between domination, lack of validation, and the destruction of a healthy strong subjectivity. Conscious knowledge is deeply connected to our ability to act on it, and our ability to act effectively in our surroundings depends on the response of others. Even more basically, individuals need the validation of others "in order to experience the truth of their own perceptions" (58). Therefore, the individual's capacity to reason and hold knowledge cannot be separated from the quality and quantity of recognition he or she has received: "Even knowledge cannot be identified with the individual thinking subject, but rather with the collective acting subject" (58). Benjamin emphasizes that it can become a matter of sanity or madness if one's perception of reality is made ineffectual by threat of punishment or if one's need to be validated is suppressed or ignored (58).

Mothers are vulnerable to losing self-knowledge in oppressive mothering contexts as they embrace the identity of satisfying others' needs over their own and are forbidden to express their anger or individuality (Moane 60). This is particularly true in cases of trauma, where others' acknowledgment is essential to healing. Unmet needs will manifest in alienated emotional responses such as anger, submission, madness, or trauma. Trauma is the ultimate consequence of the invalidation of self and self-knowledge, which is manifested in restrictive defenses like repression, silence, and dissociation. Because mothers like Sethe or the mother in *The Sea Wall* are continually denied their point of view or status as subjects in oppressive systems, their limited scope of action becomes destructive to themselves and to their children. Faced with returning to slavery, Sethe reacts violently and harms her children. Duras's mother becomes so traumatized by her defeats that she is unable to nurture her own children. And Martine's ability to nurture is distorted, even aborted, by her violent rape in *Breath, Eyes, Memory* (see discussions below).

Morrison, Duras, and Danticat express empathy and ambivalence about the fantasy of the all-powerful mother who reigns in infancy and must later be rejected by demonstrating its extremities and shortcomings (Benjamin, "Omnipotent" 140, *Bonds* 188; Dinnerstein 109, 245). In their maternal portrayals, as their characters place excessive expectations on themselves as mothers, these authors confront our fears about the mother's omnipotent role. Yet they also examine the realities that deny these characters, and women historically, social power. Their mothers' adoption of the omnipotent role is socially imposed by virtue of their sole caretaker status and by their social marginalization, and their assertions of power are fraught with contradictions because of their limited ability to act alone under oppressive circumstances. Assuming a single identity with their children, they act on their behalf, but the children often suffer physical or emotional harm from their mothers' resistance to oppressive forces. The three writers clearly admire mothers who resist and challenge their circumstances, and thus their characterizations indicate a need to extend principles of nurturing beyond the family context. They also concede, however, that mothers bear enormous guilt for not being able to save their children from adversity. This is a critical dilemma for mothers; in coercive circumstances, embrace of the omnipotent role can bring traumatic consequences.

Social and psychological theorists caution us not to accept the family system as a natural structure, but as socially mediated, absorbing, and perpetuating ideologies that reinforce social and economic structures.[7] For example, culture and families are common media for perpetuating "prejudices, fears, resentments from which few children emerge wholly uncontaminated . . . racism . . . [can be] as intimate a part of the child's familial and social upbringing as the milk he sucks in infancy" (Memmi, *Dominated* 198). Patterns of domination (for example, sexual, racial, and parental) are sustained by deeply held values learned within emotional contexts that make them particularly difficult to dislodge. Social interests and hierarchies are perpetuated by the socializing function of the family, wherein they are unconsciously absorbed and seemingly autonomously held. Similarly, notions of motherhood that promulgate maternal instinct and self-sacrifice are imposed cultural ideals used to justify social inequality and keep women as exclusive child-rearers (Barrett and McIntosh 27).

Ideologies favoring a patriarchal, nuclear structure of family life have ignored the mother's important role as cultural agent in socializing children. Sociologist Christine Everingham critiques theories of mothering that emphasize it as a "natural," private, and unsocialized activity within patriarchy performed by isolated nurturers who are instrumental in meeting the child's demands. This view, she contends, recognizes neither mothers as separate individuals nor the social nature of mothering (10). Morrison, Danticat, and Duras acknowledge this structure as a fading ideal, often irrelevant to the actualities of many poor or marginal women's lives. Consequently, they seldom depict nuclear families. Fathers are often dead or absent (Boy Boy in *Sula;* Halle Suggs in *Beloved;* Duras's father; the anonymous rapist in *Breath, Eyes, Memory*) and even when present have unproductive relations with their children (Cholly Breedlove loves but rapes his daughter; Macon Dead neglects his children).

These writers share Patricia Hill Collins's perspective on the experience of motherhood in colonized situations, in particular, minority women's experience. Such experience brings them closer to the "sociocultural concerns of racial ethnic communities" and to public policies that affect them racially, culturally, and economically than it brings them to men (58). For example, mothering has been linked to labor and economic exploitation (as in slavery), to political conquest (for Native American women), and to immigration policies. Women's work is also seen as supporting and benefiting family and community in these other cultures: "This type of motherwork recognizes that individual survival, empowerment, and identity require group survival, empowerment and identity" (59). Studies of mothers and children from other cultures indicate that in extreme poverty, attachments between mothers and children form differently or sometimes not at all.[8]

Pointing out that mutual recognition is essential to healthy nurturance, Jessica Benjamin emphasizes that the mother must have her own independent identity to be able to give the child the recognition it wants and guide its healthy development. She cannot be only a respondent to the child's demands; "she must embody something of the not-me; she must be an independent other who responds in her different way" (*Bonds* 24). If the mother or other primary caretaker(s) cannot offer enough of the "not me," overidentifications (e.g., mother = child), internalizations, and unsuccessful interactions will develop between the child and this caretaker and will affect relationships later in life as well.

But what if her social subordination problematizes the mother asserting or even having a sense of her own "otherness" or identity to present to the child or to motivate her own actions? The many competing claims on her—the child's needs, familial, and group pressures or contingencies—create conflicts between being an acting subject and a mother. Actual mothering experience is not consistent with either essentialist notions of autonomous identity or total symbiosis with the child. Rather, it reflects characterizations of modern identity as neces-

sitating many different subject positions and roles. This has special implications in colonized/postcolonial contexts, involving various in-
tercultural connections, conflicts, and positionalities therein (Bhabha,
Location 44–45). Individuals often experience stress based on the tensions between the different socially prescribed roles they adopt (Calhoun 13). "The modern subject is defined by its insertion into a series
of separate value-spheres each one of which tends to exclude or attempts to assert its priority over the rest" (Cascardi 3). Mothers have a
unique set of competing claims, including the expectations of their
own and others' children, other mothers and adults, and their own personal needs and child-rearing ideals (Everingham 32).[9]

Morrison, Danticat, and Duras join many other women writers and
scholars who are exploring and reevaluating how mothers' nurturing
and agency are socially mediated and distorted. Marianne Hirsch views
maternal subjectivity as situationally conflicted: "I see the mother as
doubly 'subjected': she is 'subject to' the institutions of family and maternity as defined by the hegemonic culture, and those institutions in
turn 'subject' her to the needs, demands, and desires both of the culture
itself and of the child whom she rears to become subject to that culture
in his or her own right" ("Maternity" 94). Even if they are powerless in
a public context, however, mothers are allowed a powerful position
within the family. As biological and psychological nurturers, they can
wield the power of life and death. Adrienne Rich describes the dual role
of mothers, where

> the helplessness of the child confers a certain narrow kind of power
> on the mother everywhere—a power she may not desire, but also of-
> ten a power which may compensate to her for her powerlessness
> everywhere else. The power of the mother is, first of all, to give or
> withhold nourishment and warmth, to give or withhold survival it-
> self. Nowhere else . . . does a woman possess such literal power over
> life and death. And it is at this moment that her life is most closely
> bound to the child's, for better or worse, and when the child, for bet-
> ter or worse, is receiving its earliest impressions. (52)

A mother's, or family's, specific relationship to the social context is
crucial in shaping mothering choices. Women's social and economic
status are deeply connected to their mothering duties, and ideologies of
materialism and dominance are already "entrenched in the internal dy-

namics of the family" (Fraser 51). Issues of race and class also strongly influence the conditions of mothering: "Racial domination and economic exploitation profoundly shape the mothering context not only for racial ethnic women in the U.S. but for all women" (Collins 56). Trauma writers strongly critique the way material deprivation has ravaged the lives of mothers and children. In their works they are responding to a profoundly important social issue, as women and children suffer the worst of the world's poverty.[10]

Morrison's Deadly Mothers

Morrison's novels *Sula* and *Beloved* particularly attend to mothers' difficult and conflicted situations, providing a compelling examination of the extent to which the sociocultural context affects the mother's ability to act and the nature of intimate relationships with their children. In these two novels, we witness mothers' passionate love for their children channeled into murderous acts. From such distorted misrenderings of love arise many questions. First, what compels a mother's will to dominate and its accompanying destructiveness? Second, to what degree is it in the nature of our conceptions of love, particularly mother-love, to refuse boundaries and to assume one can speak for or act on behalf of the other who is the object of one's love? And further, what traumatic environmental influences provoke distortions of mothering and foster the passage of traumatic legacies on to children? *Sula* and *Beloved* address these questions by pointing to the social controls dominating mothers' lives.

In Morrison's fiction the intimate love between African American mothers and their children is often infiltrated by oppressive forces. Slavery, racism, and poverty dominate the circumstances of these black families, creating psychic distortions and trauma that damage their relationships. The once-protective love of mothers like Eva Peace in *Sula* and Sethe in *Beloved* becomes desperate and possessive in a hostile environment. As mediators between their children and the world, these mothers experience a "double identity" or "self-division," wherein their ambivalent relationship to the world affects their motherly roles (Hirsch 421). This division or splitting (within the self or between self and environment) is typical of the psychology of oppression and of socially induced trauma, as mechanisms of domination such as violence and economic or sexual exploitation restrict individuals from full participation in social and personal life, alienating them from their own experience or self-knowledge (Moane 39–53, 61–62). Their children become unintentional victims of Eva's and Sethe's resistance to oppression. When threatened, they act on their children's behalf, assuming the children would share their desires or agree to their solutions. This assumption has its basis partially in mother/child symbiosis, mothers' unique physical bond to their children, and their embrace of motherhood, which all overshadow mothers' individual self-identification (Moane 59). Their actions, however, also suggest overidentification, a failure to see their children and themselves as separate. The mothers' need to act, to protect their children from what they believe is worse than death, entitles them to the power of life and death, they believe. For both characters this combination of symbiosis and the traumatic intervention of social forces makes their intense love destructive (Vickroy, "Force Outside" 29).

The conflicted interests of the motherly role are evident in the many parallels between Eva and Sethe; each is absorbed by forces beyond her control, and each ends up harming her children in trying to protect them. They are compelled to make unilateral decisions concerning their children's lives in circumstances so adverse any action could have tragic consequences. However, textual evidence and Morrison's own statements suggest that despite good intentions, these mothers victimize their children and appropriate their rights. Each mother murders one of her four children. The murders are the consequence of excessive identification between mother and children; however, it is also evident that overidentification becomes destructive *because* it is locked into a culturally based trauma.

Vowing to resist her desperate poverty after her husband Boy Boy deserts her, Eva leaves her children with neighbors and returns eighteen months later with considerable money but missing one leg. Although she has given up part of herself, she has taken control of her own and her children's lives when starvation was the alternative. This, and her attempt to save her daughter Hannah from fire, indicate Eva's willingness to sacrifice herself for them. However, the destructive side of this denial of separation between her and them is apparent when years later she murders her son, Plum, a World War I veteran who escapes his pain with a heroin addiction. She defends her actions to Hannah by explaining that she wanted him to die like a man. However, because she had also dreamt that he wanted to crawl back into her womb, her fears about control, the demands of intimacy, and the forces impinging on these are significant here as well. Even though she rationalizes this as a loving act, she violates his right to live his own life. Morrison herself has said that Eva "played God" in this instance (Syracuse lectures). Eva believes he needs the kind of control over his life with which she has defined her own life—being able to act on her own and others' destinies. Also, her dream is evidence that Eva herself was fearful of Plum's possible violation of her and that he wants to extend his childhood and her role as the nurturing mother. In effect, she desires his separation from her, but not hers from him (Vickroy, "Force Outside" 29–30). Moreover, she denies his war trauma. She cannot bear her own child's helplessness and is therefore closed off from attempting a more healing approach.

Eva is denied the ease of a life allowing mutual recognition and intersubjectivity with her children. This is evident in her reply to her daughter Hannah's question about why she never played with her children. Eva replies that she was too busy making sure they all survived.

Her identification as a powerful mother continues as she extends her mothering capacities in her sprawling house, purchased with the money from her sacrificed leg, where she reigns like a queen over her grown children and takes in orphans. She feels entitled to name all three of the orphan boys Dewey. Eva fulfills her unmet needs in being able to thus name and define their lives in contrast to her early poverty and helplessness. She only realizes her excesses as she accepts Hannah's death as God's punishment for Plum's murder.

Mothers' relative ability or inability to provide a safe, stable home not only illustrates personal traumatic legacies, but also suggests that domination in colonial relations is reenacted between mothers and daughters and that such a home can be a place of traumatic history. The living presence of a dead daughter's ghost in 124, Sethe's home after her escape from slavery (and the farm that the slaves ironically called "Sweet Home"), is indicative of the complex social and emotional baggage symbolized by this domestic space. Contained therein are Sethe's tender reunions and humbling confrontations with a terrifying and horrific past. Her home is a scene of lost love, loneliness, murder—a space of isolation and protection from the outside world. The property of an abolitionist, it is emblematic of Sethe's need to have a home of her own after being owned herself, but it gives her sanctuary from a black community that has become hostile and a place to atone for taking her child's life, even if to save her from returning to slavery. Yet, linking Sethe to an unresolved past, 124 becomes a prison, isolating her daughter Denver from the world as well. Eventually, Sethe allows the house to become an insular, exclusive space where, enmeshed with Beloved, whom she believes to be her reincarnated dead daughter, Sethe accepts the exclusion of the outside world and the diminishment of her life down to "[t]he world is in this room" (183).

Morrison's depictions of mother-love are not singly determined but fraught with irresolvable conflicts and difficulties. As each of these mothers is willing to give, so she asserts the right to take with an intensity that can be murderous and that appears extreme and even "monstrous" to some of the more moderate characters in these novels. Neither mother can acknowledge her children as separate subjects, because they cannot be freely acting subjects themselves. "How can a child see self or mother as subjects when the society denies them that status? The mother is made incapable of recognizing the child, and the child cannot recognize the mother" (Schapiro 197). Mother-love and motherly responsibility are turned into bondage by oppression. For example, when Sethe, the escaped slave mother in *Beloved*, makes the decision to condemn her children to death rather than let them suffer under slavery as she has done, she feels justified to refuse boundaries between her and them; they are, for her, "the best part of her," and it is her responsibility to offer them their fate.

Though it may seem an obvious point, it is necessary to consider the many specific ways slavery often deprived its victims of their individual humanity, their connection to their own cultures, and possible intimate relationships. The claims of slave masters (economic, sexual, etc.) could destroy, among other things, marriages, families, and self-esteem. It caused "social death," or estrangement from everything in life except slavery for slaves on many levels, according to Orlando Patterson (38). This was especially devastating for mothers, whose children were never their own but somebody's property. After the sacrifice of six of her seven children, Baby Suggs scarcely retains a sense of a surviving self or even the point of survival after her last child, Halle, has earned her freedom. "The opportunity to possess subjectivity is squelched at every possible venue as slavery denies Baby Suggs friendship, motherhood, wifehood, sisterhood, and daughterhood" (Holden-Kirwan 422–23). Further, depictions of Sethe and her mother remind readers that sexual and other bodily violations were common practices, and worse, robbed children and mothers of mothering. Deprived of her own mother, Sethe is not nurtured in a way to develop her own sense of individuality. Therefore she adopts an exclusive self-definition as a mother—considering her children as parts of herself—which offers her many consolations. She gains an identity, strength and self-determination, motivation to free her family after Schoolteacher's and the nephews' abuses, and a chance "to compensate for her own motherlessness by being a supermother to her children" (Keizer 112).

Sethe's embrace of the omnipotent mother role is always limited by a mother's status within slavery, which may allow her certain claims to power but may also lock her into an identity that may fulfill her own unmet needs while denying her own and her children's individual separateness. This is evident in Sethe's assertion of her strength and freedom, which become part of her mothering identity once she is freed:

> I did it. I got us all out. Without Halle too. Up till then it was the only thing I ever did on my own. Decided. And it came off right, like it was supposed to. We was here. Each and every one of my babies and me too. I birthed them and I got em out and it wasn't no accident. I did that. I had help, of course, lots of that, but still it was me doing it; me saying, *Go on*, and *Now.* Me having to look out. Me using my own head. But it was more than that. It was a kind of selfishness I never knew nothing about before. It felt good. Good and right. I was big, Paul D, and deep and wide and when I stretched out my arms all my children could get in between. I was *that* wide. Look like I loved em more after I got here. Or maybe I couldn't love em proper in Kentucky because they wasn't mine to love. But when I got here, when I jumped down off that wagon—there wasn't nobody in the world I couldn't love if I wanted to. You know what I mean? (162)

Feeling her strength as an individual and all-powerful nurturer, Sethe succeeds in keeping her children out of slavery but is prepared to sacrifice their lives in the attempt. Carole Boyce Davies believes *Beloved* "simultaneously critiques exclusive mother-love and asserts the necessity for black women to claim something as theirs" (45). That is, by internalizing such a role, Sethe loses her subjecthood beyond mothering and yet paradoxically must adopt this stance to achieve a sense of agency in the face of the dehumanization and objectification she undergoes in slavery.

Sethe adopts an idealized, heroic motherly role with which she resists her own and her children's objectification under slavery, but in the process she also enslaves herself to "the kind of mother-love which the society enforces for women" (Davies 54). Guilt-ridden and seeking forgiveness, Sethe allows Beloved (in Sethe's mind the resurrected child she killed) to dominate her and drain her resources. Sethe wants to become the omnipotent mother who can save her children, even bring one back from the dead, despite the cost to herself. "Rather than understanding that mothering carries with it the conflict of guilt and selfishness, holding and letting go, her needs and the child's needs, she abandons the world and her life to the demands of nurturing a child exclusively. The child becomes a succubus: bloated, unhealthy, dangerous" (55). In trying to re-create the early mother/child symbiosis Sethe missed with Beloved, she is unable to assert herself as an individuated mother who would put Beloved's excesses in check. She instead capitulates to her daughter out of her own need to atone.

Legacies of trauma can be passed on over generations as children absorb the effects of trauma from parents. Ilany Kogan's study of the second generation of the Holocaust explains the nature of this traumatic inheritance:

> The way in which events in the parent's lives were lived out often demonstrated that not only the content but also the style of trauma was re-enacted. These children's character structure, defensive and adaptive styles as well as life choices often showed the disintegrative effect of a traumatic event that could not be adequately known, understood and remembered. The trauma was retained as a discordant, encapsulated event, out of reach of reason, insight or reflection. It had the power to eclipse life or induce a break in life's procession via solitary re-enactments or permeation of life as a whole. Such transmission interfered with generalized adaptive functions such as comprehending, feeling, relating and especially taking charge of one's life and destiny. (Kogan 4)

Traumatization can be transmitted from one generation to the next through (1) the child's losing his or her sense of self, (2) the child's being exploited as a life-saving device, (3) abandonment of the child, or (4) a parent's withholding hope for a future (Kogan 26–28). This handing over of the past to the children plays a significant role in mother/child relations and in the subjectivity of daughters in Morrison's, Duras's, and Danticat's evocations of mothers' traumas.

To illustrate, the three generations of women in *Beloved* are intimately connected in collective childhood and adult traumas and in their internalizations of one another's experience. Because of this absorption of the other into oneself without acknowledging the separate, subjective existence of the other, dominance mars these connections. Again, the values, needs, and patterns passed from mothers to daughters are strongly contingent upon social forces; in this case, the brutal influence of slavery, which not only fosters sexual and reproductive exploitation but also creates a legacy of disastrous relations between mothers and children. Though very young when her mother is killed, the events of her mother's life become deeply infused within Sethe's to the point where much of her mother's experience is repeated, albeit with differences in circumstances and motivations. We learn that Sethe has re-created her mother's acts of infanticide, though out of love rather than rejecting children of rape as in her mother's case. Their bodies are used and exploited as a matter of course under slavery; their milk is "taken" for, or by, white children. Their services as breeders and wet nurses are made instrumental to the institution, traumatically removing them from more autonomous nurturance. Moreover, as her mother was repeatedly raped on the slave ship, Sethe is forcibly suckled by Schoolteacher's nephews, which for Sethe is almost worse than a rape because it violates her motherly function, her most significant identity (and she learns later, witnessing her violation will be the final unendurable trauma for her husband, Halle). Sethe's understanding of her own situation as an infant leads her to equate her own and her children's needs: "I know what it is to be without the milk that belongs to you . . . I'll tell Beloved about that; she'll understand" (200).

Sethe's desire for her mother, her identification with her . . . suggests that in regarding her children as extensions of herself and in seeing their protection as the preservation of the best part of herself, she replays her longing for a mother who would similarly protect and stay with her. Taken from her mother after a few weeks of nursing, and suckled by the one-armed Nan, who never has quite enough milk for her, Sethe is determined that she will bring her milk to her hungry babies. Through Sethe's emerging memories of her mother, Morrison suggests a genealogy of mothering under slavery that would logically produce the excesses and extreme forms of Sethe's maternal subjectivity. (Matus 111)

Marianne Hirsch believes that *Beloved* embodies the conflicted experience of mothers in that it shows the slave mother as

interpellated first and primarily into the institution of slavery: family and maternity therefore have different meanings for her. . . . Slavery heightens and intensifies the experience of family and of motherhood, of connection and separation. It raises questions about what it means to have a self, and to give that self away. It raises questions about what family means, and about the ways in which nuclear configurations dominant in the master culture (and in that culture's master narrative) prevail as points of reference even in economies in which they are thoroughly displaced and disrupted. ("Maternity" 95)

Sethe was a wounded child before she became a wounded mother. She retains a deeply hidden, unspoken horror about her own mother abandoning her (even if it is dying in the attempt to escape slavery): "nobody's ma'am would run off and leave her daughter, would she?" (203). Though Sethe knows rationally how Baby Suggs and her own mother were forced to give up any semblance of motherly agency or give up their children altogether, Sethe cannot accept this for herself. Being able to keep her children under the more "liberal" slave-owning Garners, she asserts her own power as a mother and individual in escaping, along with her children, Schoolteacher's mistreatment. On a more primal level of traumatic response, no explanation of her mother's abandonment can fill the emotional void left by that absence, no matter the cause. Claiming motherhood and subjectivity seems crazy to other characters like Paul D, who learns not to give too much of his love at one time. Sethe is able to challenge the powers of the slave system, but primarily within the context of fulfilling her own emotional needs.

Mary Jane Suero Elliot, utilizing Homi Bhabha's theory of the colonial subject, argues that Sethe's infanticide cannot be a resistant or subjective act, but rather in this context is defined by a "colonially constructed value system" and becomes an isolationist, objectifying act (190). Morrison may be supporting this position in setting up a reenactment of Beloved's murder scene wherein Sethe can act against who she thinks is the master rather than against her children. I would argue that this reenactment also breaks the cycle of trauma, always connected to oppression. This reenactment also suggests that the best form of resistance involves collective support, rather than in Sethe's traumatic response to her own abandonment (see below and chapter 5).[11]

In *Beloved* and *Sula*, patterns of dominance shape mothers' will to act and to protect. Their need to take action becomes destructive when overpowered by circumstances. Always at risk, there is no opportunity to see their children as separate or to enjoy them as autonomous individuals (Vickroy, "Force Outside" 33). Consequently, their children have not had the opportunity to grow in relationship to another who is seen as an "independent subject, not simply as the 'external world' or an adjunct of his [or her] ego" (*Bonds* 23). Sethe's daughters demonstrate both types of reactions; Denver associates her mother with the dangers of the external world and feels separated from her, but for Beloved, Sethe is part of herself. Missing here is the opportunity for balanced relationships based on mutual interaction and recognition, the ability to simultaneously acknowledge connection and difference, and thereby recognize an other's full subjectivity (25).

The most compelling evidence presented against mothers' destructive love and their denial of their children's separate subjectivity is the toll this takes on the children involved. Plum and Beloved are murdered by their mothers. Denver and Sula (Eva's granddaughter, mirror image, and surrogate daughter) survive their mothering, but are scarred by fear and alienation as a result. These children fear their death-dealing mothers: Denver has nightmares about her mother "kindly" killing her, and Sula, knowing Eva has killed Plum, has Eva put in a home rather than deal with her dangerous presence. While *Sula* and *Beloved* explore mothers' traumas and obsessions, these novels also focus at length on how the daughters who survive search for ways to live differently from their mothers. Sula leads a free life, but is disconnected from others, remains childless (so she will never experience the helplessness of the impoverished mother), and is a free spirit who is rejected for her individuality, her seductiveness (inherited from her quietly promiscuous mother), and her inability to conform. In doing this, Morrison is asserting that the forces compelling violent and desperate acts must be resisted. Therefore she creates daughters who struggle against what has overwhelmed their mothers, even while inheriting some of the mothers' qualities.

Sethe's reunion with Beloved—or more accurately, with the love and regret Sethe still carries with her—brings her some comfort but ultimately no reparation. Beloved's return initially evokes pleasant memories of connection regained, but as she and Sethe become increasingly aware of how they were separated, pain and conflict erupt. When the triad of women shuts out the world, Beloved demands an account of her abandonment, saying to Sethe, "You are my face; I am you. Why did you leave me who am you?" (216). As clues and links to the past are uncovered, Sethe tries to explain her role in Beloved's death. They become an obsessive dyad, with Sethe also accepting this exclusivity: "The world is in this room. This here's all there is and all there needs to be" (183). The repetitive cosseting and quarreling between mother and daughter witnessed by the second daughter, Denver, are obsessive recapitulations of the past with no resolution. Beloved continues to feel abandoned; Sethe repeatedly asks pardon. Their powerful love and the tragedy of separation can only be reiterated, never resolved. Despite the intentions of saving her and bringing the family "together on the other side, forever" (241), Sethe "left" Beloved. Beloved remains traumatized, locked in the past, still in many ways the abandoned infant who can neither reevaluate nor reassess her mother's actions after the fact. Nor can Sethe find resolution, unable to forgive herself or stop obsessively replaying in her mind that she murdered her daughter.

Sethe's incomplete subjectivity and absorption in the past also prove troubling for her other daughter, Denver. Denver is the only one of Sethe's children born in freedom, and Sethe renders Denver's birth story a narrative of triumph and survival, representing auspicious beginnings in freedom for Sethe and her family. This quickly falls apart, however, when Schoolteacher tries to reclaim his "property" twenty-eight days later. Most of the remainder of the novel contradicts this brief triumph, and until the end of the novel, Denver is absorbed into the past, first by Beloved's ghost and then by the appearance of the girl who seems to be Beloved. Denver feels complete, validated under the "interested, uncritical" gaze of Beloved, who she believes is her missing sister (Holden-

Kirwan 424). At this point only Beloved can provide this comfort, because she has always had a unique affinity with this ghost and the girl, who becomes her only friend after Baby Suggs dies and her brothers leave because of the ghost. Also, Denver feels her mother has turned away from her in favor of Paul D, and she carries a deeply imbedded fear of both her mother and her "unspeakable" act (killing Beloved), which Denver learns about in school and which traumatizes her into hysterical deafness for a time. For a time Sethe and her daughters form an isolated triad, where each regresses into symbiosis gone awry. Each says to one or all of the others, "You are mine" (215–17), with the speakers only approximately identified; their words and feelings become conflated, a "trialogue." Turning away from the world and spoiling Beloved leaves Sethe totally submerged in the past and in a state of near starvation, so Denver must leave the house to enter the community, and the future, if they are to survive.

As the member of the family least possessed by the past, Denver, at nineteen, must overcome her own internalization of her mother's fearful worldview, leave 124, and seek help in the community for her and Sethe to survive the demands of the past (Beloved). Sethe and Denver suffer the reality that the outside world is a potentially deadly place, as whites seem determined to spill black blood during Reconstruction.[12] The inner struggle Denver undergoes about leaving home stems from hearing her mother's and grandmother's fearful words about the world outside their yard, especially about whites ("Oh, some of them do all right by us." "Don't box with me. There's more of us they drowned than there is all of them ever lived from the start of time. Lay down your sword. This ain't a battle; it's a rout," 244). To an extent these fears are very reasonable, keeping Denver imprisoned in the house and yard, and yet, when Denver is forced from the house by hunger when her mother refuses to work to be with Beloved, she must remember the words of her grandmother, Baby Suggs—a less traumatized nurturer than her mother—in order to break the traumatic patterns of her family. Baby Suggs's words make her realize she must leave the house, know what could be out there, and "go on out the yard" anyway (244). Denver here starts to break the pattern of solitary resistance and obsession with the past. Fortunately, Denver is welcomed by Lady Jones, a teacher, and other women. Their sad story attracts the community back to the family, who in turn help lead Sethe out of traumatic stasis, and enmeshment with Beloved, who represents the sufferings of the past (see chapter 5).

Danticat: The Traumas of Mother and Daughter

Haitian American writer Edwidge Danticat spent the first twelve years of her life in Haiti and since her arrival in the U.S. has become a well-educated, successful young writer. Her works—two novels, *Breath, Eyes, Memory* and *The Farming of Bones* (a historical novel about the massacre of Haitian cane workers by Dominicans in 1937), and her story collection *Krik? Krak!*—all center on Haitian life within contexts of oppression, immigration, and history. In an interview with Eleanor Wachtel, Danticat speaks of her commitment to Haiti and her family. Knowing firsthand Haiti's culture as well as its poverty and history of political tyranny, she recognizes how important it is to write the stories that have not been told due to marginalization and persecution. The struggles and sacrifices of her own family influenced her hard work (Wachtel interview 111).[13] The support of her parents and the Haitian community in the U.S. made her accomplishments possible (degrees at Barnard and Brown, her writing) and spurred her desire to utilize an opportunity not given to many Haitians (Anglesey interview 38).

In *Breath, Eyes, Memory*, she speaks of the fragmenting experience of migration and having to re-create one's self in a new context. She also explores "the ways a young girl would become a woman on her own, without much modeling . . . how we become women in the absence of our mothers" (Wachtel interview 114). Though there are some parallels to Danticat's own life, the novel is not specifically autobiographical. Her protagonist, Sophie, demonstrates how a young woman brings together a life fragmented by separation, trauma, and culture shock by herself, "because her mother's rite of passage was this violent act, which was true for a lot of women who lived in the dictatorship [of Papa Doc Duvalier]" says Danticat (Wachtel interview 114). This novel of a troubled mother/daughter relationship testifies in personal terms to a culture traumatized by poverty, oppression, and violence. It reveals how the isolating and debilitating effects of trauma preclude change and resistance (seen in Sophie's mother, Martine). The novel also expresses hope through the protagonist, Sophie, who shares her and her mother's true-to-life story and challenges the tyranny of the past and destructive traditions.

In *Breath, Eyes, Memory*, the origins of family trauma come out of the brutal social and political repressions of the regime of François "Papa Doc" Duvalier (1957–71). At only sixteen, Martine, the mother of the protagonist, Sophie, was raped by one of the Ton Ton Macoutes.[14] These were members of a civilian paramilitary security force created by Duvalier to extend his spy network beyond the army, to maintain order, suppress civilians, and intimidate any political opponents (Laguerre 114–18). The Ton Ton Macoute forces did not follow standard practices or procedures, and sometimes their actions were based on personal animosities, but sexual abuse and violence were very common ways of controlling and silencing women, particularly those supporting opposition to Duvalier (N'Zengou-Tayo 125, 132; Charles 140). Sexual violence against women has been a pattern of modern Haiti not only under Duvalier, but also used by civilian and army forces during another regime, as recently as the early 1990s (N'Zengou-Tayo 128–29; Charles 135). Martine's rape is not instigated by any political act or opinion on her part; it is presented as a random, though not uncommon, act of terror, because we learn that it is very probable that Martine's mother underwent a similar trauma, suffering similar symptomatic nightmares as her daughter.

Breath, Eyes, Memory begins by introducing the protagonist, Sophie, a twelve-year-old girl who has not known her mother except via audiotapes that Martine has used to maintain contact with her family. Sophie is being raised by her Aunt Atie, who, although she serves as a surrogate mother, is loyal to her sister Martine in that she is willing to give Sophie back to her whenever it is possible. We learn that Martine had attempted suicide after the birth of her daughter and subsequently emigrated to New York City to escape Haiti and to recover from her devastating rape. When Sophie is twelve, Martine asks to have her daughter sent to New York. She wants so badly to fulfill her role as a mother that she hopes this will overcome the return to trauma the daughter's presence provokes. Taking Sophie after twelve years is an act of tremendous self-sacrifice, but the consequences raise the question of whether it was a wise choice for either mother or daughter.

Thereafter the narrative portrait of Martine is through Sophie's eyes. She quickly learns that her mother is still haunted by her past almost every night in the form of the same repeated anguished nightmare. Reliving the violence and feeling near death indicate that her original traumatic situation remains as real to her as when it originally happened. Martine, however, never saw her attacker's face, so her trauma remains to some extent inaccessible to her, increasing her terror, and thus remains unresolved. This anguishing lack of self-knowledge also impairs Martine's ability to remove herself from the defensive life patterns accumulated around her trauma. When her daughter wakes her up from her nightmares, Martine feels literally that Sophie "saves her life" (81). Though her daughter's return reconfigures Martine's life as a mother, it also retraumatizes her (returns her to girlhood) as the return of her nightmares coincides with Sophie's arrival. Paradoxically, the child to whom she has given life comes to mean both life and death in the form of renewed trauma, which ultimately destroys her.

The legacy of political terror can be seen in the constricted life Martine leads. She manages to have a boyfriend, Marc, also a Haitian immigrant, but primarily her life is spent working two jobs. Certainly her work is economically necessary and allows her eventually to buy a house for her and her daughter, but Danticat also suggests that work is also a form of control and avoidance; the short exposition of the intervening six years during which Martine raises Sophie indicates that mother and daughter do not spend much time together. Martine has been "unhomed," forced into exile by her rape in Haiti. She finds herself too emotionally terrified to return to Haiti until almost twenty years later: "There are ghosts there I can't face" (78). Nevertheless, she clings to a Haitian identity. She must work hard to provide a home and sets strict moral and social rules for Sophie (a religious school, no dating, no sex or any non-Haitian boyfriends) that are more appropriate to a Haitian than a U.S. context. She is not able to provide nurturance in the same way as Sophie's "other" mother, Aunt Atie, whose relationship early in the novel is shown in the fullness and closeness unachieved by the biological mother and daughter. The text represses, perhaps as Sophie does, the trauma of leaving Atie; after she is grown, Sophie expresses regret at having ever left her aunt (136). Martine struggles heroically with her own dreadful past, trying to overcome it by reclaiming Sophie despite the fact that her daughter's presence is so disturbing. Sophie's face probably resembles the rapist's, because it does not bear familiar family traits.

Even in the extended family the mother's house is prisonlike for daughters because of the rules curtailing their freedom and the virginity testing that is inflicted on and resented by all the daughters: Martine, Atie, and Sophie. Mothering in dangerous circumstances unfortunately provides more "protection" from sexual and other freedoms than from fear of violence. Atie attempts to free herself from her mother's restrictions only in middle age. The grandmother (Martine's and Atie's mother) has engaged in an overly protective mothering in a patriarchal and violent social climate. Martine has continued that stifling control in a less threatening U.S. environment; clearly, her years in Haiti and the terrors there dominate her life more than her current environment. The mothers' fears and restrictions further suppress and limit their daughters and further participate in their oppression.

Mothers' trauma-induced emotional needs direct this restrictive behavior as well. Martine's constricted life and isolation prevents her own growth as an emotionally autonomous woman and makes her incapable of acknowledging her daughter's growth and impending separation from her. Though she provides a home, on a deep emotional level Martine cannot provide the safe space for Sophie to grow apart from her mother normally; rather, Sophie has to be strong and care for her mother. Martine insists on keeping Sophie with her, agreeing only to a Haitian suitor for Sophie; consequently, Sophie must lie about seeing Joseph, the American man she eventually marries. Incapable of accepting Sophie's decisions, Martine's care for her daughter can only take the form of imposing control, because she is in fact frantic that her daughter will leave. Martine's terror and cautious living are also emblematic of a culture in trauma. Danticat has spoken of how Haitians have lived in silence, being afraid to speak, being cautious and developing survival mechanisms and codes for speech and behavior (Wachtel interview 112–13). The scary stories of the Ton Ton Macoutes, literally "bogeymen," became a reality of peoples' lives under Papa Doc (Wachtel interview 117).

A particularly disturbing aspect of passing on legacies of trauma and oppression to children is Martine's bodily violation of Sophie as she tests Sophie's virginity. In many cultures the virginity status of girls reflects on their own and their family's honor. Usually testing is performed by a doctor and the results are revealed in a public context; for example, to confirm the girl is eligible for marriage (Pelin 256–59). In Haitian culture, apparently, the mother does the testing to assure her daughter's chastity (although this is not a universal practice in Haiti and thus a point of controversy for some critics of Danticat's portrayal here ["Edwidge Danticat"]). It is a common practice in the characters' family, and although Aunt Atie and Sophie seriously rebel against it, the emotional toll is devastating.

When Martine imposes severe social and sexual restrictions on the eighteen-year-old Sophie and continually examines her daughter to see if her hymen is intact, she begins a process whereby the legacy of trauma is passed along to the daughter. Eventually, Sophie will mutilate herself by breaking her own hymen in a violent and painful manner in order to liberate herself from her mother's possessive demands. Consequently, Sophie will experience severe pain in intercourse with her husband, Joseph. There is a sense of repetition here: Sophie's sexual traumas can be interpreted as distorted examples of her mother's first sexual encounter. In various ways the mother's traumas have entered the minds and bodies of both mother and daughter, as both display similar defensive mechanisms and adaptive styles, including nightmares, dissociating or splitting off emotionally, and extreme mechanisms of self-control when faced with feeling powerless. Even before living with Martine, Sophie has nightmares where she fears her mother trying to grasp her (8, 28). Martine has left her when months old, so it could be a literary device linking them and suggesting shared trauma, but it could also indicate unconscious absorption of the mother's terror, manifested in the daughter's fear of a mother she does not yet know. Martine's fear of losing her daughter is transferred to Sophie, who says: "I feel like my daughter is the only person in the world who won't leave me" (210). Sophie is so identified with Martine that she must get over her mother's trauma before she can heal herself. Sophie's therapist says, "You will never be able to connect with your husband until you say good-bye to your father" (209), something Martine has not been able to do.

The virginity testing is a form of motherly control and self-soothing, an example of internalized oppression, clinging to a remnant of the patriarchal Haitian context in which they no longer live. It is an example of how oppressive cultural practices become enmeshed with emotional needs and crises. Clearly, Martine is anxious for Sophie because losing her own virginity was so traumatic. To reinforce virginity in her daughter is a way to reclaim her own once-intact body and mind (she begins testing Sophie after learning about Joseph). Martine feels unjustifiably betrayed when she realizes Sophie will leave her for Joseph: "You would leave me for an old man who you didn't know the year before" (85). Her response could be in part cultural, since the loss of virginity brings about separation between mother and daughter in many cultures (Holtzman and Kulish 138, 221). However, the daughter's transition into adulthood would increase the mother's dread of her own adulthood, which she will reject as she becomes pregnant again. The testing seems to be an especially self-interested bid for power because it has so much more to do with Martine's own traumas and repetitions. Not surprisingly, Martine has also been traumatized by testing; she says that her rape at least stopped the tests: "The testing and the rape. I live both every day" (170).

Danticat emphasized this practice to make a point about how legacies of trauma are passed down, especially between mothers and daughters, and also as a way to include social/political influences, as the tyranny with which Martine employs the testing seems to reflect Haitian political intimidation more than the largely supportive matriarchal system of Sophie and Martine's family in Haiti. Here again, the family unit absorbs repressive practices, since bodily violations and violent intimidation have a central part of Haiti's political regimes and their destruction of any opposition. "The Duvalier dictatorship encouraged violence against women and used rape and torture against the wives and daughters of political opponents. This violence was to be overshadowed only by the 1991–94 repression" (N'Zengou-Tayo 132).

Although Martine struggles mightily to be a mother, to be with her daughter, in many ways she has not progressed emotionally beyond the point of her rape at sixteen. She is still plagued by recurring nightmares, particularly when she forces herself to return to Haiti almost twenty years later in order to reunite with Sophie after a two-year estrangement. Martine will not be able to overcome the threat of another pregnancy, which she equates with the horrors of the first and consequently reconnects her with the terror of the past. Sophie reports to her therapist that her mother is like two people, falling apart and trying to keep together (218). No resolution seems possible for Martine, because she fears therapy, madness, being institutionalized, and is continually haunted by the image of the rapist, especially during her second pregnancy. Martine's life ends in a violent suicide, as she frantically stabs herself and the unborn child. Fear has locked Martine into a traumatic past, and her daughter has unwittingly helped condemn her by encouraging Martine to have the baby. She represents a powerful example of how some trauma victims (often documented among Holocaust survivors) kill themselves years later to be rid of their continual suffering. Further, Martine illustrates how Caruth describes the double nature of telling trauma, involving an "oscillation between a crisis of death and the . . . crisis of life" (*Unclaimed* 7). That is, both the traumatizing event *and* its survival become unbearable.

Martine's anguish and helplessness are absorbed by Sophie in many ways: "Her nightmares had somehow become my own" (193). Sophie also has suicidal thoughts, tries to deny her fears, and dissociates in sex with Joseph. She adopts defense mechanisms for coping that are similar to those of her mother. Martine worked constantly to give herself the illusion of control and Sophie becomes bulimic. However, Sophie does try individual and group therapy, attempting to end this cycle of trauma. Her therapist also points out that like her mother, Sophie has a strong capacity for denial. Living in two cultures, American and Haitian, also affects Sophie's attempts to heal and reconcile with her mother. She tries to adopt the Haitian concept of starting over with her mother, but this may also keep her from seeing how ruined her mother is. Because Sophie's daughter, Brigitte, has given her hope, she assumed it would be the same if Martine had another child, but this turns out to be a grave misconception. Each sees the other only in terms of herself, not intersubjectively, causing much misunderstanding and estrangement.

At the end of the novel, Sophie is able to contemplate all her mother went through and the connections that remain between them.

> There is always a place where nightmares are passed on through generations like heirlooms. . . .
>
> I come from a place where breath, eyes, and memory are one, a place from which you carry your past like the hair on your head. Where women return to their children as butterflies or as tears in the eyes of the statues that their daughters pray to. My mother was as brave as stars at dawn. She too was from this place. My mother was like that woman who could never bleed and then could never

stop bleeding, the one who gave in to her pain, to live as a butterfly. Yes, my mother was like me. (234)

Whether Sophie will be able to heal her sexual and eating dysfunctions remains uncertain at the end of the text. As readers, we know she is capable of taking action to heal herself, and she has a deep concern about passing on traumatic legacies to Brigitte: "It was up to me to make sure that my daughter never slept with ghosts, never lived with nightmares . . ." (203). Yet many traumatic repetitions are still pervasive in her own life; Sophie is perhaps overly dependent on her daughter as well, and the final lines of the passage above indicate both an identification with her mother and a need for self-transformation to escape the agonies of life. The question remains whether Sophie, like her mother, will seek this transformation in death. Certainly, Danticat offers readers more evidence to hope for Sophie than her mother, because unlike her mother, Sophie is able to tell the story of her pain to others. She has a sympathetic community who share her traumas.

Like Morrison, Danticat sees hope in the collective sharing of knowledge and pain. Danticat sees her writing as contributing to breaking the silence of "especially poor women [who] are often not given the opportunity to speak" (Wachtel interview 118). She does not see herself as their voice but embraces the difficult role of the writer coming from an oppressive society, where telling the truth has historically landed writers in prison, or worse. Danticat can write from the safe space of the U.S. and the place of two cultures, allowing the Haitian story to be told to a broader audience.

Duras: Collective and Familial Traumas in Indochina

Duras resisted her own colonial identity in empathizing with the oppressed. Growing up in a French family but with Vietnamese servants and friends, speaking their language fluently, Duras deeply identified with the plight of the indigenous people but also viewed their situation as exemplifying the failure, powerlessness, and solitude of the human condition (Vircondelet 40). She links their sufferings with those of her family, particularly her mother, who tried to save dying children and fought for restitution of useless farmland that she and her Vietnamese neighbors had been sold by crooked officials. Her mother and family, in reality and in her fiction, are psychologically destroyed by the broken promises of colonial life. Her focus on this empathic mother figure and destitution sets Duras distinctly apart from earlier French colonial writers such as Pierre Loti and Ernest Psichari, who enjoyed being part of the "adventure" of colonial domination (Hargreaves 16).

Largely based on Duras's mother's own life and circumstances, the mother figure who frequently reappears in Duras's work undergoes similar types of struggles involving her children's survival, her own identity, and her will to act against forces of oppression.[15] The mother's full portrait emerges over the course of several works but particularly in *The Sea Wall* and in *The Lover*. Like Sethe, she is depicted as rebelling heroically against injustice, but Duras's mother also tries to fulfill a collective struggle against oppressive systems. Both characters experience psychic disintegration and threats to their identities as mothers and as individuals. Duras's portrayal is also multifaceted; the mother is a heroic avenger of injustice, an empathic nurturer, a broken victim, and a disturbed victimizer of her children. She fights for her family's survival against colonial officials who cheat her and the elements that flood her land every year. As with Morrison's mothers, Duras gives us a portrayal of tremendous power and vulnerability. Two of Duras's novels must be considered in the context of colonization and trauma. Traumatic circumstances and the mother's resistance are emphasized in *The Sea Wall* (1952) and in a more contemporary text written thirty years later, *The Lover* (1984), wherein the traumatic consequences to mother and children are more apparent. The narrative and characterizations of *The Lover* reveal more familiarity with the workings of trauma and ways to reproduce that trauma narratively.

Duras's outrage at colonialism and its workings is most fully developed in the earlier text. She expresses her disgust with the murderous oppression of parasitical colonial officials, characterizing them as "beasts of prey" and "vampires" swimming in luxury while others starve in their midst (*Sea Wall* 167). In her detailed descriptions of the white section of the colonial city, she attacks the sense of superiority the privileged white colonials feel over nonwhites and poor whites: "They learned to wear the Colonial uniform, suits of spotless white, the color of immunity and innocence. . . . making distinctions among themselves and between themselves and the others who were not white" (135). The narrative provides detailed explanations of how officials swindled hundreds of families by selling them useless land and refusing to provide medical care or food to the peasant population.

The mother, Ma, eventually confronts their inhumanity in a letter relating how the corpses of children make the lands around them fertile, and chronicling how she and the peasants fight to reclaim the useless land so their children will not continue to starve. The mother's testimonial letter to colonial agents begins in Duras's work an important process of personally bearing witness to collective traumas. Duras recreates her mother's actual letter to memorialize and repeat her challenges to their claims to bringing progress to the Third World, to their inhumanity and to the oppressive bureaucratic machinations seen in the Holocaust and colonialism—systems described by Saul Friedlander as "dominated by political decisions and administrative decrees which neutralize the concreteness of despair and death" (53).

> When a little child dies, I tell them [the peasants]: "That will make those swine, the cadastral agents in Kam, very glad." "Why should they be glad?" they ask. And I tell them the truth, that the more children die in the plain the more the plain will be depopulated and the more your [the agents'] hold on the plain will be reinforced. I do not tell them, as you see, anything but the truth. And before a dead child I owe that to them. "Why don't they send us quinine? Why is there no doctor, why is there not one hospital clinic? Why is there no alum to purify the water in the dry season? Why is there never any vaccination?" they ask. I tell them why and even if this truth is beyond your understanding, beyond your personal claims on the plain, this truth that I give them is none the less true and you yourselves are the cause of the events that will follow . . . the lands that you covet and that you take from the plainspeople, the only fertile lands of the plain, are swarming with the corpses of children (*Sea Wall* 233).

Through Ma's direct speech, Duras creates a dialogue between her and the peasants, once addressed to their oppressors and now to readers. The mother was once the mediator on their behalf, and Duras continues to document these injustices twenty years after the fact. Thus, the personal trauma of Duras's family is linked in her fiction with the collective oppressions of colonialism, racism, and poverty.

Ma is portrayed as embracing a powerful nurturing identity whereby she attempts to provide for her family and help Vietnamese peasants and their children, who endure their own traumas, as their "misery accustomed them to passivity, their one and only defense against the spectacle of their children dying of starvation, their crops being destroyed by salt" (42). As a white, educated French schoolteacher and landowner, Ma has the resources to confront colonial policies much more directly than the Vietnamese peasants or Morrison's or Danticat's mothers of color can. She lives a hybrid existence, has a limited voice (which is soon silenced), lives in poverty, but is clearly better off than the natives, with a servant and food every day. She starts her life in the colony "desperately ignorant of the blood-sucking proclivities of colonialism" (*Sea Wall* 19), but later confronts corrupt officials and engages in many efforts to reclaim useless flood land that would sustain her family and neighbors. Like the Vietnamese, however, she is ultimately defeated by colonial powers. With the third collapse of the sea wall she and her neighbors built to protect their land, the mother is thereafter broken, despondent, emotionally unstable, and frequently abusive and neglectful of her children, who absorb her defeats. "Because of what's been done to our mother, so amiable, so trusting, we hate life, we hate ourselves . . . all three of us are our mother's children, the children of a candid creature murdered by society" (*Lover* 54–55).

A further trauma involves Ma's fruitless attempt to save a dying infant left by its mother (based on an actual incident), who symbolizes all the native children who die early from sickness and starvation: "they died in such numbers they were no longer mourned" (*Sea Wall* 93). In a colonial context of greed, want, and overabundant life, children become both life and death ("the children were always relentlessly born. It was very needful that some of them die," 93). Ma's failure to save the infant will be devastating: "The death of that child had been . . . worse than all their bad luck put together. Ma, even though she had anticipated it, had wept for days and days, working herself into a rage, swearing she would never again do anything whatsoever for children" (95). The mother's almost tireless idealism, her desire to care for others and correct injustice are deeply connected to her identification of herself as a mother who can preserve life and nurture all. Here Duras seems to be expressing a wish for mothers to save all suffering children of the world: "They played. They did not stop playing except to go and die. To die of destitution. . . . And everywhere throughout the world, as here, they died of misery. . . . There were too many, and the mothers did not take good care of them. The children learned to walk, to swim, to delouse themselves, to steal, to fish, without the mother, and they died without the mother" (259–60).

Ma's deterioration bears signs of her power and helplessness. Despite her defeats, she still tries to preserve children's lives and dedicates herself to her students' literacy even if they will be only laborers. Thus, she commits herself to social justice on a very personal level. The psychic violence she experiences from colonial officials destroys her, however. They deny not only their own misdeeds but set out to ruin her reputation, enforcing an alternative reality of the situation that not only subjects the family to a shameful isolation in poverty but also denies her voice and action. Consequently, her "powers" begin to take on destructive forms; she is described as having a primitive, elemental power as she rails at her children with the force of "the wind or waves" (109). Initially manifested in brave displays of resistance, her strength is reduced to repetitive, pathetically futile attempts to reclaim her land or to discipline her daughter long after it would be productive. As chronicled in *The Lover*, after her daughter begins an affair at fifteen with a twenty-seven-year-old Chinese man, the mother breaks violently out of her depressive inertia, violating the girl's privacy, beating her, and calling her a whore. The mother worries that her daughter will end up unmarried and victimized by the world as she has been. "Her daughter's in the direst danger, the danger of never getting married, never having a place in society, of being defenseless against it, lost, alone. My mother has attacks during which she falls on me, locks me up in my room, punches me, undresses me, comes up to me and smells my body, my underwear, says she can smell the Chinese's scent, goes even further, looks for suspect stains on my underwear, and shouts, for the whole town to hear, that her daughter's a prostitute" (*Lover* 58).

The intrusions of this scene would seem to be motivated not only by an overcompensation for her previous neglect, but also by a tragic sense that her daughter has broken away from her own and colonial society's moral precepts. The mother eventually concedes to the girl's wishes and her own impotence to stop the affair, defending her nightly truancy to one of her boarding school teachers to keep her in school. Her despondency nevertheless invades her daughter's unconscious: "[M]y mother's unhappiness took the place of dreams" (46). The girl is deeply conflicted about her mother, in some ways regretting how she has defied her and yet recognizing this defiance as a step away from her family and toward her own individuation (see chapter 4). Noticing the contrast between her once great spirit and the traumatized indifference she later exhibits devastates her children. They absorb her sense of defeat, but more importantly, she cannot give them the guidance, discipline, and "otherness" necessary for their development. In the face of her eldest son's violence toward his brother, "she never interferes . . . she's a disheartened mother" (*North China Lover* 5). She begins to realize that not placing limits on Pierre has ruined him and that she may love him more, to the distress of the other children, because he is "lost," perhaps like herself. She admits that she "couldn't be trusted" to protect Paulo from Pierre and sends the latter back to France (19). Paulo never recovers any sense of self-confidence, and Pierre remains the opium-addicted, failed colonist (see above) and becomes a shameless informer and thief during World War II.

The bungalow the mother builds on her unproductive land becomes symbolic of her struggle to survive despite her defeats: "[T]he bungalow . . . belonged to her, in full ownership, and she congratulated herself each day on having built it. Always, in proportion to her growing destitution, the bungalow, to her mind, increased in value and solidity" (*Sea Wall* 21). The contradiction of living as both a colonizer and a peasant brings out her sympathies toward collective suffering and taking action to remedy this. From her bungalow she joins peasants to fight colonial officials, yet her defeat by the officials positions her much like the peasants, and the home that is left to her becomes a desolate place of abuse and neglect. Her inability to set moral or physical limits on her children leads them to seek comfort outside the home. Their poverty leads the children to seek money from lovers and to regain their mother's love with substitutes. In both texts the daughter and son find older lovers who lavish maternal as well as sexual attentions on them as substitutions for the mother's emotional abandonment.

In Morrison's, Danticat's, and Duras's work, mothers are complicated, as their subjectivity and their circumstances fully warrant. Although these mothers are strong, courageous, and willing to take on the world to see their children survive, they often do not live up to their ideals as nurturers, either frightening or neglecting their children. Their sacrifices are heroic, almost superhuman; for example, Eva's sacrifice of her leg, Sethe's willingness to offer up herself and her children, Duras's mother's battles and loss of sanity. However, the systematized oppression under which they live underlies both their failures and the consequent psychic damage. Their motherly ideal is destroyed or distorted as it comes into conflict with forces shaping their lives, as when "Sethe's violent action becomes an attempt to hold on to the maternal right and function in a society where it defines the mother's existence" in a context of slavery (Davies 48). Again, these portrayals demonstrate how mothers are caught between many conflicting forces that direct their actions and identities as mothers and as subjects. Finally, Morrison, Duras, and Danticat demonstrate that exclusive mothering is more vulnerable to traumatization, and each notes the advantages of more collective, extrafamilial nurturing.

Morrison recognizes the benefits of a dynamic, situational and collective approach toward mothering. She also seeks understanding of mothers' conflicted positions and need to resist, exploring the difficulties arising when mothers are isolated nurturers, which can at its worst make their nurturance destructive and inappropriate, as with Eva and Sethe. In *Beloved*, Sethe has boldly but cruelly saved her children from slavery, killing one child and attempting to do so with the other three, but her pride, her grief, and her guilt over her actions alienate others from her and prevent her own healing and growth. Further, because her identity requires her children, she does not recognize that conflict and a sense of her own otherness and limits are necessary for their growth. In allowing Beloved's demands—that is, those of her own guilty past— to go unchecked, the child almost destroys her.

It is the other women in town, like Ella and Sethe's mother-in-law, Baby Suggs, and the teacher Lady Jones, who help Sethe cope with her past or offer more collective viewpoints toward mothering and nurturing. Baby Suggs has been the town's spiritual healer and nurturer, needed because all of her people have been defiled physically and spiritually. Ella has helped countless slaves escape through the Underground Railroad, recognizing that the free must help the "unfree." Lady Jones becomes a surrogate mother to Denver, helping her individuate herself by developing skills necessary to live in the world, and has educated the town's children, something systematically forbidden to slaves and necessary for their post-slavery survival. Each recognizes they share difficult situations and painful relations to their slave pasts, and many of the townswomen help Denver to recover a place in the community after living for years in fearful isolation with her mother.

Similarly, Duras depicts her family's relations as becoming increasingly more destructive the further removed they are from the French colonial community to which they once belonged. Her mother is not isolated by choice, but betrayed and socially abandoned by other colonists. Yet, she does not immediately lose her sense of being part of a community. Aligning herself with native Vietnamese, she recognizes the need for collective resistance. She becomes their spokesperson by virtue of knowing the language and systems of their oppressors. The consciousness and concern that is expressed here is from a mother's point of view. The issues of the survival of children and the callousness of those who let them die are made clearer through the eyes of a nurturer. Therefore, Duras's mother is not relegated to the private realm of mothering, but she is depicted as a woman who sees all the ramifications and interconnections between the social/political world of colonial Indochina and the tenuous daily lives of the people living under it. Ultimately worn down by fighting a system that denies her presence and her accurate charges against it, she becomes unable to care for and control her children. Thus, the mother is deprived of her potentially important role as nurturer, educator, and negotiator between cultures. Her own mother's experiences have affected Duras profoundly, making her acutely aware, from her early youth, of the injustices, inequalities, and racism of the colonial world, and by extension, the larger world (Vircondelet 21, 24). Thus, the personal trauma of Duras's family is always linked in her fiction with these larger social problems.

Danticat also creates an extensive network of mothers and nurturing women who establish a collective, worldly context of women's suffering and offer each other needed support and healing. The women in Haiti act as communal mothers as they interact with and teach children life lessons by telling them stories. Sophie's sexual phobia support group is an international mix of women who have suffered rape and genital mutilation and engage in healing rituals with Sophie. Her therapist, an African American woman, tries to help Sophie and Martine by suggesting they confront the source of their trauma. She urges them to return to Haiti and to the place of the original trauma in order to realize that they no longer need to fear the place of the rape, so that they can break the repetitive pattern of fear and realize that they are reliving the

rape emotionally. Lastly, as the novel ends, any hope for Sophie's recovery lies in her difference from her mother, that is, in her willingness
to seek help because her mother's fear and isolation have doomed her.

Duras's, Morrison's, and Danticat's works challenge both mothers'
oppression and idealization. They also eliminate dichotomies of public
and private in their work, recognizing that as mothers' sense of interaction with others and their ability to act in a larger social sense is diminished, so is their effectiveness as mothers. This is because their
own identity, their "otherness" that should have been shaped and nurtured by intersubjective relations, has also been diminished. The authors and theorists presented in this chapter raise questions about, and
help reformulate, notions of individuality and subjectivity and suggest
that these concepts are altered when considering the difficult positions
of mothers in socially mediated contexts. When contingencies are oppressive, destructive patterns of interaction and identity development
ensue and can create irresolvable traumatic responses in children, as I
will discuss in the following chapter.

THREE

THE TRAUMATIZED CHILD
AS OUTCAST IN DURAS
AND MORRISON

In their depictions of characters who exemplify social and familial dispossession and abandonment, Morrison and Duras join many scholars, theorists, and artists who have recognized the need for an investigation of the dynamics of oppression and subjugation. This need
became urgent after the political liberation of colonies worldwide in
the 1950s and the civil rights movements in this country. In particular,
scholars of colonialism, slavery, and the Holocaust, as well as psychologists, began to focus on the psychological effects of oppression and the
emotional strategies employed in response.[1] Moreover, trauma theory
has given us a deeper understanding of these effects and strategies. This
chapter demonstrates how Morrison and Duras have joined this current
of ideas in their thorough examinations of the relationship of trauma
to social oppression. Although Morrison addresses white American racial dominance from slavery to the 1970s, and Duras primarily addresses British and French control in East Asia during colonization,
their investigations share similar elements. Both have given voice to
those silenced and marginalized by oppression and probe how individuals manifest the effects of living under subjugation in the way they
carry their personal and collective histories within them. In these texts,
the protagonists are unable to tell their own stories in words—this
must be done for them—but they communicate the severity of their
traumas in repetitive reenactments.

I begin with a comparison of Morrison's *The Bluest Eye* and Duras's *The Vice-Consul* because these works address racial subjugation in a similar time period (the 1930s), introducing a new element into colonialist discourse; they both feature as protagonists young subaltern girls not previously represented in the Western literary tradition. For both writers, traumatized children provide not merely poignant metaphors but also concrete examples of the neglect, exploitation, disempowerment, and disavowal of communities and even entire cultures (e.g., African American or Third World citizens). I will demonstrate above all how these writers challenge the subordination of women and children by testifying to their experience and thereby engaging their readers in that experience.

The other texts examined in this chapter, *The Ravishing of Lol V. Stein* and *Jazz*, continue and extend many of these themes and characterizations to other contexts (such as gender oppression and American racial history) and broaden the discussion to how traumatic memory shapes identity and our views of the past and curtails one's capacity for growth or interaction. Duras's *Ravishing*, a related text because of its themes and similar renderings of traumatic responses, demonstrates how personal trauma can be reinforced by gender oppression and patriarchy, which encourage the emotional infantilism of the protagonist and create odd connections between desire and dispossession in traumatic contexts.

The Bluest Eye and *The Vice-Consul*

First, a brief reorientation to trauma should help elucidate the textual analyses to follow. Trauma is an event in an individual's life that is "defined by its intensity, by the subject's incapacity to respond adequately to it, and by the upheaval and long-lasting effects that it brings about in the psychical organization" (Laplanche and Pontalis 465). Kai Erikson emphasizes that trauma can also result "from a constellation of life's experiences as well as from a discrete event—from a prolonged exposure to danger as well as from a sudden flash of terror, from a continuing pattern of abuse as well as from a single assault, from a period of attenuation and wearing away as well as from a moment of shock" (457). Prolonged exposure to dangers and abuse have special significance for oppressed groups and constitute a pernicious form of trauma

because of the effects of the constant stress and humiliation associated
with being a person of low socioeconomic status (Brown 124–25).

In *The Bluest Eye,* several of Morrison's characters experience the
gradual psychic erosion of which Erikson speaks (457), representing the
weakening of whole communities living under an oppressive white cultural dominance. Whether the process of internalizing dominant values occurs psychologically through reinforcement and punishment, or
whether it is a reflection of what Lacan saw as a universal process of in-
scription of individual identity by the social order (Hogan 100), Morrison depicts an imposing white culture whose values are enforced
through a variety of means (violent, economic, psychological, etc.). As
she presents it, what has been seen as individualized psychopathological symptoms must be viewed differently when abuse is endured on a
larger, systematic level, as in 1930s America. *The Bluest Eye* explores
how the traumatic experience of social powerlessness and devalued
racial identity prevents the African American community from join-
ing together and truthfully evaluating the similarity of their circumstances, much less finding ways to oppose dominant forces.

The epitome of this devalued community, the Breedlove family, suffers from trauma caused by single, startling events but also in daily,
grinding oppression, where the parents pass that suffering on to their
children. Their daughter, Pecola, is especially sensitive to the fearful,
repetitively ritualized violence that her parents direct toward each
other and their children. Her further devaluation by the world, with
little relief except from her playmates and the whores who befriend her,
includes constant ridicule from other school children because of her
dark skin, poverty, and ugliness. The black boys who torment her fail to
recognize a fellow member of their community. As Michael Awkward
observes, their insults ironically reflect "their ability to disregard their
similarity to their victim; the verse they compose to belittle her ('Black
e mo . . . Yadaddsleepsnekked') reflects their own skin color and, quite
possibly, familial situations" (191). White attitudes toward blacks are
exemplified in her encounter with the storeowner, Mr. Yacobowski:
"She looks up at him and sees the vacuum where curiosity ought to
lodge. And something more. The total absence of human recognition—
the glazed separateness" (42). In this context Pecola becomes especially
vulnerable to the sudden, violent traumas of being beaten and rejected

by her mother, Pauline, and by the more horrific traumas of being raped by her father, Cholly, and then losing the baby.

Pecola's parents, furthermore, are often powerless themselves, subject to the whites who employ them, victims of their poverty and the culture that invalidates them. In addition, they themselves have been physically or emotionally abandoned by their families. Cholly was rejected by both of his parents; Pauline was made an outsider because of a limp. Traumatized children themselves, they perpetuate their psychopathology in their children by denying their own weakness in their abuse of parental power, by instilling their own fears of impotence, and by calling upon their children to fulfill their own unmet needs.

Never valued as an individual when she was a child, Pauline continues throughout her life to seek approval in others' eyes, particularly in her position as a servant for whites. She attacks her daughter (who has spilled a cobbler) in the white family's kitchen, and in turn, denies her own place in the world when she not only fails to acknowledge Pecola but also comforts the white family's child. Pecola's desire for blue eyes is in fact an inheritance from Pauline herself; vulnerable to accepted ideals of white beauty completely disconnected from herself and her blackness, Pauline wants to look like Jean Harlow. Pauline and Pecola, like the rest of the black community, have internalized the pervasive standard of whiteness—in the white dolls they buy their children, in the movies they watch and emulate, and in their privileging of the light-skinned black child, Maureen Peal, over the darker children. Donald Gibson points out that even through narrative, in the use of the school primer as a structuring device, Morrison has foregrounded the way that their lives are "contained within the framework of the values of the dominant culture and subjected to those values" (21). More subtly, she uses the motif of trauma to suggest the overwhelming power the larger white culture wields in its relentless obliteration of the value of blackness. Her characters affirm the dominant perspective because cultivating awareness of their own collusion would bring incredible pain, no readily available form of action, and increased hopelessness.

Cholly's traumatized past ultimately leads to consequences that are even more devastating for his daughter. After being abandoned by his parents, the most formatively brutalizing incident in Cholly's youth was the interruption of his first sexual experience by armed whites. The experience of being forced by white hunters to continue relations with his partner constitutes a trauma not only in its humiliating intensity, but also in the impossibility of his being able to react to the situation. The displacement of his anger onto his fellow victim, Darlene (Gibson 28), reveals the extent and depth of his trauma: "Never did he once consider directing his hatred toward the hunters. Such an emotion would have destroyed him. They were big, white, armed men. He was small, black, helpless" (119). Their actions have an overwhelming effect on Cholly, who cannot assimilate the truth of his subjugation without being annihilated by a sense of his own powerlessness.

When the environment sustains him, that is, when his marriage and work are stable, Cholly copes well, but when these sources of support and stability are taken away, his past returns to plague his present actions. Psychological research indicates that stress causes "state dependent returns to earlier behavior patterns" (Van der Kolk and Van der Hart 444). A stressful situation will cause thoughts to travel along the same pathways as those connected to a previous traumatic event, and if immediate stimuli recall this event, the individual will be transported back to that somatic (bodily) state and react accordingly. Responding as if faced with past threat, and losing "the mental synthesis that constitutes reflective will and belief, [the individual will] simply transform into automatic wills and beliefs the impulses which are momentarily the strongest" (445). Such is the process that accounts in part for Cholly's rape of Pecola.

When Pecola makes a gesture that reminds him of the tender feelings he once had for Pauline, Pecola's sadness and helplessness and his own inability to make her happy provoke a repetition of the violent impotence and the helpless fear that he and Darlene felt with the white men. His angry response toward Darlene returns and becomes confounded with feelings of love for Pauline and Pecola, and also with self-hatred, because Pecola is like Cholly once was, small and impotent. His pessimistic attitudes toward life, himself, and his capacity to love return to this traumatic context, and he loses the ability to approach life or his daughter positively. One way for him to rid himself of his fears is to project them onto Pecola, and in part he tries to destroy those fears by raping her.

This type of projection as a manifestation of the trauma victim's dissociation from the truth of his or her situation is not unique to

Cholly. The community in which the Breedlove family lives also projects its own sense of devaluation onto the Breedloves, dismissing them for being "low," ugly outsiders, when actually they are merely extreme examples of the larger group's own abasement by white culture. An important example of this projection may be seen in the way that another member of their community, Geraldine, separates herself from "trashy" blacks like Pecola, who she believes threaten her position with regard to whites: "She looked at Pecola. Saw the dirty torn dress, the plaits sticking out on her head, hair matted where the plaits had come undone, the muddy shoes with the wad of gum peeping out from between the cheap soles . . . She had seen this little girl all of her life . . . [children like Pecola] crowded into pews at church, taking space from the nice, neat colored children . . . Like flies they hovered; like flies they settled. And this one had settled in her house" (75).

In her poverty and blackness, Pecola represents everything Geraldine is "fighting to suppress," and in telling Pecola to leave her house, she is "attempting to rid herself of her fears of her own unworthiness, of her own shadow of blackness" (Awkward 194). Geraldine's disregard of Pecola represents what Donald Gibson sees as Morrison's acknowledgment of the black community's participation in its own oppression (21). Geraldine and others fail to recognize that they are outsiders in a white world. Not recognizing that they themselves are what Morrison calls a "pariah community," they reject and revile their own members, like the Breedloves; whereas they should examine the condition of such despised members as "useful for the conscience of that community," so that they can realistically evaluate their own subjugation (Tate interview 129).

Although not specifically addressing trauma, many critics of Morrison's work, in particular Cynthia A. Davis, analyze how oppression is represented in the form of "psychic violence"—the destructiveness of a white racist society that is not always physically brutal, but destroys by engaging in "the systematic denial of the reality of black lives" (323). Roberta Rubenstein also sees Morrison's work as illustrating that the "constriction of the growth of the self is implicitly linked to restrictive or oppressive cultural circumstances" ("Pariahs" 126). Like Davis and Rubenstein, I believe the role of scapegoat that is assigned to Pecola reveals the connection between her devastated life and those of the other individuals in her community. Not psychically able to acknowledge their own lack of power, their seeming lack of sympathy with Pecola is really a displacement "onto the Other all that is feared in the self" (Davis 328). To avoid a sense of their own victimization, the community projects its sense of inferiority onto Pecola, who "is the epitome of the victim in a world that reduces persons to objects and then makes them feel inferior as objects." In order to escape from a similar fate, their response is to act within "the interlocking hierarchies that allow most to feel superior to someone" (330).

The traumatic context of Duras's *The Vice-Consul* is Third World destitution endured by one native character and observed by European colonists living in India. The novel opens with Peter Morgan, the British colonist narrator and character, imagining the thoughts and actions of a beggar woman he has seen. He gives an extended account of the beggar, who as a girl becomes pregnant through her own ignorance and is subsequently driven away from home by her mother, who says, "If you come back I will kill you" (1). She is identified as one of many who have been driven from their homes. The narrative follows the beggar's wandering on the roads from Cambodia to Calcutta, surviving despite the experience of being outcast and pregnant and of giving birth to numerous subsequent children whom she abandons out of madness and destitution. Throughout the narrative, she longs to be a child again, imagining a return to her mother and clinging to all she has left of the safety of childhood and home, that is, scraps of memories and a word, the name of her town.

Interspersed with the beggar's story is that of a group of European colonists who are appalled at the apparent breakdown of one of their own—specifically, the eponymous vice-consul, Jean-Marc de H. A colonial official, he has shot at a group of East Indian lepers in the Shalimar Gardens. This incident is not only harmful to his career, but it also disrupts the veneer of control the colonials have constructed amidst the extreme poverty, disease, and misery that lie just outside the walls of their enclaves. The other male colonials, Peter Morgan, Charles Rossett, Michael Richardson, and the French ambassador, Stretter, avoid and abhor the vice-consul's instability and betrayal of their social and psychological order. He gets marginal sympathy from the ambassador's wife, Anne Marie Stretter, who, like Jean-Marc, is affected deeply by the misery around her, but who also helps distract and protect her many lovers in the colony from the realities of the Third World; with her, they believe, "all the sorrows of the world wash over them in waves" (93).[2] Though they never meet her, Jean-Marc and Anne Marie are both textually linked to the beggar in several ways—by geographical proximity, in being abandoned by parents early in life, and by their manifestations of madness and sorrow. She also contributes elements of the beggar's story, such as how she sold her child. The other men try to keep Anne Marie away from the influence of Jean-Marc, because his influence would bring on despair and compromise her role as an emotional buffer for them. On at least a subconscious level all these Europeans approximate the traumatic responses of the beggar in their denials of and dissociations from reality.

Both Morrison and Duras portray adults as preying on children and destroying their innocence: Pecola is raped by her father, and the fate of Duras's beggar began when she was a young Cambodian girl who became impregnated by a neighbor. "I went into the forest with him," the girl says simply; "I am too young to understand" (10). Like Pecola, the girl is still a child, but menstruating, and so she is treated as an adult for adult needs. When the Cambodian girl's mother rejects her for becoming pregnant and forces her out into the world to beg because of her "adult" behavior, she is refusing to see the girl as still a child and is choosing on behalf of the survival of her younger children. The mother's ruthless detachment from her daughter, like those in Pecola's community, could also be a strategy of survival, an avoidance of the pain of knowing that one is powerless to change one's situation because this truth is too overwhelming. Although the mother inflicts a traumatizing emotional and physical isolation upon her daughter, the text leaves open the possibility that though the mother's anger, like Cholly's toward Pecola, is directed at the daughter, it may stem from the impossibility of any other kind of action, given her own destitute situation and belief in sexual taboos.

The child victims created by Morrison and Duras are the embodiment of traumatic knowledge that, once understood and articulated, would reveal fearful truths about the other characters' lives. This knowledge, denied by victims and observers alike, sets individuals apart from one another and underlies separations by skin color, cultural affiliation, class, and other factors that help to maintain hierarchies of power. The "communities" depicted in *The Bluest Eye* and in *The Vice-Consul* possess the same inability to recognize themselves and their own experience in the outcasts they shun. They illustrate what Judith Herman so aptly describes as the communal expedience of forgetting such truths: "Repression, dissociation and denial are phenomena of social as well as individual consciousness" (9).

Neither her family nor community can offer Pecola support; the latter are embarrassed or revolted by her incestuous pregnancy and madness. They blame the "dog" Cholly but cannot offer her comfort, because her situation is an extreme of their own unacknowledged powerlessness. The narrator, Claudia, admits, "All of us felt so wholesome after we cleaned ourselves on her. . . . Even her waking dreams we used—to silence our own nightmares. . . . We honed our egos on her . . . and yawned in the fantasy of our strength" (159). It is this lack of understanding and response that Morrison attacks, the toleration of isolated suffering, which in fact not only reflects but also perpetuates collective suffering. For all the Breedloves, trauma stems from their devastated, love-deprived lives, from a barren cultural landscape, a "soil [that] is bad for certain flowers. Certain seeds it will not nurture, certain fruit it will not bear, and when the land kills of its own volition, we acquiesce and say the victim had no right to live. We are wrong of course" (160).

According to Claudia, in 1930s America the oppressed and traumatized cannot help one another, because the only power they have available to them is that of feeling superior to the weakest. This is especially evident in the treatment of children. Child psychoanalyst Alice Miller stresses that the kind of contempt and violence shown to children is really the weapon of the weak to mask their own feelings of helplessness and loneliness (67–69). Morrison's work often recognizes the mistreatment of children (e.g., *Sula* and *Beloved*), and though attributing it to adults who have also been brutalized, she nevertheless does not condone their abuse of power.

The madness brought on by the victimization of the two child protagonists frightens others. The people of her town avoid Pecola and exacerbate her separateness by removing her from school because of her uncanny, staring eyes. The beggar in Duras's novel similarly terrifies other characters, such as the British colonist Charles Rossett. When she approaches him covered with mud, her "unwavering smile is terrifying" (163) as she bites the head off a live fish in his presence. Unable to endure the reality of her madness and her filth, he runs terrified toward the safety of the fence that encloses his hotel, and that separates the whites from the people of color, the rich from the poor, the colonists from the colonized. Rossett is afraid of her because he cannot tolerate that which he cannot act upon, that which would make him despair—madness, hopelessness, poverty, the forces of nature—all of which the beggar represents. He and the other colonists do not want to acknowledge they might also be vulnerable to these forces. Hence, the beggar—but also the vice-consul, one of the few colonials in the novel who can empathize and give up the illusion of emotional control—become the objects of others' fear or scorn in order that these others can avoid their own role in the oppression and destitution they witness. In *The Bluest Eye*, avoidance of these individuals enables those in the larger group to mask their fears and their collusion in systems that degrade themselves. In *The Vice-Consul*, the colonizers mask their fear, their privileged status, and their weakness in the face of abjection through denial and avoidance.

In their discussion of trauma, Van der Kolk and Van der Hart explain that "a feeling of helplessness, of physical or emotional paralysis, is fundamental to making an experience traumatic: the person was unable to take any action that could affect the outcome of events," because as appropriate categorization of experience is impaired, traumatic experience cannot be integrated into memory as with normal events (446). A failure to make sense of these past experiences results in fixed ideas that create repetitive and impotent activities around attempted re-creations of the event, and leads to dissociation, where the individual becomes "emotionally constricted and cannot experience a full range of affects" (432). At its worst, personality development is arrested and "cannot expand any more by the addition or assimilation of new elements" (432). In a traumatic experience the past remains unresolved and lingering, because it is not processed in the way that normal information is, either cognitively or emotionally. Nontraumatic memories lose their force, for when new ideas and information become stored, they "are constantly combined with old knowledge to form flexible mental schemas," and once an event is within a larger scheme, it can no longer be accessed as an individual element. In contrast, traumatic memories are those that are frozen in time, not subject to a previous context or to subsequent experience, and are therefore reexperienced without change (441–42). The reality of the traumatic event "continues to elude the subject who lives in its grip and unwittingly undergoes its ceaseless repetitions and reenactments" (Felman and Laub 69). Moreover, Van der Kolk and Ducey affirm that "a sudden and passively endured trauma is relived repeatedly, until a person learns to remember simultaneously the affect and cognition associated with the trauma through access to language" (271).

In a traumatic context, repetition can be an attempt to attack one's own fears, as in Cholly's rape of Pecola, but it can also be a sign of being caught in stasis, of not being able to move on and resolve the initial trauma. Pecola's compulsion to repeat begins after her rape. In her conversations with her imaginary friend, her obsessive but ineffectual questioning of herself and what happened with her father—"He just tried, see? He didn't do anything. You hear me?" (154)—exhibits some of the repetition and dissociation common in the victims of such experience. This coupled with her mother's denial ("She didn't even believe me when I told her," 155) cuts Pecola off from any reconcilable knowledge of what she endured. Pecola takes her other "voice" (a split-off part of herself) to task for continuing to question her about what happened with Cholly, expressing a desperate need to be believed, to understand, and yet to forget and deny as well. Her response is very much like those of many trauma victims, who, as Robert Jay Lifton has observed, feel compelled both to confront and to avoid traumatic experience (162–63).

Pecola's desire for blue eyes becomes obsessive after her rape, and her conviction that Soaphead Church (the man who promises her a miracle from God) has given them to her indicates a complete psychic disintegration. Her own negative reflection in others' eyes has been the continual source of her pain, and her main wish is that her reflection be desirable. The extent of Pecola's obsession and pathology at this stage is presented through hallucinations, through her resistance to blinking, and her delusional view that others envy her gift. "Look. I can look right at the sun . . ." she says, "I don't even have to blink. . . . He really did a good job. Everybody's jealous. Every time I look at somebody, they look off" (151). Her obsessive return to the mirror for reassurance that her "blue eyes" are the bluest and the nicest—"How many times a minute are you going to look?" her "friend" asks (150)—also represents a textual repetition of the destructive power of judgment based solely on appearance and prejudice.

A predisposition toward aggressive differentiation characterizes the colonial mentality, wherein myths of ethnocentrism, privilege, progress, and race highlight differences and block recognition of the other. Frantz Fanon described the psychopathology of racist whites who created myths about blacks that originated in their own regressive fears and illogical feelings; for example, eroticizing or demonizing them or using them as scapegoats or projections of their own unwanted traits (*Black Skin* 155–61). Consequently, those thus mythologized develop a split, or dual consciousness, torn between others' definitions of them and their own possible identities ("a negro is forever in combat with his own image," 194).[3] For example, Fanon witnessed black West Indian children lose the battle as they depicted themselves in school essays as "rosy cheeked." Such self-description is evidence of how dominating cultural practices create physically distorted self-conceptions and "a permanent duality" within individuals living in two radically different cultural viewpoints (142–144; Memmi, *Colonized* 105–6). Fanon's assessment suggests how this duality could have traumatic consequences. The gradual wearing down of one's personal and cultural identity can create a crisis of subjectivity.

With repeated themes and imagery, Morrison underscores her critique of the way that an individual's entire being is reduced to and determined in a glance, just as she is deeply critical of insubstantial and superficial images that lead to the creation of false selves and that assign such power to the gazer. Pecola's belief that she has blue eyes represents her pitiable attempt to feel agency, for she is now the one who looks, but more importantly, this belief symbolizes the trauma of not being loved. She defends against her pain by reexperiencing others' gazes with what she believes is an acceptable, if not lovable, appearance. Ironically, this delusion makes her more of an outcast, because her madness spooks everyone, including her mother. In our last glimpse of Pecola, her potential gone, she wanders in a regressive animal-like state punctuated by useless, repetitive movements: "The damage done was total. She spent her days, her tendril, sap-green days, walking up and down, up and down, her head jerking to the beat of a drummer so distant only she could hear. Elbows bent, hands on shoulders, she flailed her arms like a bird in an eternal, grotesquely futile effort to fly.

Beating the air, a winged but grounded bird, intent on the blue void it could not reach—could not even see—but which filled the valleys of the mind" (158).

Duras's beggar acts in an even more repetitive fashion, particularly after the loss of her first child. The successive abandonment of her children is but one scenario connected with her own abandonment. In order to survive and obtain food, she must prostitute herself to other fishermen; thus she reenacts the original loveless sexual encounter that led to her pregnancy and rejection. Her somnambulistic, interminable walking also exhibits reenactive and dissociative responses to trauma. In wandering, she is obeying her mother's early commands to leave. As she is about to leave the first child behind, she feels that the word for her home village, "Battambang," will protect her; it is a word she will repeat, the only word remaining to her that is understandable to the narrator, signifying a desire to return home to her mother and to the past (46, 48–49).

This unproductive traumatic activity is also subtly linked by both Duras and Morrison to metaphors of fecundity gone awry. Pecola, just become a biological woman at age eleven, cannot sustain her father's unwanted seed. In *The Vice-Consul*, like the cloyingly sweet custard apples, children are obscenely abundant beyond what can be sustained and are consequently wasted (just as in another of Duras's novels set in Indochina, *The Sea Wall*, where the dead bodies of children are said to make the land fertile). Each girl (Pecola and the beggar) carries a child (or children, in the beggar's case) that is lost or left behind, and these losses create dissociation and deterioration from which they never recover. In the beggar girl's rejection of her first, and subsequent infants, Duras represents in "the abandonment of a child the scandalous limit of dispossession: the limit of misery, of unawareness, of madness" (Borgomano 489, my translation). When babies do not survive, the future is cut off; so the loss of these children is a powerful symbol of an ultimate loss of the future.

The most severe traumatic loss of the beggar girl's life is having to give up her first child, a girl. Although she knows she will never be able to find work with a child in tow, she has heard that whites sometimes take in children (38). Accordingly, she pursues a French woman and begs her to take her ill, starving child, which the mother does (40–43) and as Duras's own mother once did (Vircondelet 37; Borgomano 491).

While the French foster mother consults with a doctor and cries over the obviously doomed infant, the baby's girl-mother observes: "It no longer concerns me. It is the business of other women now. You [the baby] in addition to myself, an impossible association, yet how hard it was to separate us" (49). Dramatizing this dissociation, the narrative shifts to the third person: "The doctor approaches the newly-washed infant, and gives it an injection. The child gives a feeble cry. . . . Unconsciously, she mimics the grimace on the child's crumpled face. For the rest of her life she will feel, between her shoulders, the pressure of the child's weight, her exact weight now. Alive or dead, for her the child will never exceed that weight. The girl leaves the spot from which she has been watching. She turns her back, now bare of its burden, on the window. She leaves" (49–50).

Speaking for and about her, Duras's narrator, Peter Morgan, predicts that the girl will in turn abandon all her other children after this one, that she will put them aside, miss them briefly, and forget them. This detachment from them can be explained as a way of coping with the loss of the first child; in order to keep that original pain at bay, she shuts down affectively and separates herself from them both physically and emotionally. In doing so she also repeats her own traumatic separation from her mother (Hofmann 70).

When individuals are exposed to trauma, in other words, a frightening event outside of ordinary human experience, they experience "speechless terror" (Van der Kolk and Van der Hart 442). Traumatic memory, psychoanalyst Judith Herman explains, is "wordless and static" (Trauma 175) and initially iconic or visual (175, 177); it also manifests itself in "behavioral reenactments, nightmares [or] flashbacks," because traumatic experience "cannot be easily translated into the symbolic language necessary for linguistic retrieval" (Van der Kolk and Van der Hart 442–43). Traumatic experience at its worst creates a "loss of voice, . . . of knowledge, of awareness, of truth, of the capacity to feel . . . and to speak" (Felman and Laub 231–32). In order to help the individual to reexperience the past fully and affectively, it is therefore necessary for the therapist to encourage the victim to construct a completed narrative of the event, including "a full and vivid description of the traumatic imagery" (Herman 177). Duras and Morrison are "textual" therapists, who attempt to recover traumatic experience from the silence and repression that attend it.

They engage in a kind of therapeutic process in their narratives by working through the traumatic process—not for these protagonists, who are imprisoned psychologically, but for readers to see the social and personal costs. They do this by providing knowledge of their dilemmas and a means of analyzing traumatic effects through the thoughts of narrators and the behaviors of the protagonists. Like many autobiographies and testimonial literature of this century, Morrison and Duras share the pain of these situations with readers (Henke xix), and through the hopeless stories of Pecola and the beggar, Morrison and Duras take us through the mistakes and collusion in exploitative systems that exacerbate individuals' sufferings and, by extension, collective suffering. We are offered these stories through the voices of observant others who demonstrate for us as readers and outsiders what we might or might not do as potential witnesses to abuse. Would we condone it? Deny it? Participate in it? Fear it? These writers take us through the process of analyzing the costs of inaction and conformity. Thus they become writers of testimonio in attempting to speak for the marginal in works of moral and political urgency that are concerned with "problematic collective social situations" (Beverley 95–99) and in resisting those situations by intending to stimulate at the very least public beliefs and opinions, if not actions.

In both novels there is an attempt to speak for victims virtually silenced by the process of trauma. First, this takes the form of trying to articulate the victims' own words, suggesting their traumatized condition through the narratively dissociative yet emotionally overdetermined quality of these words. For example, the only word left to the beggar, the name of her hometown, "Battambang," is repeatedly invoked to emphasize her desire to return home (though there is some indication she would no longer recognize it) and to symbolize the safe place of childhood. Even though this is the place where her mother rejected her, she longs to speak in her own language (she has strayed, symbolically, out of her own country). The narrator informs us that the beggar speaks to her absent mother now that she no longer has the child to hear her, but she remains silenced in effect because her word(s) remain incomprehensible to others.

Julia Kristeva asserts that in Duras's texts the sense of loss or void left by traumatic abandonments are presented as "unused affects and in a discourse emptied of meaning" (146), but that her texts also speak a "discourse of blunted pain," which represents "the trace of an absence" (140, 146). That is, all that is left for these dispossessed individuals is a profound sense of absence of self or of significant others. Kristeva does not directly link Duras's characterization and discourse to traumatic re-actions, but I would argue that these traces also correspond to the left-over emotions and the inarticulateness common to victims of trauma, and that if such emptiness is in keeping with Duras's general philoso-phy, it is also important to acknowledge that this philosophical con-ception is born in a context of trauma and takes the form of a psycho-logical critique of oppression.

Pecola similarly seeks comfort in words. In part she seeks under-standing of what her father has done to her, but her conflicted dialogue with a split-off persona of herself also illustrates how much she has been isolated and how her pain and need to speak are ignored by her community and even her family. To characterize this self-splitting, Morrison utilizes an interchange of voices: "How come you don't talk to anybody? *I talk to you* . . . I just wondered. You don't talk to anybody. You don't go to school. And nobody talks to you. *How do you know no-body talks to me?* They don't. When you're in the house with me, even Mrs. Breedlove doesn't say anything to you. Ever. Sometimes I wonder if she even sees you" (*Bluest Eye* 153, italics in original). Hence, both writers are faced with two important issues when speaking for these protagonists: First, there is the necessity of communicating their expe-rience so that it will be known; second, there is the question of how this can be done when the characters are cut off from linguistic connections or from dialogue with others. They address this dilemma by creating other voices to compensate for the gaps.

Outsider narrators are employed by both writers to supplement the victims' voices and to construct suggestive if unmasterly narratives that are essential for their stories to be told and for the therapeutic function of such telling to occur. By demonstrating the limitations of their narrators, however, both writers also acknowledge the problem of the further oppression that might result from the attempt to give voices to oppressed victims. They problematize their narrators but also their own roles as writers and ours as readers of this material. We are enticed into the material but also asked to contemplate its implications.

Carefully observing the silencing effects of trauma, Morrison recog-nized that as the most traumatized character, Pecola will not be able to tell her own story. Consequently, she provides Claudia and a third-person narrator to testify for her: "[S]ince the victim does not have the vocabulary to understand the violence or its context, gullible, vulnerable girl friends . . . would have to do that for her, and would have to fill those silences with their own reflective lives" ("Unspeakable" 22). Claudia, who has been Pecola's friend, realizes the harm done to Pecola by the community, including herself in that complicity: "She seemed to fold into herself, like a pleated wing. Her pain antagonized me" (61); "We tried to see her without looking at her . . . because we had failed her" (158). Not only is Claudia sympathetic toward Pecola, but she is also self-conscious and self-critical about her own complicity. In this way, through her narrative we are slowly exposed to the dynamics and effects of racism. Similarly, if Claudia is an insider in the way she experiences some of the same pain as Pecola, she is also an outsider and privileged in the sense that having been loved, she possesses the strength to have her own desires. Outsider and insider at the same time, she is aware enough of the need to recognize her community's role and their own defeat in Pecola's disintegration. Thus, she illustrates to some extent the reader's double position as an engaged yet separate witness. Claudia plays out our own potential roles in either exacerbating trauma or as part of a healing process.

Duras's use of a male narrator to tell the story of an abused girl is equally effective in drawing attention to the suspect position of speaking for (i.e., defining) an other. Peter Morgan tries to understand the tragedy of Calcutta through the narration of the beggar's story, and his hope is that "wisdom may start to grow out of bitter experience" (18). In his narrative appropriation of others' suffering, however, Morgan indulges in what Eric Santner would call "narrative fetishism," which he defines as "the construction and deployment of a narrative consciously or unconsciously designed to expunge the traces of the trauma or loss that called that narrative into being in the first place" (144). As Duras portrays him, Morgan, like most of the other colonists, keeps himself remote from the horrors of deprivation surrounding him by creating a narrative about a dispossessed beggar woman he sees in Calcutta. Only by focusing in on one case of destitution in a fictional form can he approach the woman's condition from a safe distance: "I am drunk with the sufferings of India. Aren't we all, more or less? It's impossible to talk about such suffering unless one has made it as much a part of oneself as breathing. That woman stirs my imagination. I note down my thoughts about her" (124). The identification with suffering that Morgan claims for himself is actually truer of two of the other characters, the vice-consul (who Morgan studiously avoids), and Anne Marie Stretter, who are both immediately and emotionally affected by India, and almost driven mad by it. Thus Morgan's approach reveals the fear, denial, and repression characteristic of the colonists' position, and though he uses his own memory and others' accounts to "explain the madness of the beggar woman of Calcutta" (54), he remains out of touch with the sources and contexts of her madness.

With these characters Duras makes readers consider different possible reactions and positionings, as well as the pain involved even in just empathizing. Duras's creation of the speculative narrator illustrates Doris Sommer's notion about texts that resist allowing readers to have full knowledge of a situation they will never experience (408–9), leading us to contemplate, and experience like trauma victims, our own uncertainty. Also, resistance avoids misuse or misinterpretation of information. For example, readers' knowledge could give them power over victims, or cause them to misjudge because of cultural differences or ignorance of the ethical, social, or psychological implications of victims' situations (417–18).

Morgan's attempt to identify with this woman and with India through language is also problematic because she has no available language with which to express herself and her sufferings. Up to a point Morgan is aware of this problem: "How to put into words the things she never said? . . . How to describe the things that she does not know she has seen, the experiences that she does not know she has had? How to reconstruct the forgotten years?" (55) Duras displays here an awareness of possible appropriation and a simultaneous need to understand associated with any narrative. That is, although Morgan's narrative is useful to establish the story's context and the voices of the colonists, Duras follows the beggar further than Morgan does and allows her to surpass the definition and containment of Morgan's narrative when she is described toward the end of the novel by an unidentified neutral narrator. Here, the beggar emerges in an almost triumphant madness, as if in panoply; she ceases here to be the one who helps another (Morgan) to understand himself and becomes someone whose presence demands recognition in and of itself. By bringing her into contact with the obsessively rational Englishman Rossett, Duras forces a colonist to directly confront the awful reality of the beggar—one of their colonized subjects—and he is horrified by the encounter (163–64).

I have focused on the beggar and Pecola together because their stories are so interwoven. They powerfully exemplify many of the social, political, and identity issues that concern Morrison and Duras. Their stories are only a beginning, however. Many of Morrison's and Duras's other texts offer similar characterizations and patterns of behavior and extend the threads of traumatic experience, including abandonment, repetition, and transference, incapacity to feel for oneself, and fractured relationships. These other texts also explore the social position of the traumatized and develop mediatory relationships whereby characters are enabled to experience or feel through others as part of an important process of witnessing and (re)constructing the past through narrative. Such mediation represents a significant connection to trauma in foregrounding transference relationships, substitutions, and repetitions that are characteristic of traumatic stasis and being engulfed by the past. Mediations, however, also involve witnessing, whereby isolating individual experience can be grasped by others with the goal of creating collective knowledge and healing (see chapters 4 and 5).

The Ravishing of Lol V. Stein

Duras already explored the theme of abandoned, traumatized children in *The Ravishing of Lol V. Stein*, written two years before *The Vice-Consul*. In *Ravishing*, abandonment by a lover instead of a mother brings these issues out of the context of family and colonialism into the realm of power and desire in gender relations. Lol's story fits with the circumstances of Pecola and the beggar for several reasons—not only because she is abandoned, but a childlike regression informs her adult life, and in the false desires created out of traumatic defenses, we see with Lol the most devastating emotional consequences of trauma that can take shape even in the mundane life of a middle-class French housewife. The characterization of Lol prefigures the beggar's appearance in her fiction; each reenacts her own abandonment, each manifests her madness and desire in repetitive acts, and each seems untouched by time. Both characters live in a deathlike traumatic stasis, retaining youth even after motherhood, and remaining more deeply affected by the past than the present. Repetition becomes the driving force of their lives. Their continual wanderings reenact connection to the past as much as they annihilate conscious memory of it, but these roamings also reflect and sustain desire. In reference to the repetitive walking of Lol in *Ravishing*, again as she reappears in *L'Amour* (1972), and in "La Femme du Gange" (her 1973 film of *L'Amour*),[4] Duras notes: "Here we are in a world totally corporeal. It is in walking that another memory comes to her and that a memory leaves her, that *the transference takes place*" (*Les Lieux* 98, italics added). That is, those memories lodged most deeply in the unconscious can only be realized in physical activity, in the body. In making this connection between a French woman and a marginalized Third World beggar, Duras demonstrates how her experience of Third World poverty continues to inform her view of the world while also serving as a way to link the human sufferings of very different people and circumstances.[5]

Like the beggar, Lol is locked into a repression so impenetrable that she loses touch with conscious memory of the origins of her trauma. She watches with morbid fascination as her fiancé, Michael Richardson, becomes infatuated with another woman at a ball and deserts Lol. Yet although Lol forcefully denies and represses her devastation for years, she never recovers from this incident and it permanently marks her inner being and desires. Lol cannot remember the original scene, even when confronted with the actual room late in the novel, and she eagerly forgets individuals connected to that scene, even very important people in her life, including her mother and her best friend, Tatiana. South Tahla, the town where this occurred and to which she later returns, has been erased from her memory such that she sees it all as new. In this small town, where everyone knew of her lover's abandonment, she strongly defends herself against this knowledge. Her memory of it is reversed; walking through the town, it becomes less rather than more familiar to her ("she began to recognize less," 33). Thus Duras illustrates Lol's disconnection from her past, her loved ones, and from her life in any deep sense.

While watching Michael betray her with Anne Marie Stretter (two other textual links with *The Vice-Consul*), Lol instinctively recognizes their implacable desires and almost immediately begins to dissociate, to distance herself emotionally through identification with them, and to reposition her own role in the situation so that she can be part of that experience and "unhurt" by it. She watches them dance "the way a woman whose heart is wholly unattached . . . watches her children leave her: she seemed to love them" (8). She becomes upset only at the end of the evening when she wants to prolong the dance, begging the couple not to leave. Already, there is comfort in repetition. Lol will spend the time between the ball and her marriage (to another man) by repeating the phrases she used to try to keep the couple from leaving. Afterward, all that will remain of the moment when Lol knew the night of the ball was over "is time in all its purity, bone-white time" (37). Thus, the traumatic incident remains static, unchanged by time for Lol, the bone image connoting a kind of changeless death in life for her.

After a ten-year absence, years seemingly filled with obsessive attention to domestic duties, Lol returns to South Tahla and begins daily, habitual walking, which will ultimately bring her another kind of contact with her past. The narrator describes the "mechanical movement" of Lol's body while walking, emphasizing its automaticity and her lack of self-awareness. Her walks remove her from the confining space of her house and her outward life of uneventful duty, through which she also mechanically "walks." The narrator also says that her walks produce "a welter of thoughts, all rendered equally sterile the moment her walk was over—none of these thoughts had ever crossed the threshold with her into her house" (35). Neither the narrator, Jack Hold, nor the reader are privy to these thoughts; however, we do know that her wanderings lead her to Hold and to fulfillment of her original desire through reenactment and replacement.

Ravishing is the first Duras text where trauma indicates not only dispossession but also connects desire with abandonment, self-effacement, and replacement (connections more fully developed in *The Lover*). Lol's self-effacement originates from the fixed idea she develops at the ball that she can only have Michael by watching him with another women, from outside, hence her desire to be present as he undresses and makes love to Anne Marie. This desire underlies her wanting to reconstruct this triangle, now with Jack and Tatiana, which both includes and excludes herself. She picks them because they are already illicit lovers (Tatiana is married), and she projects Michael's qualities onto Jack, transferring her desires to him because she can feel pleasure only through the mediation of the triangle ("she loves the man who must love Tatiana," 122). Jack also enhances his own sexual pleasure with Tatiana by thinking of Lol waiting outside the hotel where they rendezvous. Although Jack prefers Lol, she makes him promise never to leave Tatiana, because she can only love the man who "betrays" her. Ironically, though Jack enters into Lol's fantasies self-interestedly, he will come to realize that he functions only to keep alive Lol's desire for another man.

Ravishing concludes with the impossibility of re-creating or representing an original traumatic scene; Lol is left with mere repetition and echoing (Willis 87). The proof that resolution is never achieved and that the past is unrecapturable for Lol is evident in her return to the ballroom. There is no sudden climactic realization at the originary site of trauma; she experiences no memory or response. The closest she can come is in replacement through Jack and Tatiana; her desire is rooted in repetition.

Lol displays many characteristics of traumatization. Lol is described as a ghost—inscribed in the past—and someone who empties the spaces in which she lives. Devoid of spirit and volition, Lol feels she has never chosen her life but cannot conceive of another ("One day . . . Lol Stein found herself married to John Bedford," 21). Jack describes her as "she who so constantly takes wing away from her living life" (156). Like Pecola and the beggar, she needs disconnection from the contiguous relations of past and present and from desiring unachievable emotional ties. She has lost connection with her feelings, telling Tatiana that she does not know if she still thinks of the ball and claims not to have suffered. Repression usually predominates over remembering, but Lol occasionally reveals some hidden awareness, as when Hold realizes Lol is "repressing some frightful pain to which she fails to yield, which, on the contrary, she cultivates with all her might, on the edge of bringing it to climactic expression" (121). Jack is convinced that she pretends forgetting at times because she denies having ever suffered but shows emotion and resistance when he questions this.

Lol's silence and inarticulateness indicate the extremity of her condition; she maintains traumatic silence because there are no words to express her feelings, Jack realizes.

Lol does not probe very deeply into the unknown into which this moment [the end of the ball] opens. She has no memory, not even an imaginary one, she has not the faintest notion of this unknown. But what she does believe is that she must enter it, that that was what she had to do, that it would always have meant, for her mind as well as her body, both their greatest pain and their greatest joy, so commingled as to be undefinable, a single entity but unnamable for lack of a word. I like to believe—since I love her—that if Lol is silent in her daily life it is because, for a split second, she believed that this word might exist. Since it does not, she remains silent. It would have been an absence-word, a hole-word, whose center would have been hollowed out into a hole, a kind of hole in which all other words would have been buried. It would have been impossible to utter it, but it would have been made to reverberate. Enormous, *endless, an empty gong*, it would have held back anyone who had wanted to leave, it would have convinced them of the impossible, it would have made them deaf to any other word save that one, in one fell swoop it would have defined the future and the moment themselves. (38, italics added)

Lol's silence reflects her helplessness to find the word or gesture that would have affected the events that have forever changed her. Much like the beggar with the name of her town, or Pecola with her blue eyes, Lol tries and fails to find a sign, a word, that will bring solace and make her life meaningful. The overwhelming meaning of those impossible events is never known to her and hence cannot be articulated. But the events continue to reverberate in her life, as "endless, an empty gong." Silence represents the loss, repression, inarticulateness, and shock associated with trauma; Lol was speechless at the ball, distancing herself from the desire and pain associated with Michael, and she later reenacts this same process with Jack. Lol says to Jack, "[I]n a certain state of mind, all trace of feeling is banished. Whenever I remain silent in a certain way, I don't love you, have you noticed that?" (128–29).

Trauma and its effects provide the means for Duras to critique conventions of identity, gender, and relationships in *Ravishing*. For example, through other characters' reactions to Lol's behavior Duras demonstrates how traumatic repression suits conventional social, gender, and marital relations. The people of South Tahla help Lol retain her repression. They do not greet her when she returns after ten years, believing that she wants to forget her tragic past. Her sober, conservative appearance makes them mistakenly believe that "she had emerged forever from a traumatic experience" (32). Duras critiques gender roles in

presenting male characters who find Lol's somnambulism not only con-
venient but appealing. Her husband, John Bedford, never questions her
about the past and likes both her "obsessive orderliness" in running
their household (another manifestation of the automaticity of her life)
and her passivity (which he considers gentleness). He is attracted to her
wounds and incompletion, having a "penchant for young girls, girls not
completely grown into adults" (20). When she first meets him at nineteen, she looks fifteen, and the narrator says she still carries this "mor-
bidly young" look ten years later, after marriage and motherhood. For
Bedford, she is the "sleeping beauty who never offered a word of com-
plaint" (24). Again, his self-interest discourages recovery of her lost
self or her development as a woman, much less a fully functioning person. Her marriage encourages her passive state, wherein she makes no
choices and lives an imitative life of false order.

For Duras, Bedford is clearly an example of how many men enjoy dominion over emotionally removed and inarticulate women, keeping
them childlike and acquiescent. The limited space of her monotonous
married life, mostly glossed over in the text, contrasts markedly with
the intense passion she seeks to re-create and the relatively freer space
of the town where she wanders. Jack Hold similarly wants to possess
and contain her and attempts to appropriate her obsessive passions for
his own sexual fulfillment. Hold is attracted to Lol's body, "made taut
by her constant effort to efface herself . . . the body of a grown-up school-
girl" (104). Again, as in *The Bluest Eye* and *The Vice-Consul*, children
or the childlike are a focus for desire and exploitation by others.

Significantly and conversely, it is women who care for Lol the most.
Both her mother and Tatiana are concerned about her feelings and do
not accept her lack of emotion as healthy. Lol's rejection of her mother
emphasizes her denial and repression of Michael's betrayal. When the
mother arrives at the end of the ball, expresses anger toward the couple,
and tries to comfort Lol, her daughter knocks her down. Lol thereby defends herself against what her mother feels *for* her, that is, in her stead.
Lol will thereafter try to forget her mother because she had identified
with what should have been Lol's heartbreak: that which Lol had to repress at all cost, even her sanity. Her mother's death later on will not
visibly affect her, because she continues to resist any awareness of her
own pain, which her mother represents. She similarly represses her
friendship with Tatiana, who also supported her during the ball, until

knowing her again becomes associated with her desire to reenact a passion that no longer exists between her and Michael or Michael and Anne Marie.

The prevalence of dissociation in this text, in Lol's character and in her limited, obsessional view of life indicates severe traumatic response and a fragmented sense of identity. This fragmentation brings her closer to her desires and removes her from conventional roles, but it also precludes awareness and integration of her past, present, and future. Lol's splitting articulates the great distance between her actual life and her desires. When asked to consider leaving her husband, she says about herself: "Lol has always returned home safe and sound with John Bedford" (126). Splitting dictates Lol's relationship to Jack as well. In bed with Hold, Lol's obsessive delusion about him and Tatiana divides her identity between herself and Tatiana. Even her desire becomes conflicted as she alternately seeks his body and seeks to flee (179). He comes to recognize that "she was beside me and separated from me by a great distance, abyss and sister" (156). The fear she expresses in sharing identity with Tatiana as Hold's lover indicates a fear of directly experiencing sexual passion. Splitting extends to the narrator as well; both he and Lol refer to themselves in the third person. He is deliberately split to conceal his identity from the reader or to dissolve it into Michael's to please Lol, but he also recognizes her desires divide himself as well, as he knowingly describes the process of how he is becoming a substitute for Michael (102–4).

As Duras describes Lol, she has the same relation to memory as the beggar, both propelled by the past and oblivious to it: "[S]he is haunted, she is like a haunted place. She cannot make a compromise with memory, she is crushed by the memory which, each day, each day of her life is new, recaptures its freshness, a kind of original freshness. That's it, Lol V. Stein is someone who each day remembers for the first time and this all repeats itself each time as if there were fathomless gulfs of forgetting between the days of Lol V. Stein. She does not get used to memory. Neither to forgetting, moreover" (*Les Lieux* 99, my translation). Lol is incapable of reflection according to Duras: "She stopped herself living before reflection. This is perhaps what makes her so dear to me, finally, so close . . . Reflection is something which I find questionable, which annoys me" (*Les Lieux* 98, my translation). For Duras, Lol is blessed because memory and reflection are antithetical to passionate desire, which originates and continues only in the unconscious realm of the transference. Traumatic memory enables her to cling to and continually, insatiably, restage a dead passion that remembering and working through would only destroy.

Duras embraces the excess of emotion connected to transference of originary loves and abandonments. As Carol Hofmann notes, madness does not have normally pejorative social connotations for Duras, but rather "signals the release from a repressed, constrained memory," and forgetting "means the destruction of social constraints" in which Duras reveled (53). Traumatic withdrawal and fantasy remove Lol from the void of her daily life but also preclude new relationships or experiences unattached to her past. Duras describes here a world so oppressive to women that madness becomes their only refuge, escape can be only an interior process.

L'Amour takes place seven years after *Ravishing* (Hofmann 129). It portrays Lol again, unnamed, completely removed from social roles and constrictions, her whole days spent wandering a beach in South Tahla and conversing with two men who seem to correspond to Jack Hold and Michael Richardson. Richardson, the lover she lost seventeen years ago, has returned, intending to commit suicide. He speaks of her illness after the ball, but although she knows him and the hotel, she claims not to know what happened there. This work is created from other Duras texts; what happens here would have no reference point without *Ravishing* and *The Vice-Consul.* This is also a Beckettian, socially dissociated text; the actions and words of the characters are very distanced from normal social intercourse, which has receded to the past with the husband Bedford's death.

This other Lol's life and self express an even more radical dissociation and dislocation than in *Ravishing,* and her characterization resembles that of the beggar as much as Lol. She is described as living outdoors like a vagrant, immobile like a corpse in sleep, her body is "abandoned," but she will go with any man who will have her and seems to be continually hungry, pregnant, and nauseated like the beggar. Further, it is said that she has had many children and given them away. We are not really sure if children are being born in this context, however, because the characters' words could be expressions of desire rather than fact. In *L'Amour,* Duras immerses readers in the starkly arid existence of the most severely traumatized, unembellished by social

roles or concerns. Here, pain is not shared but endured in mutual isolation and individuals are driven by automaticity not choice, experiencing radical dissociation from everything but their pain.

The Dispossessed Children of Morrison's *Jazz*

Morrison views deprivation of identity in less positive terms than
Duras, and her characterizations reflect a view of identity as multifaceted and constructed both within and apart from one's social group. She
also insists, though, that responses to subjugation and neglect—that is,
detachment, physical and emotional isolation—have been devastating
to African Americans and their community. Her characters suffer
greatly when deprived of their identity either as blacks in a white-dominated America or when constricting racist or moral attitudes deny
them their familial origins or healthy reciprocating relationships. Such
deprivation distorts the characters' desires and sense of connection and
responsibility to others throughout their lives.

In Morrison's *Jazz*, the reader is confronted with a collectivity of
abandoned children. As in *Beloved*, Morrison links the severing of intimate ties to issues of ancestry, slavery, and racism, but this more recent
novel covers the time period from slavery to the 1920s rather than ending during Reconstruction. Their abandonments are frequently linked
with the consequence of racial intolerance manifested in physical violence, taboos, or economic warfare. In one case the missing parent is
mad. The common circumstance of these characters' lives is being
deprived early in life of guiding influences necessary to identity and
forming attachments. As in *Ravishing*, dispossessions carry repercus-
sions well into the characters' adult lives as they entertain murderous
thoughts, engage and avoid questions of regeneration and attachment,
search insatiably for love, and attempt to fill voids with substitutions
for what they have lost.

Four of the major characters in *Jazz* are deprived of parents in their
formative years. Joe Trace is the child of a "wild" woman who lives in
the woods and will not acknowledge their bond: "Too brain blasted
to do what the meanest sow managed: nurse what she birthed" (179).
Worse than the most dissolute mother, in Joe's eyes, her "indecent
speechless lurking insanity" provokes his murderous thoughts and his
frequent searches for her in the woods. The cause of her insanity is unknown, but her cunning ability to survive in nature and giving up a

child recall Duras's beggar. Wild is another extreme example of dispossession made more disturbing by her failure at mothering. Joe's outrage at being abandoned will emerge again with his lover, Dorcas. Violet Trace's mother, Rose Dear, shuts down emotionally and eventually commits suicide after everything the family owns is confiscated, after whites have run her husband off, most likely as a punishment for his racial activism during Reconstruction. Violet does not want to be like her mother, and both she and her husband, Joe, bury themselves in work, do not mourn her miscarriages, and believe that by not having children they will never be put in the position of being unable to take care of their needs. In this way they also avoid thinking about lost attachments, which will leave them unconsciously vulnerable to unmourned loss. Dorcas, Joe's young lover, loses her parents as a child when their home is burned down in an unprovoked attack by white racists during the East St. Louis riots of 1912. Dorcas immediately dissociates, suppressing thoughts about her parents' deaths by imagining how fast her dolls would have burned in the fire: "She went to two funerals in five days, and never said a word" (57). Only later, in her late teens, will her desperate need for love surface in her affairs with men. The last similarly dispossessed character is Golden Gray, the son of a loving, attentive white mother and a black slave father whose identity is kept a secret until the boy is grown. The mother, Vera-Louise, was banished by her slave-owning parents for this pregnancy, although her father has clearly practiced miscegenation himself. Golden does not suffer until he learns, at eighteen, of his father's existence, which creates a huge sense of loss and a void in his life. Golden is linked to both Joe and Violet's pasts in that he rescues Joe's mother and has been raised by True Belle, Violet's grandmother, who fills her imagination with stories of his pampered, idyllic childhood. All these characters continue to suffer from the emotional gaps in their lives.

In midlife Violet is crushed by "mother-hunger [that] had hit her like a hammer. Knocked her down and out" (108), such that she sleeps with a baby doll. Up until then, much of her life involved substitute mothering tasks like hairdressing and caring for birds (O'Reilly 370). Although Violet fills her days with tasks so her emotions will not reach the surface, she is prone to bouts of "public craziness," which she has trouble identifying as her own—sitting down in the street for no apparent reason, or taking another's baby out of its carriage and beginning to walk away with it. Violet loses connection with her life, as if she is watching it from a distance. She experiences an extreme self-division, identifying the behavior from which she wants to dissociate as done by a double of herself. Carolyn Jones describes the cracks or gaps in Violet's consciousness as spaces Violet cannot fill with the story or testimony of her life, and secondly, as a form of knowledge (485). This unspoken, alienated knowledge is in fact the emergence of traumatic memory, which cannot be assimilated until she seeks the help of Alice, whose critical voice acts as a catalyst to mourning. This splitting of herself resembles Pecola's in its repression of unbearable knowledge; Violet tries to remain distanced from her pain by remaining apart from the "crazy" acts that are a response to it.

Violet is the last of three generations of women deprived of a mother's care and love, beginning with her grandmother True Belle, who spent most of her life in slavery. True Belle is taken from her own children to help Vera-Louise raise Golden Gray. Consequently, it is implied that Rose Dear possesses little sense of self or a will to survive. After her mother's suicide, Violet grows up hearing Golden Gray stories from True Belle. Andrea O'Reilly argues that Violet's "fatal attraction" for Golden Gray "is responsible for her emotional scarring; the pain of unrequited love damages her selfhood. Further, she learns to value that which is not herself (maleness, whiteness) and tragically, "[t]he mother love that rightly belonged to the daughters was lavished on a white boy [Golden]" (368). Violet will eventually go through a process, with Alice's help, of evaluating her own unconscious actions and recognizing her temporary alienation from her own life. In a therapeutic conversation with Felice (Dorcas's friend), she explains what led to her actions— a sense of wanting to be "White. Light. Young again" (208), everything she is not, and forgetting her own strength and ability to survive up to the point of her breakdown, including exile from the South and a new life as part of the Great Migration north.

Dorcas, at eighteen, becomes a substitute who fills in many gaps for Joe and Violet. Each sees what they need to see in her. Both Dorcas and Joe feel unloved when they meet, and each fills a void in the other's life. Joe wants to recapture the love that he and Violet had when they were young, because Violet has become so preoccupied with needing a child. Even Violet cannot decide whether Dorcas is a temptress or "the daughter who fled her womb" (109). When Dorcas rejects Joe, he stalks her as he once did his mother. Finding her in the arms of another man awakens the feelings of love, betrayal, and abandonment that he felt toward his mother, and he shoots Dorcas. After the funeral, the couple obsesses on a photo of Dorcas, with Joe trying to keep his memory of her alive and Violet trying to understand who she was. Joe nurtures his guilty grief; forgetting is also traumatic for him. Joe's defensive strategy of becoming a new man to fit his situation no longer works for him. As he mourns Dorcas every day with tears, he is also mourning his mother's loss. Violet also mourns her own past through looking at Dorcas's picture.

It is Dorcas's guardian and aunt Alice, and friend Felice, having known Dorcas better, who are able to bring information and perspective and eventually heal the couple's grief so that they can recover their love for one another. Alice fulfills the role True Belle once had in Violet's life, as guide and advisor. Alice urges Violet to stop focusing on her own hurt, to love what she has and recognize that people like Dorcas take because they are desperately needy as well. When Violet asks if she shouldn't fight for what is hers, Alice replies, "Fight what, who? Some mishandled child who saw her parents burn up? Who knew better than you or me or anybody just how small and quick this little bitty life is? Or maybe you want to stomp somebody with three kids and one pair of shoes. . . . Somebody wanting arms just like you do" (113). Alice's insights point out the consequences of collective loss in the black community. Their deprivations, meshed with a precarious hold on love and security, along with the harsh looseness of life in the city, produces repeated abandonments as well as violent conflicts over love and possession of the beloved.

It is in the figure of Golden Gray, the blonde mixed-race boy/man that Morrison links these characters with a slave past as well as continued oppression after Reconstruction. Golden's appearance as he looks for his father, Hunter's Hunter, coincides with Southern whites running black farmers like Joe off their land, forcing them to move and change jobs and eventually to migrate north. When Golden learns at eighteen that his father is black, it initially makes him "loose, lost," and then he begins to understand how his father's absence affected him, which Morrison expresses with an image of mutilation for loss. "Only now, he thought, now that I know I have a father, do I feel his absence: the place where he should have been and was not. Before, I thought everybody was one-armed, like me. Now I feel the surgery" (158). With True Belle's encouragement he seeks his father, hoping thus to recover his identity and place in the world: "When I see him, or what is left of him, I will tell him all about the missing part of me and listen for his crying shame. I will exchange then; let him have mine and take his as my own and we will both be free, arm-tangled and whole" (159). Upon meeting his father, Golden Gray wants to kill him but does not; Hunter's Hunter tells his son that he is welcome to stay but not to chastise him, because he did not know he had a son. Presumably their relationship does not continue since Hunter's Hunter never mentions Golden Gray to his protégé, Joe, but Joe finds Hunter's and Golden's possessions mysteriously present in the wild woman's lair.

Again, we are made to understand how racism and slavery have broken families apart and the difficulty of filling that void once created. Morrison tackles here the countless traumas, denials, and avoidances this country has endured concerning miscegenation. She says that for her the past is infinite and full of such stories. She raises questions that remain pertinent about the interconnections of identity and history for ancestors of slave masters and slaves. This has been a source of anger and agony for decades, fueling perceptions and conflicts over skin color and racial identity that are still felt and debated today.[6]

Morrison's statements and textual evidence indicate that Wild is the pregnant Beloved who disappears at the end of *Beloved* (O'Reilly 372–73; Cutter 67–69). Morrison again uses this figure to embody African American dispossession with a young woman who in not nurturing her child, symbolizes the shattering of African and African American family relations from the Middle Passage to Reconstruction and beyond. In this inability to nurture, which negates the future, she also resembles Pecola and Duras's beggar. Beloved and Wild represent the displaced, the unclaimed, the dangerously free. They are also haunting reminders of lost origins and the price of disconnection from ancestors. *Jazz* concludes optimistically with Violet and Joe working through their past conflicts and engaged in mourning. Roberta Rubenstein concludes that *Jazz* is an act of "cultural mourning" on Morrison's part "that ultimately serves as an expression of grief for lost loves and possibilities and as a form of re-appropriation of lost (appropriated) cultural creations" ("Singing" 149). Morrison does this "through the use of literary techniques that inventively borrow from blues patterns and the structure of jazz performance" (149). Blues and jazz can testify to traumatic loss and pain, but they can also help in redefining the self, creating a sense of life as improvisational and unpredictable, and thus counter trauma in expressive healing.

All the characterizations examined in this chapter enable Duras and Morrison to express the condition of traumatic dispossession, its causes and effects. For Duras, the beggar became an externalized symbol of oppression and of the sufferings she witnessed in her childhood in Indochina; she becomes what Madeleine Borgomano has called the "generating cell" of Duras's work. In her more autobiographical novels, the beggar is also internalized into the workings of the narrator's identity and Duras's relation to her family. According to Maria DeBattista, the beggar "comes to symbolize for Duras the negative interpenetration of figure and world, indeed represents . . . the possibility of representing the sufferings of the world, the brutalities of colonialism . . . and it is here, and here only, that literature stops and writing becomes sacred— here where it rejoins the world as a transgressive text insistent on its sins but penitent for its self-absorption" (295). In many of Duras's texts, the characters are caught in madness and pain without social context, and these works would seem to reinforce Kristeva's argument that in Duras's writing political life becomes unreal, that "madness represents a space of antisocial, apolitical, and paradoxically, free individuation" (143). Certainly, in many of her texts traumatic events are measured in the context of individualized human pain. Yet, to focus on the victims' pain does not remove the influence of the world; rather, it emphasizes the human consequences of its machinations.[7] In *The Vice-Consul*, and in later works where the contexts of colonized India and Indochina are specified, it is precisely through Duras's rendering of the effects on individuals of such contexts that we can measure the traumatic impact of world events and practices. The "generating cell" that fuels her need to write is part of a real childhood memory, of her mother buying a dying infant from a beggar woman: "The act has remained with me in an opaqueness from which I will never emerge . . . the event recurs to me as a problem to resolve with the only means that I have, that is, writing . . . I have tried to put it in literature . . . and I have not succeeded" (cited in Borgomano 491, my translation). Much of her writing has been an attempt to understand this woman's act, which has continued to haunt her, and cannot be separated in her mind from the larger context of the colonial Third World. This and other traumas of her youth became the lens through which she was able to see other contexts of oppression as well, such as World War II, Hiroshima, and gender and social oppression.

Morrison's work also shows a strong awareness that victims of trauma are mentally imprisoned and isolated by their traumatic experience, and yet she also makes it clear that disturbed relationships reflect and interconnect with a broader social context. Focusing on traumatized characters preoccupied with an unresolved past, she suggests that our ability to change the nature of our attachments to others depends on whether we evaluate the past and examine our behaviors and relations in it. Thus the message that underlies her focus on the traumatized is not merely that they are oppressed, but that correcting the situation cannot be achieved by solitary individuals who are psychologically and even physically immobilized. More than Duras, Morrison emphasizes collective knowledge, solidarity, refusal, and resistance as ways out of traumatic stasis. Even the "outcasts" of her works are never completely outcast; others tolerate, respond to, react against, and sometimes even help them. These gestures of tolerance and sense of community represent the best aspects of African American traditions for Morrison but are also part of her solution to counteract how oppression diminishes and isolates individuals. For her, trauma is not simply a personal tragedy, but often a clear signal that larger destructive forces are at work. For Morrison, creating such characters and the act of narration are means in the process of collecting and sharing knowledge heretofore held by "discredited people," a means of resisting the urge to see collective suffering only as individualized ("Memory" 388; Davis interview 146).

There is a tendency for both those involved and outsiders to want to forget or cover up real traumas. To become aware of extreme abuses leads us "into realms of the unthinkable and . . . forces us to face human vulnerability and our capacity for evil, forces us to bear witness to horrible events" (Herman 7–8). Duras and Morrison want their readers to confront the unthinkable, to be able to demystify what's denied or rationalized, unfolding for readers those "unspeakable things unspoken" that Morrison refers to in discussing the exclusion of African Americans from American literary and cultural history ("Unspeakable" 1). What can be the writer's rights and goals in describing such misery? Can such abjection and disconnection be understood? Morrison and Duras are very sensitive to how the social construction of identity and the internalization of inferior status can be formidable and brutal. They suggest that oppression and resulting psychic vulnerability will be perpetuated unless memories are collectively articulated and shared. This is where the greatest value of their work lies: in helping readers empathize with and share victims' experience from the victim's point of view, and in insisting via the positions of their narrators that we all must explore our own role in perpetuating traumatic isolation, whether our guilt takes the form of direct responsibility or complicity. In depicting trauma within its larger social contexts, Morrison and Duras urge their readers to remember and evaluate the wrongs of the past. They recognize what Shoshana Felman calls the importance of testifying about what has been forgotten or repressed: "[T]o testify is thus not merely to narrate but to commit oneself, and to commit the narrative, to others: to take responsibility—in speech—for history or for the truth of an occurrence, for something which, by definition, goes beyond the personal, in having general (nonpersonal) validity and consequences" (204). Both writers acknowledge that inarticulate victims can be spoken for only inadequately, can be understood only partially, and yet they need such interpretation from outside because they cannot do it alone. In giving each of their characters the opportunity to speak or to act in his or her own right, however briefly, Duras and Morrison give us a sense of the victim's limited ability to communicate and act, and his or her need to find empathetic ears.

The characters in this chapter were depicted as unable to tell their own stories, and this failure pointed to their disintegration and inability to see and articulate their losses and problems. In chapter 4, writers create self-narrating characters who use stories or create alternative views of self that help them survive better than the devastated characters in chapter 3. The protagonists I have discussed in this chapter are emblematic of personal and cultural defeat. The narrators/protagonists discussed next will be able to construct forms of self-creation, resistance, and negotiation in postcolonial or less isolating circumstances.

FOUR

"A LOVED VERSION OF YOUR LIFE"

Healing and the Provisional Self

*Two or three things I know for sure, and one of them
is what it means to have no loved version of your life
but the one you make.* DOROTHY ALLISON

*We do not choose themes because they are topical
or timely, they choose us because they are the very
stuff of our lives.* NADINE GORDIMER

In chapter 3, the legacies of trauma defeated children who were unable
to survive extreme deprivation and loss with an intact ego structure.
This chapter presents traumatized children who grow into a more elaborated and adult consciousness and develop more adept survivor skills,
including a greater capacity for symbolizing their experience, than the
protagonists in chapter 3. The subjects of this chapter—the protago-
nist/narrators of Jamaica Kincaid's *The Autobiography of My Mother*
(1996), Marguerite Duras's *The Lover* (1984), and Dorothy Allison's *Bastard out of Carolina* (1992)—employ a variety of defensive strategies to
help them survive their losses. The loss of the mother or primary love
object, through death or in an emotional or nurturing capacity, is the
basis of traumatization, and the daughter/protagonists manifest a typical array of defenses against reexperiencing such painful loss, including
emotional stasis, repetitive acting out, dissociation, splitting, denial,
and overcompensation. These defenses play an important role in how
the protagonists' memories, subjectivity, and relationships to others
are constituted and in the ways their experience is represented. Each
protagonist also creates a constructive narcissism that provides a semblance of control, a possible subjectivity, and gives readers a sense of human agency amidst a devastating emotional void. The word "narcissism" is used in a positive sense here, as an overinvestment in the self,
a focus on self-love (or at least self-soothing) that is part of a survival-

based process of self-creation or reconstitution of the ego when faced with the fragmentation caused by inadequate nurturance. This reconstitutive process involves both an identification with mothers' defeats as well as confrontations with forces devaluing mothers.

What I am calling a constructive narcissism working in these texts involves sexual, imaginative, and alleviating aspects.[1] Each female protagonist becomes fascinated with her own body and its effects on others, each seeks substitutions for motherly attentions or sexual stimulation as her body becomes a vehicle for self-soothing. They survive by learning to love unique aspects of themselves, though their own needs impede developing a capacity to love or trust others; their narcissism also involves a greater need to be loved than to love in turn. Defenses are also manifest in powerful transferences; in Kincaid and Duras, the daughters' erotic relationships are largely substitutive and reenactive of traumatic family relations. Further, each protagonist is the narrator of the respective novels, representing a component of self-creation in the face of possible effacement through writing or storytelling that emphasizes for readers trauma survivor experiences and defensive attempts to heal.

All three texts create complex representations and imagery that aid readers in understanding the contexts and consequences of trauma as they affect identity, agency, and relationships. The ability to symbolize involves a recognition of differentiation and is associated with the processes of separation and individuation a child goes through in the first months of life: "Symbols are created in the internal world as a means of . . . recapturing . . . the original object" but are not equated with this object (Segal, "Notes" 55). Sigmund Freud noted that symbolization brings at least the illusion of control and mastery after observing his grandson's "fort/da" spool game that represented his mother's comings and goings. Later, object relations theorists Melanie Klein and D. W. Winnicott established use of symbols as crucial to the formation of an individual's relation to the world and to the interchange between external reality and personal psychic reality; symbolism, fantasy, and imagining are all important to self-construction ("Importance of Symbol Formation" 97–98; *Playing and Reality* 96–97). Similarly, the capacity for metaphor (separation of signifier and object) is related to ego integrity and boundaries that can be broken down in traumatic circumstances (Grubrich-Simitis 305–7). In addition, symptoms of cognitive and emotional stasis and an inability to integrate the traumatic event with other memories can cause regression to earlier modes of symbolization, disturbing the recognition of symbols as differentiated or metaphorical.

Disturbed symbolization processes emerge out of poor early object relations, trauma, or other psychic upheavals where the individual never develops or loses the ability to distinguish between inner and outer reality. Such disturbances are indicated in individuals' use of symbolic equations, which indicate a defensive fusion between self and object, or object and symbol. "Symbolic equation is used to deny the separateness between the subject and object [while the true] symbol is used to overcome an accepted loss" (Segal, "On Symbolism" 316). With the decreased ability to separate one association from another, random exposure to anything remotely associated with a trauma could return the victim to that experience; for example, fog may recall a fire (Garland 111). Victims become obsessed with any associations that can be linked to the trauma, even if they exist within different contexts. This recalls the omnipotent thinking common to early stages of life, where self and object are still so inseparable that particular elements (words, images) become overdetermined, as in dreams where one element can be traced to multiple psychic causes. In each of these texts, the authors create complex metaphoric/symbolic structures that mirror the complexities of thought and memory accompanying trauma. Characters become locked into particular associations with their traumas, and these associated symbols gather disparate concepts into an intensely narrow focus. In Kincaid's work, for example, a concept like blackness becomes multipurpose, linking various aspects of the narrator's life, being, and environment.

Writing in colonized contexts with similarly positioned narrators, Kincaid, Duras, and Allison express crucial issues surrounding trauma in deeply personal ways by exploring intense mother/daughter relationships.[2] This chapter will focus on how these texts engage readers around a number of important social and psychological issues, that is, trauma as a multicontextual social issue, how trauma narratives raise questions about how we define subjectivity, and how characters' dilemmas confront us with ethical questions as well as many of our own fears—of death, of dissolution, of loss, of loss of control—and provide a potential space within which to consider these issues. My analysis will pay particular attention to (1) how the defeat and loss of the protagonists' mothers influence the daughters' identities and worldviews, and (2) how the daughters' defenses establish subjectivity but prevent deeper connections to others.

"The Person I Did Not Allow Myself to Become": Surviving the Mother's Absence in *The Autobiography of My Mother*

How one might survive trauma with limited emotional resources is a key theme of Kincaid's novel *The Autobiography of My Mother*, which asks readers to imagine what it would be like to live without a mother: how an individual could survive without the crucial early object relations with a maternal figure who can act as a safe psychic container, helping the child to fantasize, imagine, remember, and in short, process her experience of the world before taking it on herself (Ingham 106). Kincaid's narrative demonstrates how the loss of this safe inner place usually provided by the mother can devastate the subject's ego structure, worldview, and future relations. However, Kincaid's traumatized daughter responds to this devastation with a keen consciousness, intelligence, and a resourceful capacity for survival.[3]

The protagonist and narrator, Xuela Claudette Desvarieux, sees the world, her life, and her relations to others all in the context of the traumatic loss of her mother, who dies giving birth to Xuela. Further defining this context are the emotionally inadequate early relations with her distant father and the first two mother surrogates, women of color, one of whom is merely insensitive, while the other, her stepmother, attempts to kill Xuela. Moreover, Xuela lives in the postcolonial context of Dominica (an island off Antigua), where the lingering effects of colonization exacerbate her losses and discourage hope. The isolation and disconnection between many of the characters reflects a country fragmented by contrasts of rich and poor, class and racial barriers, and exploitation by neocolonizers from their own population, such as the protagonist's father. Xuela does have cause to feel abandoned and internalizes a sense of being unrelated because her father gives her to another woman in infancy. Although he takes her back when she is seven, her feelings of mistrust and hopelessness have already firmly formed her worldview. Neocolonialism, her rejection by her father's second family, and her knowledge that her mother was one of the last of a dying people all further contribute to the structuring of her bleak inner world that justifies to some extent her view of the world as a tainted and hopeless place.

This postcolonial setting retains the vestiges of British imperialism that underlie the false relations and identities that Xuela quickly realizes plague the people, both British and Afro-Caribbean, around her. The subjugations and exploitations of her people under colonialism resurface in the everyday and intimate relations between or among all these peoples. Consequently, they and Xuela become "hopelessly trapped in history" (Simmons 107). Kincaid has frequently condemned both colonizers and her own Antiguan people in her work. She demonstrates how her people have embraced the corrupt and destructive aspects of British rule, but not the constructive ones, such as keeping up the libraries.[4] Xuela notes early in life that her people are taught self-hatred and mistrust for one another:

> You cannot trust these people, my father would say to me, the very words the other children's parents were saying to them, perhaps even at the same time. That "these people" were ourselves, that this insistence on mistrust of others—that people who looked so very much like each other, who shared a common history of suffering and humiliation and enslavement, should be taught to mistrust each other, even as children, is no longer a mystery to me. The people we should naturally have mistrusted were beyond our influence completely; what we needed to defeat them, to rid ourselves of them, was something far more powerful than mistrust. To mistrust each other was just one of the many feelings we had for each other, all of them the opposite of love, all of them standing in the place of love. It was as if we were in competition with each other for a secret prize, and we were afraid that someone else would get it; any expression of love, then, would not be sincere, for love might give someone else the advantage. (47–48)

Xuela also becomes skeptical about the way her people seem to value the British above themselves. Diane Simmons concludes that Xuela is trapped in "a prison of history" and will never discover a true self, because "her deepest self . . . even her innermost being, has been determined by British power" (111): "That the first words I said were in the language of a people I would never like or love is not now a mystery to me; everything in my life, good or bad, to which I am inextricably bound is a source of pain" (*Autobiography* 7).

What she learns in school helps to shape her conflicted identity, wherein she absorbs colonial power but also seeks cultural authenticity. The schools are British, so obviously they inculcate those values, as the first words Xuela learns to read are "The British Empire," on a school map. The schoolteacher, a potential role model, instead models the self-denigration of the African-based population: "My teacher was a woman who had been trained by Methodist missionaries; she was of the African people . . . and she found in this a source of humiliation and self-loathing, and she wore despair like an article of clothing . . . a birthright which she would pass on to us. She did not love us; we did not love her; we did not love one another, not then, not ever" (15). To this teacher, Xuela's unusual quickness and intelligence and her partial Caribe heritage (she has the looks of an almost extinct people) make Xuela "evil." Her father wants her to be educated, presumably to help him in his rise as a neocolonial master in his own right. Education creates bewildering dilemmas, offering the promise of opportunity given few women, and yet fills her with unanswered questions, anger, and humiliation about her people's history. Education enables her to question and at the same time tries to instill forgetting and rejection of her own culture.

Xuela's early relations with parental figures, actual and surrogate, are tainted by power relations and expediencies that prevent her from developing a valued sense of identity as a Dominican or as someone capable of giving or taking love freely. Failure to nurture is a major theme in the novel and is linked with white colonialism, but also patriarchy, as women are devalued in both Anglo and Afro-Caribbean cultures. Ma Eunice, the first surrogate, a washerwoman of color who receives Xuela when she is born, fails to love her own kind and idealizes the British. This is demonstrated in the plate she worships, depicting Heaven (really "a picture of the English countryside idealized," 9), which Xuela breaks. Afterwards, Ma Eunice punishes Xuela by having her kneel and hold up her hands (Xuela will not apologize), a punishment Xuela says is "redolent . . . of the relationship between . . . master and slave . . . the powerful and the powerless" (10). And yet, from her description of Eunice's ragged clothes and frustrated poverty, we see the sad irony and devastation that attends internalizing a powerful other.

These mothers of color are fertile but often fail as mothers because they denigrate themselves and their daughters. Kincaid demonstrates how these mothers internalize their own self-effacement, as in Xuela's stepmother's preference for her son over her daughter: "That she did not think very much of the person who was most like her, a daughter, a female, was so normal that it would have been noticed only if it had been otherwise: to people like us, despising anything that was most like ourselves was almost a law of nature" (52). The stepmother's attitude illustrates Kincaid's frequent depictions of mothers as teachers of cultural imperialism and patriarchy, very much part of her own upbringing.[5]

The white women such as Lise LaBatte and Moira also fail to nurture; they are symbolically barren (i.e., colonialism cannot sustain life). These white "mothers," who demonstrate a degree of maternal care toward Xuela, perhaps sensing her losses in light of their own maternal deprivation, win more of her sympathy than her surrogates of color. When Xuela begins to work at the LaBattes' at age fifteen, Lise seems to offer Xuela a kind of mothering (bathing and sympathy) that Xuela does not fully trust but accepts. Xuela, however, is too old to be a child, and what Lise really wants is Xuela to bear a child for her. Thus she initiates Xuela into adulthood by encouraging sex with her husband. Monsieur LaBatte has sex with Xuela in a room full of his money; he never speaks to her, nor is he present when the other two women are together. Cherene Sherrard argues that this three-way relationship suggests a repetition of the "master/mistress/slave triangle" and "demonstrates the complexity and the distortion of neocolonial motherhood. Madame LaBatte represents the white female colonial's desire to direct the fate of her former subject. Yet the hopelessness of her marriage reveals the contradictory victor/victim status with which patriarchy invests white women" (130–31). The relations between these two women are complex. One can argue that Lise tries to exploit Xuela, but she is also caught in a dead marriage and Xuela recognizes her defeat in her husband's physical rejection of her. Her life becomes a warning to Xuela not to be vulnerable to men. The two women speak in French patois, "the language of the captive, the illegitimate" (74). Xuela is extremely uncomfortable when Lise puts her in one of her old dresses, as though a surrogate for herself, and Xuela later refuses this role in aborting the child of this coupling (discussion below).

Xuela sympathizes with the powerlessness of all the women in the book and resists the sense of inferiority to men the others have internalized. She asks herself at one point, "Why do women hate each other?" (159) and suspects this relates to their competition over men ("Why is the state of marriage so desirable that all women are afraid to be caught outside it?" 171–72). She prefers to "possess myself" rather than a man (174) and challenges this self-effacing mentality: "I came to love myself in defiance, out of despair because there was nothing else" (56–57). Xuela recognizes marriage as a kind of colonization for women that she resists in sexual freedom and by refusing the role of the virtuous, demure, selfless woman, but eventually she marries an Englishman.

A sense of unalterable loss pervades this narrative of her life from the vantage point of her later years: "[E]verything in my life, good or bad, to which I am inextricably bound is a source of pain" (7). What she knows of her mother is of her own creation, a fantasy she uses to "mother" herself. As a child she continually looks for her mother to reappear: "I missed the face I had never seen; I looked over my shoulder to see if someone was coming" (5). And in repeated self-nurturing dreams her mother appears to her, floating down feet first, but Xuela never sees her face. Throughout her life she has felt unprotected: "[M]y whole life I had been standing on a precipice" (3). Her pervading sense of death in life permeates the text with images of death, often associated with blackness ("the black room of the world," 3), and as she fears death from pregnancy, she is "standing in a black hole" (81–82).

There are also numerous real and imagined threats to her life. Because of her mother's absence and the failure of others to sufficiently validate her worth, she must fight off a fear of annihilation, both hers and her mother's, because her mother's people are the Caribes, a virtually extinct people whose legacy Xuela will not continue because of her refusal to bear children. Fear of death is the fundamental anxiety experienced by trauma victims (Herman 33; Lifton, 1991 Interview 153; Garland 110), and this fear weighs in more with the absence of the mother who would provide the basis for a strong sense of identity. Xuela's thoughts of facing eternity begin the novel.

My mother died at the moment I was born, and so for my whole life there was nothing standing between myself and eternity; at my back was always a bleak, black wind. . . . at my beginning was this woman whose face I had never seen, but at my end was nothing, no one between me and the black room of the world. I came to feel that for my whole life I had been standing on a precipice, that my loss had made me vulnerable, hard, and helpless; on knowing this I became overwhelmed with sadness and shame and pity for myself. (3–4)

Kincaid creates a complex web of symbols and metaphors that establish symbolic equivalencies between death and life, as the mother—and Xuela's relationship to her—represents both death and life. Even in nature, Xuela is threatened with being swallowed up in the "black waters" of her country (88). Blackness is a particularly overdetermined (i.e., having many causes and connections) trope, at various points connoting the void, death, race, ignorance, pregnancy, fear, and nature. Blackness can be a multivalent signifier of the social context and interior life if neocolonialism is now less based on race than on behavior and status. Giovanna Covi identifies blackness as a continually shifting signifier used to disrupt identity and as a decolonizing element in Kincaid's *At the Bottom of the River* (47). Leigh Gilmore notes that for Kincaid the ubiquity of death is a reminder that writing and creating stave off death (119). Kincaid says in *My Brother*, an account of her brother's death from AIDS, "When I was young . . . I started to write about my own life and I came to see that this act saved my life. When I heard about my brother's illness and his dying, I knew, instinctively, that to understand it, or to make an attempt to understand his dying, and not to die with him, I would write about it" (196).

Turtles are prominent symbols of Xuela's feelings of helplessness and the defensive postures she takes to survive. The first instance of this symbol is when Xuela reenacts her own sense of entrapment and desire for agency on her pet turtles. At this point in her childhood, she has been deprived of a mother's love, cut off from her father, and is living with the surrogate mother he has chosen for her and to whom she does not feel close. She tries to confine and control her turtles, but because they do not obey her, she kills them by stuffing their head holes with mud (11–12). Here she reenacts the leftover colonial relations of domination and subordination that surround her. This is the first instance in the novel readers witness her seeking the dominant role. Later in the novel this symbol shifts, referring to the "protective shells" worn by Xuela and her father, neither of whom is able to fully face their own pain or the consequences of their behavior on others (192).

Xuela suffers a severe traumatization in her teens that frames and redefines the original trauma of losing her mother at birth. Xuela aborts her baby by Monsieur LaBatte at age sixteen and feels an overwhelming sense of emptiness and loss. She undergoes a lengthy period of mourning, where she withdraws from other people and effaces her sexual identity. At this point she has a fantasy of omnipotence, imagining herself as the creator and destroyer of many children. Fantasies are theorized by psychoanalysts as scenarios imagined by individuals that dramatize desire and bodily sensations and facilitate defensive processes such as projection or reversals of self (Laplanche and Pontalis 318). Fantasies are initiated in infancy to express instinctual impulses and help to facilitate a child's relations to others and objects in their environment (Hinshelwood 32–38). A defensive reversal is evident, as the mortal dangers the children in Xuela's fantasy face are the dangers she has felt herself.

Her fantasy is also an obsessively repeated symbolic equation of birth and death, of mother and daughter; because her birth has meant her mother's death, Xuela fears her own death if she gives birth. The brink of life and death is contained in her own and her mother's bodies. The cognitive and emotional stasis common to the severely traumatized prevents them from recognizing symbols as differentiated, or metaphorical; that is, they tend to equate one association with another (Garland 111). This kind of symbolic equation sometimes replaces the differentiated symbol for the traumatized; therefore, exposure to similar associations (symbols) could return the victims to the traumatic events. In this case, Xuela sees no essential difference between herself, her mother, and each other's suffering in procreativity. Xuela's statement "I would condemn them [the fantasy children] to live in an empty space frozen in the same posture" (97) represents her own emotional stasis, a sense that her life is an irreparable loss, common to trauma survivors. Moreover, after throwing the imaginary children "from a great height" (suggestive of the precipice she feels she lives on), the children's bones will not heal, a figuration of her own unhealed wounds. Such fantasy also acts as a defense against trauma. In the omnipotent role of destroyer, she can approximate self-possession and counteract her sense of being near annihilation herself. This role may also suggest the dis-placement of her rage at being abandoned by her mother onto the imag-inary children.

She concludes her fantasy with a seemingly narcissistic self-asser-tion of her barrenness: "It is in this way that I did not become a mother; it is in this way that I bore my children" (98). Despite the emphasis on "I," she again really seeks connection with her mother, because her mother is the one who bore a child but did not live to mother her. As her mother was also abandoned, an orphan, to not have children would connect Xuela to her mother's experience and continue the repetition of broken ties between mothers and daughters. Though deprived of her mother, Xuela cannot think of herself as separate from her either. Her fantasy becomes the space "in which the introjected object [mother] is merged omnipotently, in phantasy, with a part of the self" (Rosenfeld, qtd. in Hinshelwood 357).

Xuela's deadly thoughts and actions, from her point of view, para-doxically sustain her life. Given the traumatic context and the similar-ities to symptomatology of failed early object relations, Kincaid em-phasizes the potentially self-sustaining function of unconscious fantasy as linking the body to the symbolic world. The frozen posture and bro-ken bones of children viscerally and symbolically represent her own emotional brokenness. The fantasy expresses feelings of rejection, yet a sense that she shares her mother's experience and can create a provi-sional sense of her own agency. This illustrates how trauma survivors' defenses often include some incorporations of the traumatic context, embracing some of what is threatening in order to exercise some con-trol over it. This type of defense, though not curative, has some com-forting effects as it prevents feelings of total helplessness (Herman 109). These fantasies can also be metaphors for the possible but problematic paths of resistance open to the subjugated.

The nature of this fantasy and her subsequent reactions reveal a split sense of self. Splitting off from part of oneself or one's experience, a form of dissociation, is a primary defense mechanism against the ago-nies of reexperiencing trauma. Xuela's fantasy cuts her off from the full experience of her losses by putting herself in the omnipotent creator/ destroyer role, when actually the dangers the children face are closer to her own inner fears. She may be getting too close to dangerous material, her worst fears about herself as helpless and destroyed, when she indicates, "I came to know myself, and this frightened me," and in the next line acknowledges she is proceeding away from deeper insight: "To rid myself of this fear I began to look at a reflection of my face in any surface I could find" (99). Thus begins another construction of a more comforting view of herself. Fearing her inability to love and her destructive impulses toward herself and others, she focuses on the solace her appearance and her body bring her, again splitting into inner and outer selves: "I began to worship myself. . . . It was this picture of myself . . . I willed before me. My own face was a comfort to me, my own body was a comfort to me" (100). Narcissistic self-assertion becomes the focus for her continued attempts to defend against her fears.[6] She evades the torn-up inner world her fantasy reveals and focuses on her outer being, with a glimmer of awareness that this self-involvement would cut her off from others: "I allowed nothing to replace my own being in my own mind" (100). Xuela's situation raises the important question of the role of defenses as both necessary to survival and a sense of psychic well-being, yet capable of distancing us from the good as well as the bad in our lives.

Xuela's ambivalent relations to her father reflect a number of unresolvable complexities in her life: her feelings of abandonment; an unconscious equation of mother and father, life and death; and the contradictions of power and powerlessness living under neocolonialism. Her imagined relation to her mother is frequently conflated with her father. For example, she addresses a letter to her father expressing her loneliness, which she intends for her mother, and when her teacher sends it to him, this happily leads to the reuniting of father and daughter when she is seven. The father has abandoned Xuela emotionally for the first seven years of her life, giving over her care to Ma Eunice, and he puts her in a dangerous position with his second wife, who attempts to kill her. His abandonment exacerbates the loss of her mother and frames her traumatic isolation from her parents. "He believed he loved me, but I could tell him how untrue that was, I could list for him the number of times he had placed me squarely within the jaws of death; I could list for him the number of times he had failed to be a father to me, his motherless child, while on his way to becoming a man of this world" (113). Despite his neglect, he does save her from depression and danger at times, facts she downplays.

Like her father, she is both a victim and a colonizer; they live out their personal traumas in complex postcolonial identities, seeking control over others and in doing so denying their own vulnerability. She disdains her people's oppressors but also emulates them; she speaks their language, English, but at the same time says it is a language alien to her, of "a people I would never like or love" (7). The language of her narrative is this alien one, implying a lack of self-knowledge, because the means to express identity is limited. Like his daughter, Xuela's father has survived by creating a provisional self through which he identifies as a colonizer, and comes to hate his own people so as to avoid being associated with the poor and defeated (187). Xuela is more concerned with avoiding others' domination of her rather than dominating herself, though arguably she dominates her husband.

Xuela's father personifies Kincaid's observation that the ex-colonized often appropriate the worst rather than the most positive aspects of colonial rule, preferring to wield power over their own people rather than educate them, for example (Vorda interview 84–85). Clearly, dominating others has given Alfred Richardson purpose in his life, an identity among the winners, not the losers. This character embodies Kincaid's views of the new rulers in Antigua.[7] Richardson's disdain for his poor compatriots is documented numerous times, particularly when he refuses nails to a desperately poor man, Lazarus, and then violently chastises Xuela for trying to help the man. She describes how he has internalized his policeman's role so much that his uniform becomes his "skin," how he made others fearful, and how "he came to despise all who behaved like the African people: not all who looked like them, only all who behaved like them, all who were defeated, doomed, conquered, poor, diseased, head bowed down, mind numbed from cruelty" (187). However, she also recognizes that he has suffered his own traumas. In his youth he gave over his life savings to his father for a voyage to England, which ends in the loss of his father and his money. His subsequent greed and corruption could be a repeated fruitless attempt to compensate for this initial loss. In raising this possibility, Kincaid problematizes any simple definitions of postcolonial identity or motivations.

Xuela's own rigidity, her desire for control over others and particularly over nature, link her with neocolonizers like her father. The English desire to master nature, represented in the Englishman Philip's collection of boxed, dead animals contrasts greatly with the Antiguan noncontrolling sensibility, where nature can overwhelm the senses and the imagination. Nevertheless, Xuela "masters" nature by refusing to love and to give birth, Kincaid suggests. Going against nature also goes back to the loss of her mother. Though Xuela realizes her mother could not help dying, "[H]ow can any child understand such a thing, so profound an abandonment? I have refused to bear any children" (199). This is a refusal of the ultimate natural force, death. Her insistence on standing alone against the world, a kind of tragic parody of Western individualism, brings with it a sense of futility, emptiness, and doom.

It is this fear of the void that provokes Xuela to find comfort in her own body. Sexuality, the instinct for life, fends off death. In one instance, Xuela hears the sounds of animals preying on one another in the night: "And it ended only after my hands had traveled up and down all over my own body in a loving caress, finally coming to the soft, moist spot between my legs, and a gasp of pleasure had escaped my lips which I would allow no one to hear" (43).

Though she has survived, her relations to others and her connections to life (having children) have been severely debilitated. She seeks out sexual comfort from men in part as substitutes for the love and recognition she lacked early in life. Her need to be loved and her sexual desire are caught up in her sense of incompleteness and emptiness. As Xuela is about to make love to Philip for the first time, she describes within herself "a sweet hollow feeling, an empty space with a yearning to be filled, to be filled up until the yearning to be filled up was exhausted" (154). Her focus on her breasts during sex, wanting them sucked, and then the hysterical pregnancies she experiences throughout her life, indicate deeply felt maternal desires manifested in the body. Xuela creates substitutions for the maternal function she rejects by trying to raise an infant with her sister (had by her sister's husband with another woman), but the child dies. Moreover, Philip becomes a substitute for the children she never had, and she takes control over his life: "I mediated for him, I translated for him. I did not always tell him the truth, I did not always tell him everything. I blocked his entrance to the world in which he lived. . . . He became all the children I did not allow to be born, some of them fathered by him, some of them fathered by others. I would oversee his end also" (224). Like her father, she has decided to be the master rather than the mastered, as all relationships she has witnessed seem "an attempt to mimic colonial rulers, to entice, to ensnare, to dominate, to enhance one's own sense of power and importance by taking advantage of those who are innocent or weak" (Simmons 114).

Xuela's apparent immersion in the language and behavior of colonial power relations would appear to support Spivak's contention that the subaltern cannot speak because unmediated resistance is impossible. Female voices in particular cannot be heard because of the array of cultural beliefs that would silence or misconstrue them (Spivak 90–104). There is some question if Xuela is a subaltern; she attempts to speak for her mother, who seemed to have this status far more than her daughter. However, the fact that Xuela recognizes power relations and gender exploitation, seeks the less vulnerable role, and rejects social and gender categories indicates her rejection of the notion of absolute hegemony. Xuela's multicontextual consciousness and identity would seem to suggest a cultured being involved in the "uneven, incomplete production of meaning and value, often composed of incommensurable demands and practices, produced in the act of social survival" (Bhabha, *Location* 172). Although Xuela engages in resistance, it is often destructive, isolated, and not useful to her people collectively. Kincaid's portrait of her is a warning against repetition of such destructive relations and how they leave largely unfulfilled the promise of a dynamic, contestatory, hybrid sense of culture and agency that avoids binarisms, suggested by Homi Bhabha and Stuart Hall in their postcolonial cultural analyses.

Splitting off from her feelings toward others is an important aspect of Xuela's defensive posture, her self-protection from feeling and hurt. Consequently, Xuela convinces herself not to love her father but idealizes her mother, who is really the recipient of much of her unconscious anger. Though she identifies with her mother—"I am of the vanquished, I am of the defeated" (215)—her continual idealization of the mother is undermined by hints of unconscious anger when Xuela projects her own aggression onto her actions as a fantasy mother. Her potential for emotional involvement and her avoidance of it are particularly conflicted in her relationship to her white English husband, Philip. An important instance of how Xuela refuses to own her feelings is described as strong emotions emerge from her in sex with Philip, who is initially her married lover: "[I]nside, the room grew smaller and smaller as it filled up almost to bursting with hisses, gasps, moans, sighs, tears, bursts of laughter; but they had a deep twist to them, a spin, an edge, that transformed these sounds from their ordinary selves and would make you cover your ears unless they came from inside you, until you realized that they came from inside you; all these sounds came from me" (155). She describes her responses from a distance, divorced from herself, with a sense of shame, and she is never really able to analyze her own feelings completely.

She will regard this relationship, which lasts for decades, as two people bound to each other who did not belong together (for various racial, class, and personal reasons): "I could not mean peace to him, it would have been dangerous for him if that had been so, the temptation to see him die I would have found overwhelming, I would not have been able to resist it" (155). Her violent feelings toward him have two possible sources. First, because he provides in some way the physical closeness she did not have with her mother or father, so the vague sense of anger could be connected to her feelings about the love they were unable to provide her. Second, in identifying so strongly with her mother and rejecting her father's own brand of colonialism—importantly, Philip is a business associate of her father's—Xuela deprives herself of fully feeling the connection she has to the European man with whom she lives most of her life. Only much later will Xuela acknowledge that Philip gave up his white status and expressed his devotion by marrying her. His sacrifice has problematized her all-encompassing rejection of colonialism, has complicated the fact that people live out racial difference in intimate relations and must recognize each others' humanity, which she resists: "I realized that many things which reminded me that he, too, was human and frail caused a great feeling of anger to swell up in me; for if he, too, was human, then would not all whom he came from be human, too, and where would that leave me and all that I came from?" (219–20). She holds off their intimacy by claiming that their differences make their relationship impossible, and yet she remains with him until the end of his life.

Xuela and Philip are shunned by his peers once it is clear that Philip is not exploiting her but loves and marries her after his English wife, Moira, in whom Kincaid symbolizes colonial privilege and barrenness, dies. Xuela maintains emotional distance from Philip, avoiding his total humanity: "I was capable . . . of making his suffering real to myself, but I would not allow myself to do it" (219). She does, at times, realize he had the ability to condemn himself; yet she fears intimacy and feels contempt for him as an inheritor of conquest. She cannot break away from the rigid, dichotomous thinking that partakes of her and her mother's positions as traumatized victims, but also partakes of the colonizers' thinking, which separates and defines colonizers and colonized as separate entities. "He did not look like anyone I could love, and he did not look like anyone I should love, and so I determined then that I could not love him and I determined that I should not love him. There is a certain way that life ought to be, an ideal way, a perfect way, and there is the way that life is" (152). And yet her protectiveness of him, her passionate physical responses to him contradict this. In a reversal of colonial positionings, she describes his hair as like an animal's. Here Kincaid offers a critique demonstrating that such reactive role reversals perpetuate rather than eliminate the colonial mentality. "With this marriage, Kincaid paints a tragic portrait of the ongoing relationship between the descendants of Europeans and the descendants of Africans whom they have enslaved and colonized. The colonial relationship and the legacy of slavery dictate the inner sense of self for both ruled and ruler. Turning the tables of domination is only a cold comfort, as both groups are still tragically cut off from themselves, locked into the destructive terms of their mutual history" (Simmons 115).

Speaking of conquerors and the conquered, Kincaid recognizes that there are no absolutes with regard to these positions and that the human capacity to be either is always there: "I have to be in the position to bear in mind that they were wrong and they could be me, and that is an ambivalence and that's what's complicated. At any moment you are anyone. You are the victim. You are the victor, at any moment. And so it is not clear. It is not straightforward who is who, and it does have many truths and sometimes they contradict" (Ferguson interview 184).

In particular moments of insight, Xuela recognizes the complex and sometimes contradictory functions of her marriage. First, "it allowed me to make a romance of my life, it allowed me to think of all my deeds and of myself with kindness in the deep dark of night, when sometimes it was necessary for me to do so. Romance is the refuge of the defeated; the defeated need songs to soothe themselves . . . for their whole being is a wound; they need a soft bed to sleep on, for when they are awake it is a nightmare, the dream of sleep is their reality" (216). And yet there is a sense of love experienced, if denied:

I married a man I did not love, but that word, "love," that idea, love—what could it mean to me, what should it mean to me? I did not know, and yet . . . I would have saved him if ever he needed saving, as long as it was not from myself. Was this, then, a form of love, an incomplete love, or no love at all? I did not know. I believe my entire life was without such a thing, love, the kind of love you die from or the kind of love that causes you to live eternally, and if this was not actually so, I cannot be convinced of an otherwise. (216–17)

Though she protects him from her inner rage, she also denies him her full self. Her marriage illustrates what for Kincaid is an "obsessive theme" in her work: "the relationship between the powerful and the powerless" (Ferguson interview 176). It is a relationship that falls in on itself, because as the assertion of power precludes real intimacy, the need for power here is also born out of a feeling of powerlessness and abandonment for Xuela. Because Xuela can only envision her marriage in these terms, she limits her potential to appreciate the depth and complexity of her husband and the possibilities for intimacy between them.

Xuela in many ways enacts the creation of the "impromptu self" that Holocaust and other trauma survivors create out of necessity in adverse circumstances (Langer, *Testimonies* 121–61). In adopting this identity, survivors inevitably feel tainted by their guilt over survival, or regret of a better self lost under duress. Further, there is a moral breach because of having to live in extreme situations with few choices (124). One could argue that Kincaid's scenario does not match the extremity or brutality of Holocaust experience. However, the violence of the colonial context, and particularly the psychic violence visited on peoples whose heritage has been destroyed and whose sense of future (embodied here by Xuela's aborted children) is potential unfulfilled, is expressed and seemingly felt by Kincaid's protagonist in equally devastating terms.[8] In preserving parts of herself, she comes to realize at the end of her life the chances for connection that she has lost:

This account of my life has been an account of my mother's life as much as it has been an account of mine, and even so, again it is an account of the life of the children I did not have, as it is their account of me. In me is the voice I never heard, the face I never saw, the being I came from. In me are the voices that should have come out of me, the faces I never allowed to form, the eyes I never allowed to see me. This account is an account of the person who was never allowed to be and an account of the person I did not allow myself to become. (227–28)

The book's title, *The Autobiography of My Mother*, implies both a fantasized omnipotence on the part of the daughter who never knew her mother but who nevertheless speaks to an identification with the dead mother so complete that the protagonist's own life becomes effaced. She becomes her own mother but no one else's, and this prevents her own deeper development. In admitting the costs of her refusals, Xuela reveals how she has participated in the continued legacy of colonization, which destroys the lives of the colonizers and colonized alike.

"Waiting Outside the Closed Door": Writing the Anguished Past in *The Lover*

The Lover is considered to be a largely autobiographical novel of Marguerite Duras's traumatic youth in Indochina, particularly her last two years there, between the ages of fifteen and seventeen. The focus is primarily on the difficult process Duras, or the "girl" (as she often refers to herself), undergoes in differentiating herself from her family and entering into a complex, passionate, and doomed affair with a Chinese man in his late twenties. Her family's psychological brutalization under colonialism and poverty foster her mother's madness and the neglect of her children. It also cultivates the brutal tyranny and addiction of the older brother, who persecutes and psychologically destroys the younger brother ("poverty had knocked down the walls of the family and we were all left outside, each one fending for himself," 45). While Duras's *The Sea Wall* examines the mother's trauma (see chapter 2), *The Lover* deals with the traumatization of the children. In particular, it explores the formation of the daughter's identity and is perhaps her most penetrating attempt to resist and understand the influence of a devastating past through her writing.

The traumatizing emotional defeat of the mother is pivotal to the development of Duras's protagonist/narrator, who seeks escape from her ravaged family. The family is characterized by their emotional dissociation or frigidity, a "family of stone," and the daughter is depicted as emotionally detached and distrustful, because the mother was at times "unable to wash us, dress us or sometimes even feed us. Every day my mother experienced this deep despondency about living . . . every day the despair would make its appearance" (*The Lover* 14–15). Like Xuela, Duras's protagonist is haunted by her mother, whose suffering is absorbed so completely by her daughter that it fills her dreams: "[W]hen I was a child my mother's unhappiness took the place of dreams. My dreams were of my mother, never of Christmas trees, always just her, a mother either flayed by poverty or distraught and muttering in the wilderness . . . telling of her innocence, her savings, her hopes" (46). Daughters' close identification and obsession with their lost mothers is evoked repeatedly in both texts. The narrator describes this intense identification when her mother loses herself in madness: "that identity irreplaceable by any other had disappeared and I was powerless to make it come back . . . There was no longer anything there to inhabit her image. I went mad in full possession of my senses. Just long enough to cry out. I did cry out. A faint cry, a call for help, to crack the ice in which the whole scene was fatally freezing" (85–86). The girl avoids the "ice" (emotional paralysis) into which her mother sinks. To fill this emotional void, the daughter creates herself as a writer to tell her mother's story. She survives by becoming a witness who can empathize with this madness and yet separate herself from it, though she feels so little sense of separation from her mother that she fears she herself will become mad too. Represented here is a symbolic equivalence of mother and madness, mother and daughter, similar to the equivalence of mother and death in Kincaid's text. And yet there are differences here, because Duras's protagonist is differentiated, yet empathetic.

Duras's heroine also attempts to fill the void left by the mother's absence through an active creation of self, a constructed narcissism that aids her in seeking emotional substitutes in a sexual relationship. Like Xuela, the girl claims an identity based on her newfound ability to attract desire. As she launches herself into adulthood, sexual desire becomes a substitute for mother-love, the only tolerable kind of intimacy, a place where affect emerges within the sexual act but is contained by a fear of intimacy manifest in her emotional distance from her lover. Yet, as with Kincaid's heroine, Duras's girl attracts the love/desire she desperately needs with sexual aggressiveness and provocation; it is very important that the men in their lives love them and less important that they love in return. Like Xuela, the girl defends against her emotional vulnerability. She is the focus of the Chinese lover's life: "He gives me my shower . . . he puts my make-up on and dresses me, he adores me. I'm the darling of his life. He lives in terror lest I meet another man" (63). He functions completely according to her desires: to be loved without distraction. However, most importantly, his attentiveness and instinctive skill at physical pleasure combine to create the girl's love ideal, both motherly and sexual (Vickroy, "Filling the Void" 126).

Duras's narrative tries to recapture the passion that fends off defensive suppression, numbness, and other dissociations from feeling in response to trauma. The images of ice and stone that refer to the family's deadened emotions are juxtaposed with the flow of sexual energy between the lovers, their passion associated with the power of water: "And, weeping, he makes love. At first, pain. And then the pain is possessed in its turn, changed, slowly drawn away, borne toward pleasure, clasped to it. The sea, formless, simply beyond compare" (38). The free flow of natural and sexual energy combats the stasis of trauma. The lover is a catalyst for emotion in contrast to the closed off, destroyed family, and the sensual passion between the couple becomes the only outlet for the intense emotions she hides from her family. Although the girl does not speak to him when she is with her family, her feelings emerge when alone with him: "[K]isses on the body bring tears. Almost like a consolation. At home I don't cry" (46); "Our first confidants . . . are our lovers" (60). He becomes her witness, as she is for her mother, embracing her passion and her agony: "His face against hers he receives her tears, crushes her to him, mad with desire for her tears, for her anger" (101); "He lays his head on me and weeps to see me weep" (46). Despite this, she is unable to express her love for him until after they have parted, not understanding at the time how her love for him is so closely tied with her love for her family (yet Duras clearly acknowledges this love in writing her text).

Duras explores contradictions, or as she puts it, "all contraries confounded" (8) in her complex use of imagery, which maintains past patterns but also reveals and breaks with those patterns with new, displaced contextual elements. For example, the image of water, particularly the sea, condenses many elements of past and present. When used as a metaphor for the passion between the lovers ("all is swept away in the torrent, in the force of desire," 43), the sea expresses the inexpressible, it describes the power and wildness of lovemaking and is thus connected with the girl's differentiation from her family. In this context it is a gesture of freedom, toward being, and away from the futile desiring associated with this image in connection with her mother: the sea defeats the girl's mother every year as it floods her land. Ultimately, the wild force of water displaces the girl's passion from the rest of her life when it expresses her relations with her lover, yet it also reconnects that passion to her obsession with her mother and loss. As with her love for her lover, this image is simultaneously liberating and regressive, pleasure-giving and pain-inducing (Vickroy, "Filling the Void" 133). With the many associations suggested in her use of water imagery, Duras concedes the impossibility of finding stasis in identity, time, or experience (131). It is possible only to recover particular moments, or glances: "[T]he act of remembering is emblematic of the textual process itself: the impossible task of recuperating in words the fleeting experience of emotion" (Murphy 171–72).

As in Kincaid, multiple references to death permeate *The Lover.* The section of the novel detailing the couple's first assignation contains many such references (36–45), connoting traumatic annihilation of self (both physical and psychological), loss, the void, and grief. The daughter fears that her mother's continued misfortunes are leading to her death. Her passionate attachment to her mother is imbued with fears of loss: "I couldn't leave my mother yet without dying of grief" (40). Though the girl's relations with her lover are meant to aid the mother financially before she is completely destroyed, her mother would want to kill her if she learned of her transgression. The lovers' passion is life-changing, cutting her off from family, and it is unendurably painful because, doomed from the start, their union will never be accepted and he does not have the courage to give up his family's money for her. Her developing sexuality and relationship to her lover bring the death of her childhood. Her choice of words for describing moments of sexual passion—using the phrase "*à en mourir,*" which means to do something a lot, but literally "to death"—is telling, especially with the many other references to death in this section. "I asked him to do it again. Do it to me. And he did, did it in the unctuousness of blood. And it really was unto death. It has been unto death" (43). Their passion always rests on the brink of the void. As the book ends, he confirms for her decades later that "he could never stop loving her, that he'd love her until death" (117). Death is a powerful symbol in Duras's narrative, providing a sense of absoluteness to the intensity of traumatic loss and to the passion meant to combat it. Writing as a remembrance of dead or lost loved ones is also a resistance to the annihilation of memory, and of the self, of a particular time.

The connections between losing the mother and gaining a lover is emphasized in *The Lover*, as the sometimes brutal passions of the mother (who hits her daughter because she cannot control her and is worried about her reputation) and the lover toward the girl are rendered similarly to indicate the transferential link between the girl's love for her mother (and brothers) and her passion for the Chinese man. Transference, or the attempted re-creation of previous emotional experience, though a common psychological phenomena, is also a powerful indicator of attempts to repeat and resolve traumatic situations. The girl's love for this man is a logical extension of her love for her mother, whose desperation motivates the girl to take a lover and whose presence is also felt when the two make love (39, 100). Thoughts of her mother appear adjacent to sections in the text where the couple is making love in his bachelor room ("The image of the woman in darned stockings has crossed the room," 39), and she is discussed ("their mother was a child. Their mother never knew pleasure," 39) a reminder that the mother is the author and first object of her daughter's desires, even her desires to surpass her mother (Vickroy, "Filling the Void" 127–28). An important indication that a kind of transference has taken place in Duras's text is that the lover is given the role the mother could not fulfill. He is maternal in his attentions to the girl; he compensates for the mother's depression-induced neglect by washing and dressing her. The Chinese man is further connected to the mother in the narrator's emphasis on the incestuous aspects of their love: "I had become his child. It was with his own child he made love every evening" (100). In her portrayal of him, the girl questions his masculinity, emphasizing his softness and gentleness. She identifies with this man particularly in their sorrow over their futile relationship and their powerlessness to change anything. The men the girl loves most have a gentle quality, are vulnerable, soft, and have no desire to hurt others. They are as defeated, doomed, and powerless as her beloved mother and younger brother, thus suggesting the repeated symbolic equivalence of mother-brother-lover that will be further elaborated in a later novel, *The North China Lover*, where Duras reveals her incestuous relationship with this brother.

Because of their nonconformity in situations unsympathetic to difference, there seems to be little future in these intensely passionate but ambivalent relationships, and the power dynamic is very complex in both texts. The lovers, Philip and the Chinese man, have social advantages, money, and power, especially within these colonized contexts. The differences and conflicts that arise between them and the young women regarding age, race, and class also indicate some mutual exploitation. However, the narrators depict themselves as wielding sexual power over these men, even if they are considered socially inferior to them.

The girl's identification with her family, her internalization of their demands and values, causes contradictory feelings toward her lover. She ignores him when they are with her family. They deny his existence while at the same time eating the expensive meals he buys them. From the family's perspective, because he is Chinese, the son of a rich man who exploits people in their circumstances, because he "pays" to see her, and because they are white colonials with no power, influence, or money, she is expected to despise him. This family is a closed unit detesting all outside of it, emotionally abusive among themselves and to others. They (the first loves) and their attitudes take precedence over this new relationship (even as they help to form it). In their presence she no longer attends to her lover and, like her brothers, does not speak to him. The older brother is depicted as masculine and domineering, and in his strong presence her inability to resist his "sinister attraction" (53) particularly effaces the Chinese man (Vickroy, "Filling the Void" 128–29).

> In my elder brother's presence he ceases to be my lover. He doesn't cease to exist, but he's no longer anything to me. He becomes a burned-out shell. My desire obeys my elder brother, rejects my lover. Every time I see them together I think I can never bear the sight again. My lover's denied in just that weak body, just that weakness which transports me with pleasure. In my brother's presence he becomes an unmentionable outrage, a cause of shame who ought to be kept out of sight. I can't fight my brother's silent commands. (52)

In this context, she exploits him as do the others: "[I]t's taken for granted I don't love him, that I'm with him for the money, that I can't love him, it's impossible, that he could take any sort of treatment from me and still go on loving me. This because he's a Chinese, because he's not a white man. The way my elder brother treats my lover, not speaking to him, ignoring him, stems from such absolute conviction it acts as a model. We all treat my lover as he does" (51).

Duras's analysis of colonialism in *The Lover* associates it with desires formed from a degraded sense of self and within family relations, and how these relations encourage colonizers' values, which favor homogeneity and traditional forms of gender and racial identity. Duras portrays these values as inculcated and perpetuated in regressive familial patterns of behavior, creating the "model" she speaks of in the quote above. The childish and frighteningly self-centered older brother, who has been allowed the position of patriarch within the family, imposes his will, his masculinity, and his racism upon the rest of the family. Their domination and exploitation of the Chinese man is the family's one success as colonial subjects (129).

The girl's involvement with her lover—a transgressive act on several counts—breaks racial, social, sexual, and familial taboos. The regressive homogeneity of her family is displaced by the heterogeneities and nonabsolutes of this love affair. The affair is illicit, described as incestuous, miscegenational. However, the girl's transgressions cannot overcome the family's taboos, which induce the girl to ultimately abandon her lover. Indeed, the ideologies or attitudes from their respective cultures cause each to feel "lonely in love" (37). As a down-at-heel colonial she identifies with his exclusion from her society. She also both desires and resents him for his wealth. He in turn is also a colonizer (his father is a rich landlord) who cannot sacrifice his fortune or disobey his father to run off with her. Social status, represented by race or money, causes both to feel shame about their relationship. Transgressions and learned patterns are intimately connected yet also clash, acting both to fuel their love and to defeat it.

The general lack of emotion and depression the girl frequently displays indicate her emotional withdrawal from pain and abuse. Duras portrays herself as a precocious girl whose passionate sexuality in her lover's room is tempered by her detached awareness of the world around them, the impersonality she sometimes adopts with her lover ("I'd like you to do as you usually do with women," 37) and keeping some distance even in the same bed ("We can't stop loving each other . . . I sleep with him. I don't want to sleep in his arms," 63). Such shifts acknowledge pleasure and pain and yet keep them at arm's length. Another example is the girl's response to hearing how her lover and his father have gotten rich building crowded compartments, or housing for the poor, with whom she identifies: "Suddenly I have a pain. Very slight, almost imperceptible. It's my heartbeat, shifted into the fresh, keen wound he's made in me, he, the one who's talking to me, the one who also made the afternoon's pleasure. I don't hear what he's saying, I've stopped listening. He sees, stops. I tell him to go on. He does. I listen again. He says he thinks about Paris a lot. He thinks I'm very different from the girls in Paris, not nearly so nice. I say the compartments can't be as profitable as all that. He doesn't answer" (48–49). Her changing affect reflects her conflict in loving a man who exploits those whom she and her family have come to resemble. Duras here seems to be capturing the distance with which trauma victims observe their own pain or learn to live split between being "I," or functioning subject, or "she," that is, victim. Because trauma often remains repressed and inaccessible to memory, its victims perform a doubling of themselves, into a self who is altered by trauma and another self who carries on, and though integration of the two is necessary for recovery, it is often not possible (Lifton, 1991 Interview, 164; Langer, *Testimonies* 23, 35).

In *The Lover*, Duras also constructs a pivotal moment of subject formation that focuses on the protagonist's ability to look at herself with loving eyes because that loving gaze is not provided in the family context. Early in the text the girl describes herself at fifteen as she is about to meet her Chinese lover, wearing provocative yet sexually ambiguous clothes, largely given to her by her mother, including a transparent silk dress, a man's fedora, and gold lamé high heels.

> I . . . look at myself in the shopkeeper's glass, and see that there, beneath the man's hat, the thin awkward shape, the inadequacy of childhood, has turned into something else. Has ceased to be a harsh, inescapable imposition of nature. Has become, on the contrary, a provoking choice of nature, a choice of the mind. Suddenly it's de-

liberate. Suddenly I see myself as another, as another would be seen, outside myself, available to all, available to all eyes, in circulation for cities, journeys, desire. (12–13)

This is a crucial instance of her development as a woman, where she is able to look at herself from outside, imagining herself in the male gaze but also as something other than the childhood she is trying to shed. Her self-representation also reflects her own sexual desire and a need for emotional reparation (perhaps a lover will give her what her family cannot). Although there are economic as well as emotional issues underlying her "circulation," Duras gives her protagonist considerable agency in reinventing herself and taking steps away from her disturbed family. A positive narcissistic self-assertion brings her to other experiences, notably to her lover and to writing, that will in the end take her outside her family and yet will also be shaped by her obsession to understand the family's destruction.

Assuming multiple roles and positions as the subject, object, and witness to her past life, Duras's narrative employs dialogism, or a "constant interaction between meanings" or viewpoints (Bakhtin 426), which provides a medium for re-creating the past, reshaping its significance, and playing out conflicting tendencies within Duras's narrator/protagonist. Dialogism is significant in the positioning of the narrator as both engaged and detached and in a dual subject position as she alternately refers to herself as "I" and "she." These subject shifts could indicate that the narrator is looking back in time, but they are frequent and not always consistent with chronology. Rather, this dialogue between inside and outside experience creates possibilities for uncovering inaccessible memories that would not be possible from only one of these positions, because trauma creates a "loss of voice, . . . of knowledge, of awareness, of truth, of the capacity to feel . . . [and] to speak" (Felman and Laub 231–32). The first splitting of I/she comes with the pivotal description of herself as she invites men's attention in the man's hat, silk dress, and heels. Her statement "I see myself as another" (13) begins her separation from her family and indicates her dual role as observer and object of study. Her new alluring clothes represent her coming adulthood and her future, both of which are associated with her need to write, and as she reimagines herself in these clothes she notes the desire within her younger self: "I want to write" (21). Her adult desires will take her away from her family; only she, and not her brothers, has the intelligence and skills to leave and succeed. There is also a profound sense of sadness and separation from them as she takes these steps. Her involvement with the Chinese man marks a permanent separation from them: "As soon as she got into the black car she knew: she's excluded from the family for the first time and forever" (35). Her subject position changes again during the narrator's first sexual encounter, indicating emotional withdrawal and then connection. Referring to herself as "she" in the initial context as she loses her virginity, she then switches to first person within a page as the couple become more intimate lovers and she is able to describe to him her family's desperation (38–40).

Suzanne Chester argues that the I/she dichotomy is a way for Duras to assert a position of control regarding who is observing and observed, for example, as she directs her gaze (and ours) onto the feminized body of her lover (445–48). As the narrator, Duras takes the position of observer and interpreter, but also as a victim of her family's emotional deprivation and physical punishment. This duality within the narrator, Janice Morgan effectively argues, also creates a necessary "tension that exists in the written text between intimacy and distance, deception and sincerity, language and silence [which] is, in fact, intrinsic to the experiences as she lived them" (273). Given the traumatized context from which this story has been told, and Duras's obsessive returns to it throughout her work, I would also contend that the narrative incorporates the responses of splitting and self-numbing, which reflect the trauma survivor's struggle "with how to cohere and how to absorb and in some measure confront what one has had thrust upon one, what one has been exposed to" (Lifton, 1991 Interview, 163–64). As Suzette Henke has observed about women's contemporary autobiographies, Duras feels compelled to reconstruct and reassess the past and reinvent the self in narrative. Moreover, the narrative of *The Lover* re-creates the sense of dislocation inherent to traumatic experience, which resists direct access to memory of it (Caruth, *Unclaimed* 8) through a creation of present and past selves that are simultaneously split and connected.

Duras structures her narrative not linearly, but in fragments that sometimes stand alone as memories of particular moments, as partial portraits of herself and others, or as needed information offered to the reader to clarify chronology as her narrative shifts frequently between past and present; she is retelling part of her youth from the distance of old age. More importantly, such fragments represent a re-creation of the uncertainties and gaps in traumatic memory. She uses particular foci— such as a face, an image, or a feeling—to provide connections between the fragments, so that the text does not read like random thoughts, but the connections are implicit from the standpoint of Duras's memories. To illustrate, the first three pages of the text consist in four fragments that describe her face in old age, two images of herself when she is fifteen and is about to meet her Chinese lover on a ferry, and the process of aging her face underwent between the ages of fifteen and nineteen. These different views of herself are the crux for the workings of her memory in this section, where the connection between the processes of aging and identity formation is implicitly made.

> I often think of the image only I can see now. . . . It's the only image of myself I like, the only one in which I recognize myself, in which I delight.

> . . . I grew old at eighteen. . . . My ageing [*sic*] was very sudden. . . . The people who knew me at seventeen, when I went to France, were surprised when they saw me again two years later, at nineteen. And I've kept it ever since, the new face I had then. . . .

> So, I'm fifteen and a half.
> It's on a ferry crossing the Mekong River.
> The image lasts all the way across. (3–5)

The connections between these images of her face are more firmly established as she begins to explain how she got that face. "Something occurred when I was eighteen to make that face happen" (7). Her face reflects her inner turmoil and the hatred she feels toward her elder brother and toward her mother, expressing the desire "to punish her for loving him so much, so badly" and to save her younger brother from the elder one, who followed an "animal law, filling every moment of every day of the younger brother's life with fear, a fear that one day reached his heart and killed him" (7). Her face will also entice the Chinese lover on the ferry and reflect how the family's neglect will in part bring about her attraction to him: "At the age of fifteen I had the face of pleasure, and yet I had no knowledge of pleasure. There was no mistaking that face. . . . That was how everything started for me—with that flagrant, exhausted face, those rings around the eyes, in advance of time and experience" (9). We also assume her eighteen-year-old face reflects the loss of her lover.

The daughter's narrative is depicted (and performed) by Duras as an attempt to recover traumatic memory as well as locating the family's life in images. The mother had desperately tried to construct an image of the family with photographs she had had taken of her children. Supposedly they were images for posterity, but they became merely illusionary depictions of a family increasingly doomed to chaos and insanity. The daughter's "images," however, are not fixed, but fleeting recovered moments. The narrator's presentation of the absent photos of herself enact remembering (Murphy 171). Her narrative images differ from the mother's picture-taking strategies in that she desires to reveal rather than conceal the family's madness. These contrasting images indicate the radical difference between surface and internal memory.

The plentiful gaps in the text highlight individual moments but also provide silences in the text, evidence that there are missing details— what is of necessity repressed because it is too painful or memory is too unreliable for the past to be fully known or reconstructed. She indicates that what is most important cannot be told in a conventional, detailed narrative. "The *story* of my life doesn't exist. Does not exist. There's never any center to it. No path, no line. There are great spaces where you pretend there used to be someone, but it's not true, there was no one. . . . Before, I spoke of clear periods, those on which the light fell. Now I'm talking about the *hidden stretches* of that same youth, of certain facts, feelings, events that I *buried*" (8, italics added). In presenting this story as both a witnessed narrative and distorted memories, Duras is also acknowledging what Shoshana Felman refers to as a "crisis of truth" with regard to traumatic experience (5–6), that remembering and narrating it are urgent but necessarily incomplete efforts.

In self-consciously evaluating the writing process in the midst of retelling her past, she admits the limitations of such an attempt because of her own uncertain recollections and how the past can linger on in us years later without our understanding why. She tries to explain here the impossible task of fully understanding oneself, much less an other:

[I]n the books I've written about my childhood I can't remember, suddenly, what I left out, what I said. I think I wrote about our love for our mother, but I don't know if I wrote about how we hated her too, or about our love for one another, and our terrible hatred too, in that common family history of ruin and death which was ours whatever happened, in love or in hate, and *which I still can't understand however hard I try, which is still beyond my reach, hidden in the very depths of my flesh, blind as a newborn child. It's the area on whose brink silence begins. What happens there is silence, the slow travail of my whole life.* I'm still there, watching those possessed children, as far away from the mystery now as I was then. I've never written, though I thought I wrote, never loved, though I thought I loved, never done anything but wait outside the closed door. (25, italics added)

A silence born of pain, grief, forgetfulness, and bewilderment insinuates itself, and she attempts to break the silence with words but knows she can only partially succeed. Here, the purpose of this style of narrative becomes clearer. By shifting from silence to words and recovering memory through images linked to being and feeling, as traumatic memory would actually emerge, she is able to more honestly evoke a limited experience of the past with brief glimpses, intimately connected and yet distanced ("I'm still there, watching"). This passage is an important instance of her use of the notion of an "overpowering narrative," wherein one describes the past yet is still locked into it. In referring to her memories as "hidden in the depths of my flesh," she recaptures the experience of the traumatized, who "become themselves the symptom of a history that they cannot entirely possess" (Caruth, "Introduction" I 1991, 4). Memory lies in the body, as with Xuela's hysterical pregnancies.

In *The Lover*, the writing process becomes a physical manifestation of the psyche. The girl's connections to her mother and brothers arise not only in physical union with her lover, but in the physical act of writing, another manifestation of desire. Speaking of remembering and writing about her family so much later, the narrator says:

They're dead now, my mother and my two brothers. For memories too it's too late. Now I don't love them any more. I don't remember if I ever did. I've left them. In my head I no longer have the scent of her skin, nor in my eyes the color of her eyes. I can't remember her voice, except sometimes when it grew soft with the weariness of evening. Her laughter I can't hear any more—neither her laughter nor her cries. It's over, I don't remember. That's why I can write about her so easily now, so long, so fully. She's become just something you write without difficulty, cursive writing. (28–29)

No memory lingers, only haunting from the deepest reaches. This passage suggests that writing has become a physical process, no longer constrained by conscious memory or even the senses. This flow of the pen brings to mind the flowing of water (that which cannot be contained), that ubiquitous image in Duras's work. This flowing also suggests an outpouring of something buried so deeply and known so intimately that it has been absorbed into the body and into movement. She expresses this not as mastery of the object of one's writing in the sense of explaining or defining, but as an absorption of it as part of one's own affect, to be transferred onto the page.

Duras offers the reader different positions here as well—of absorbing or internalizing the roles of victim, empathic witness, and interlocutor. As Duras increasingly struggled to recover memory in her work, the role of the reader became more prominent. In interviews late in her career (1970s and 1980s), she expressed a need to connect with her audience and a need to risk exposing intimate details of her life to them to establish this connection and further motivate her writing (Armel 70, 92, 94). At the same time, she does not offer any simple avenues into her troubled past. Even as she tries to write personal history, she challenges autobiographical forms. In this more personal disposition, Duras is constructing narratives that attempt to draw the reader into the experience of the traumatized through partial reconstruction of shame-filled events. The reader is intended to be the empathic witness to a testimony of mourning that becomes a "space in which loss may come to be symbolically and affectively mastered" (Santner 25). She acknowledges her readers as those who have read her previous attempts to describe her past ("Before, I spoke of clear periods, those on which the light fell. Now I'm talking about the hidden stretches of that same youth," 8; "Yes, it's the big funereal car that's in my books," 17). As such, she recognizes her readers as important witnesses, who, if they connect with the text, reading it becomes a personal and emotional experience for them as well. "Are my books difficult? . . . Yes, they are difficult . . . You can't understand these books anyway. That's not the right word. It's a matter of a private relationship between the book and the reader. They weep and grieve together" (*Practicalities* 107). Duras's texts also involve readers by bringing them into the disoriented positions of the characters through shifts back and forth in time, memory and affect. These shifts emulate the characters' and narrator's memory functions and experiences ("On the ferry, look, I've still got my hair," 16), prompting readers to occupy positions both inside and outside the narrative, provoking them to both feel and evaluate as the narrator does.[9]

Readers can recognize the silences of the narrative as well, for "the speakers about trauma on some level prefer silence so as to protect themselves from the fear of being listened to—and of listening to themselves . . . while silence is defeat, it serves them both as a sanctuary and as a place of bondage" (Felman and Laub 58). What is not said or cannot be remembered is equally revealing of traumatic memories; these gaps help readers to join her in the process of either reconstructing or gaining more understanding of her experience with each succeeding text. As testimonial witnesses to Duras's painful past, she hopes readers will carry forth her memories as well as their own.

"Love Was a Curse": Surviving Adult Betrayal in *Bastard out of Carolina*

Dorothy Allison considers the crucial issues of personal survival in adversity and what role the creative imagination can have in a process of healing. Her novels, stories, and essays have dealt with incest and rape, salvation and redemption, and the strong but breakable bond between mother and child. Her writing remembers her poor working-class family, her mother's struggles, and her own sexual abuse.[10] Admitting it is a presumptuous goal, Allison says that for her, writing literature is a commitment "to push people into changing their ideas about the world, and . . . to encourage us in the work of changing the world, to making it more just and more truly human" ("Believing" 165). Seeking understanding is an imperative of her writing, challenging and yet trying to overcome readers' resistance while humanizing disturbing aspects of traumatic experience. In fictionalizing her own past, she engages this process of discovery through scriptotherapy with inventions and reconstructions of the past that allow reassessment and criticism (Henke xvi). In *Bastard out of Carolina*, Allison explores how defensive reactions shape trauma survivors' identities and problematize their relationships to others. She demonstrates how psychological defenses, although necessary for survival, are constricting and indicative of the difficulty survivors, perpetrators, and others have in facing situations that defy our normalized conceptions of reality, ethics, and human agency. Allison deals with many of these difficult issues by engaging and testing readers' sympathies in her portrayals of Bone, her mother Anney, and her stepfather Glen, through a child's point of view.

Bastard out of Carolina (1992) is a semiautobiographical novel intimately chronicling child abuse. The novel focuses on the life of the protagonist, Bone, up to age twelve. From a poor South Carolina family, she becomes the object of her stepfather, Glen's, physical and sexual abuse. Bone is also the narrator, and through a young girl's perspective Allison effectively conveys the confusion, shame, and sense of the world as cruel and futureless that abused children often feel (Meiselman 41–47; Ulman and Brothers 67). Her perceptions of the world and herself (as evil, defiled, an outsider, etc.) are particularly strong indicators of traumatic effects (Herman and Hirschman 96–99; Meiselman 46–47). In detailing how Glen abuses Bone, Allison highlights both the daily terrors of such a situation as well as their effects on Bone's sexual development, behavior, and imagination. In addition, the novel explores the costs of adults' betrayal of her. Bone's ability to survive is contingent in part upon her imagination, but also upon the occasional loving support of other adults.

The novel carefully establishes the social, familial, and emotional environments that shape her identity, the forms of her abuse, and her responses to it. The struggles involved with the family's lower socioeconomic status create stresses and humiliations that exacerbate the stepfather's abusive behavior. Her extended family of maternal aunts and ne'er-do-well uncles, the Boatwrights, provide Bone with strong family supports and colorful family histories, but also teach her exacting gender roles that to a certain degree set up and attenuate the abuse she suffers. The women in her family indulge their men and grow old fast taking care of them and their children with few material resources. They indulgently look at their men as "overgrown boys," and Bone learns early that "men could do anything" (23). It is no accident that one of Bone's loving but wildly dysfunctional uncles brings Glen into her mother's life. The women in Bone's universe often view the world from a more stoic but passive position, while the men are more likely to take action, even if it is foolhardy and destructive. Bone learns early that women tolerate and are even attracted to male immaturity and violence: "Men could do anything, and everything they did, no matter how violent or mistaken, was viewed with humor and understanding" (23). Many of the women in Bone's family, including her own mother, define their worth by a man's love. Her aunt Ruth explains to Bone that Glen is jealous of her, wants to be her mother's baby himself, and that this is how men are and that women put up with it. Allison suggests here that women's acceptance of these rigid gender roles puts them at risk for abuse. In an interview, Allison considers why her mother and the other women in her family remained in such brutalizing situations.

> The hardest thing for me to understand was why my mother stayed in this bad, bad marriage with a brutal man. . . . I didn't really understand it fully until I started going to meet the few of her sisters who were still alive. Looking at the choices they made and seeing how powerfully caught they were in the things they were supposed to do . . . keep kids safe, find a good man, save him, and hang on for dear life. The concept of giving up and leaving was so alien to them. They believed that they could tame and heal the men in their lives with love. In some cases that works, which is kind of extraordinary. (Megan interview 76–77)

The traumatic loss of the mother, Anney, transpires slowly over the course of the novel. The first wedge between Anney and Bone is the secrecy Bone and Glen maintain about his abuse, and the split widens as Anney continues to jeopardize Bone by not recognizing the severity of Glen's behavior unless directly confronted with it. Anney understands Glen's pain, loves but fears him, and stoically tries to endure, only standing up to him when they have no food in the house or when he is especially abusive to Bone. Allison clearly establishes Anney's struggles, good motherly qualities and intentions in the first three chapters. She has her first child, Bone, illegitimately at age fifteen with a young man who cannot or will not take responsibility. After trying to survive the death of her first husband when she is nineteen, she then struggles, largely successfully, to support and be a good mother to Bone and her sister, Reese. In telling her mother's story, Bone recognizes how the losses and adversities of their lives make Anney and Glen emotionally needy. Allison observes that "being poor in this country is about being constantly hungry, because the thing that you get, the emotional sustenance you get is never enough, so that hunger becomes a way of life, that longing for something never had" (Megan interview 77). Not surprisingly, Anney is described in the novel as needing Glen "like a starving woman needs meat between her teeth" (41).

As in Duras's portrayal, the daughter feels a powerful identification with her mother's life and suffering, recognizing Anney's powerful need to be loved and to have a happy family. Bone keeps quiet about Glen to protect her mother and to maintain the veneer of unity and happiness in the family. Though this unity is a myth, it is one Bone knows her mother (and she herself to an extent) needs to preserve; Anney could not endure a conflict between loving Glen and loving her daughters. Bone also displays the characteristic abused child's need to preserve faith in the parents, necessitating strong defenses against awareness, such as dissociation, rationalization, or denial (Herman 107; Meiselman 44–46; Freyd 85–89). To illustrate, Bone says of her mother, "More terrified of hurting her than of anything that might happen to me, I would work as hard as he [Glen] did to make sure she never knew" (118). In trying to preserve a bond with her mother, she inadvertently plays a role in prolonging her own agonies, until her situation with Glen cannot be ignored and ultimately destroys the connection between mother and daughter.

Bone's tendency to keep family secrets typifies why children usually do not report their abuse, keeping strict allegiance to their families. Even when invited to tell her story by an outraged doctor who recognizes she has been beaten, all she wants is the comfort of family and fears any disruption her telling would create. This exemplifies how seeking help for abuse may put victims at odds with others close to them and at odds with their own hopes and ideals (Herman 178). Allison illustrates the many barriers to uncovering the realities of abuse in family units—defensive systems and pressures to play particular roles, for example—that are often unexamined aspects of all family structures, even if incest or other traumas are not an issue (Laing 121). By illustrating these defenses and relational dynamics through a child's consciousness, readers might more readily accept the complexities involved.

Allison's portrayal of Glen draws parallels with Bone's suffering and confronts readers with the destructiveness psychological trauma can bring about. Though much less sympathetic than the protagonist because he directs his own pain into murderous violence toward others, a case could be made that he is the most traumatized and most miserable of the characters. As with many adult survivors of childhood abuse, Glen has trouble with trust, autonomy, and initiative (Herman 110). Continually scapegoated as the unsuccessful member of his family, particularly by his father, who, Bone notes, regularly recites "all the things Glen had done wrong in his long life of failure and disappointment" (99), Glen's life is spent in a repetitive and self-defeating quest to measure up to his family's expectations. He fails miserably, however, because every setback or perceived insult sends him into violent rages. Though these bring him some release, this classic dysfunctional control-seeking behavior prevents him from breaking the destructive patterns of his life (Meiselman 19–23). He is still a "prisoner of his childhood" (Herman 110) in that he has absorbed his father's edict that he is a failure.

Glen's life exemplifies that purposeful action is made impossible in traumatizing situations and that bonds with others are broken and one's belief in self-competence is translated into shame and doubt. Glen's totalitarian control and imposed social isolation of his family (very typical of abusers, Herman and Hirschman 71–73) are directly connected to Glen's own shame: shame about poverty, unemployment, the miscarriage of his baby son, and his inability to pay for a grave for the child. Because he fails as a patriarch in many ways, he claims his family and his stepchildren as his only real "property." His attitudes reflect patriarchal aspects of Southern culture, as Minrose Gwin suggests in her discussion of incest narratives, that since the days of the Old South there has been a relation between "white male dominance, property ownership, and the control of women's bodies" (417).

Like many who are traumatized, he clings to fixed ideas that do not coincide with reality. For example, although his birth family is the cause of much of his shame, rage, and sense of helplessness, he cannot confront or reject them. He feels the pain of family life, yet defends against it by "one moment complaining of how badly they treated him and the next explaining it away" (99). Like Bone, he too cannot bear the idea of separation, even from an abusive family. He recognizes himself in Bone, another scared but angry child, who in turn sees in Glen an unsure, frightened, yet enraged child who trembles underneath the surface of his macho posturing when with his father: "He would pull at his pants like a little boy and drop his head if anyone asked him a question. It was hard to put that image of him next to the way he was all the rest of the time—the swaggering bantam rooster man who called himself my daddy" (99). Continually unemployed because of his violent attacks on fellow employees, it is no coincidence that his inability to provide financially for the family escalates his abuse of Bone.

Despite the horrors of Glen's violence toward Bone, including a vicious rape, Allison does not want readers to completely demonize Glen. She makes it clear that his violence is a function of his own feelings of helplessness and need for control. Caught in the trap of his own destructiveness, he alienates everyone except his wife. Glen seems to have no capacity for self-reflection upon the consequences of his violent behavior. He is trapped in his emotions, displacing his anger, failing to recognize the source of his rage, and thus he never confronts or resolves his own pain and conflict. For him and perhaps for Bone's mother, Allison's epigraph from James Baldwin rings very true: "People pay for what they do, and still more, for what they have allowed themselves to become. And they pay for it simply: by the lives they lead."

Bone comes to resemble Glen in many ways, as an abuse victim and in absorbing the emotional environment and worldview he provides. They both feel unloved, rageful, and helpless. When they visit his relatives, who clearly disdain them for being poor and "trashy," Bone feels an "aching lust to hurt somebody back" (98) that we imagine Glen feels. He shapes her perspective about men outside her family too, such that all male authorities, like the insensitive sheriff who tries to question her about her rape, seem to resemble him.

Glen's status as a stepfather and Bone's awareness of his flaws and weaknesses make this a somewhat different situation than typical father/daughter incest. Bone does not seem to expect him to be a father figure and keeps silent to protect her mother more than him. Some incestuous elements emerge as Bone is initiated into sexuality by Glen's caresses and responds in some ways because it is the only affection she gets from him. As with other incest victims, her response is most disturbing to her, because she wants affection but it makes her feel responsible (Meiselman 30).

Bone's thoughts represent many uncomfortable aspects of how abuse affects the inner psyche of a child. Bone feels at times that she is complicit with her stepfather Glen's abuse (standing passively when he caresses her, for instance), but as in any such terrorizing situation, agency is curtailed and refusal is impossible (Herman 35). When Bone is ten, the stresses in Glen's life shorten his temper and he begins to regularly and relentlessly pursue, fondle, and beat Bone, usually when her mother is working. At this point in the novel, Bone begins to realize she cannot avoid his rage and already wishes Anney would leave him. Here she feels the most helpless and traumatized.

> I did not know how to tell anyone what I felt, what scared me and shamed me and still made me stand, unmoving and desperate, while he rubbed against me and ground his face into my neck. I could not tell Mama. I would not have known how to explain why I stood there and let him touch me. It wasn't sex, not like a man and woman . . . but, then, it was something like sex, something powerful and frightening that he wanted badly and I did not understand at all. Worse, when Daddy Glen held me that way, it was the only time his hands were gentle. . . . Fear. It might have been fear. . . . I only knew that there was something I was doing wrong, something terrible. He said, "You drive me crazy," in a strange distracted voice, and I shuddered but believed him. (109)

Bone's interior monologues convey the perplexed thoughts of the traumatized child who feels guilty, helpless, and shamed. Completely in his control, she keeps their encounters secret because he has confused her about her own involvement and offers her only this context for tenderness. Her thoughts also express confusion about her relationships to him and to her mother, about the power of adults and the strangeness of their actions, fear of approaching her mother, belief in the adult abuser's irrational explanations for his behavior, and identification with him because he is also a source of comfort. She also voices feelings of complicity and guilt because she does not fight him off and responds to being caressed. Here Allison demonstrates the early sexualization of incest victims and being held hostage psychically by their abusers. If they feel any type of arousal or closeness to the abuser, they feel some allegiance to that person, or in this case, fear to hurt the mother or disrupt the family by telling the truth. A confused sense of their own sexuality is illustrated in Bone's partial consciousness of her mother and Glen having sex, and she begins to speculate: "Sex. Was that what Daddy Glen had been doing to me in the parking lot? Was it what I had started doing to myself whenever I was alone in the afternoons?" (63)

The taint of abuse deals a crushing blow to Bone's identity and emotional development because it prevents her finding comfort from her mother and debases her self-concept. Bone's consciousness is permeated by Glen's degrading view of her, until her aunts, especially Ruth and Raylene, give her some perspective about Glen and bolster her own value:

> When I saw myself in Daddy Glen's eyes, I wanted to die. . . . Everything felt hopeless. He looked at me and I was ashamed of myself. It was like sliding down an endless hole, seeing myself at the bottom, dirty, ragged, poor, stupid. But at the bottom, at the darkest point, my anger would come and I would know that he had no idea who I was, that he never saw me as the girl who worked hard for Aunt Raylene, who got good grades no matter how often I changed schools, who ran errands for Mama and took good care of Reese. I was not dirty, not stupid, and if I was poor, whose fault was that? (209)

Bone also experiences fragmentation of her personality because she must hide her relationship with Glen from her mother. Glen frightens her mother and Reese at times, but because they are not as severely abused, they view their home situation more optimistically than Bone. She also experiences confusion and loss of identity as the family moves frequently from place to place, so much so that she lies about her name in school with the assurance that she will have moved on before anyone knows. Consequently, developing a clear sense of reality and who she is beyond Glen's hurtful definitions of her behavior is extremely difficult. She looks to her own fantasies, or to gospel music and religion, to give her a sense of order and belonging. Until she forms a close bond with Raylene, only her dying aunt Ruth inquires whether Glen abuses her, tries to offer her information and comfort, but is hindered by Bone's fear and shame about telling.

Her identification with Glen and especially Shannon Pearl, a school friend who is albino, emphasizes the defensive strategies Bone adopts to survive. All three lash out from being in pain, seeking revenge rather than a path toward healing. Noting that Shannon is constantly ridiculed and isolated by schoolmates because of her appearance, Bone recognizes her own pain in the other girl: "Was it possible she could see the same thing in my eyes? Did I have that much hate in me?" (161) Analogous to Bone's fantasies of punishing Glen (see below), Shannon creates violent retributive tales of the gruesome deaths of innocent children—fantasized revenge on the cruel children who torment her. Shannon projects the tough defensive exterior Bone cultivates, but so much so that her suffering makes her unable to sympathize with others and she embraces fanatical religiousness and bigotry.

Another connection between the two girls is that Shannon's parents organize concert tours for gospel singers, coinciding with Bone's fascination with religion and gospel music. She wants to be one of these singers so she will be loved, and these records evoke the strong emotions she feels about Glen and that her aunt Ruth feels about her own impending death. The music expresses her feelings of guilt and shame ("make you hate and love yourself at the same time, make you ashamed and glorified," 136). Hoping religion will redeem her, she is "almost saved" by fourteen different churches she approaches, evidence of repetitive acting out, which does not bring her resolution or absolution. She wants vindication for her suffering, but because she feels tainted and is unable to forgive herself, she embraces the familiar moment of "sitting on the line between salvation and damnation with the preacher and the old women pulling bodily at my poor darkened soul" (151). This moment reflects best her own conflicts about needing recognition yet also feeling complicit and unredeemable. Her attempts to convert her uncles reveal her need to be cocooned by narrow, predictable thinking. Bone's religious detour represents a stage in the process of her developing awareness of her internal struggles and what might bring her comfort.

Like Shannon, Glen, and her male relatives, Bone spends much of the novel grasping at any illusions of control available to her. Living in an increasingly dangerous and totalitarian environment where everyone's actions are subsumed to Glen's moods, she consoles herself with rigid thinking, such as convincing herself that she has some sense of agency if she does not cry when he beats her. She also develops a tough

exterior and violent posture like her uncles and Glen, wanting to emulate their power in physical violence when they feel slighted. Her own
smaller versions of this violence—her invention of aggressive revenge
stories and acting out her rebellion in various small crimes like breaking into Woolworth's—gives her some brief sense of the same potency
her uncles and Glen share. This forcefulness is an illusion of course, because even if it is momentarily satisfying, it also undermines these
men's lives (e.g., Glen loses jobs, her uncles land in jail). Such attempts
are revealed as repetitive, emotionally static actions, dissociating these
characters from others and from awareness of their own hurt feelings.
Not until she realizes that she does not have any control over Glen's or
her mother's actions can Bone overcome her defenses and accept her
own sorrow in a lengthy process of mourning beginning as the novel
ends. Allison's portrayals demonstrate the short-term relief of dissociating from pain and loss as well as its long-term futility for healing.

The symbolic structure Allison employs to create Bone's fantasies—
storytelling and accompanying imagery—highlight a consciousness in
distress. First, Bone has revenge fantasies wherein she combats her own
helplessness with Glen and the secrecy surrounding her abuse. In one
fantasy, Bone visualizes people watching Glen beat her: "In my imagination I was proud and defiant. . . . Those who watched admired me
and hated him" (112). She acknowledges the consoling, narcissistic,
and erotic aspects of these daydreams: "Yet it was only in my fantasies
with people watching me that I was able to defy Daddy Glen. Only
there that I had any pride. I loved those fantasies, even though I was
sure they were a terrible thing. They had to be; they were self-centered
and they made me have shuddering orgasms. In them, I was very special. I was triumphant, important. I was not ashamed. There was no
heroism possible in the real beatings. There was just being beaten until
I was covered with snot and misery" (113). Allison's reference to the
self-centeredness of these fantasies calls attention not only to Bone's
disconnection from others and her mother's failure to comfort her—at
this point in her life, only her body is a means of comfort—but also in
that preoccupation with the self, which will not bring healing. Only the
words and acknowledgment of others will do that, as her aunt Raylene's
nurturance will demonstrate. Therapists who deal with trauma note
that revenge fantasies are not effective means of coping, that in fact,
they may actually increase feelings of torment, horror, and degradation.

As victims can never really "get even," therapy is most effective when it focuses beyond the victim's relationship to the perpetrator to mourning losses (Herman 189). Bone begins to do this at the end of the novel as she mourns the loss of her mother.

Bone's dreams, fantasies, and made-up stories bear witness to the intermixing of sex and violence that she has internalized from her abuse. Her perceptions of the world and herself (as tainted, evil, etc.) and her inability to articulate her experience to others are particularly strong indicators of traumatic effects. When she is ten, Glen's physical and sexual abuse (fondling at this point) becomes more frequent, and she is most isolated and confused. His actions and perceptions dominate her inner life so completely that she associates her own sexual pleasure with danger and entrapment. She begins to masturbate excitedly to a fantasy of "struggling to get free while [a] fire burned hotter and closer. I am not sure if I came when the fire reached me or after I had imagined escaping it. But I came. I orgasmed on my hand to the dream of fire" (63). Ann Cvetkovich emphasizes the relation between sexual trauma and sexual pleasure for Bone, pointing out how Bone is unclear about whether she gives into or overcomes her own annihilation in her fantasy (388–89). Karin Meiselman says that for girls who are victims of incest, such as Bone, "the humiliation and helplessness of their incest experience, along with premature sexual stimulation, can lead to attempts at mastery and reassertion of personal power in sexual ways" (49). This example also demonstrates how incorporating aspects of abuse into a pleasurable context can also be a victim's defensive action to mitigate terror (Herman 109). Any sense of control, even if it is self-abusing or ineffectual, is necessary to building a perception of an integrated identity. The ego must avoid feelings of total helplessness, or a sense of self will disappear; these feelings are cited by trauma survivors as the most damaging of their experiences (Van der Kolk and Van der Hart 446; Langer 6–16, 197; Herman 47).

Bone's perceptions form a complex picture of pleasure and shame: "I was ashamed of myself for the things I thought about when I put my hands between my legs, more ashamed for masturbating to the fantasy of being beaten than for being beaten in the first place. I lived in a world of shame. I hid my bruises as if they were evidence of crimes I had committed. I knew I was a sick disgusting person. . . . How could I explain to anyone that I hated being beaten but still masturbated to the story I told myself about it?" (113). Her sexuality develops as a means of self-soothing but is paradoxically associated with violence. Bone's stories and her "desires, wishes and passions are entrenched in sadomasochism," which marks the occurrence of trauma (Horvitz 43, 4). Glen's violence also infiltrates her imagination, imprisoning her body and her mind. "[Bone] is unable to disentangle the beating that she hates from the fantasy about it that she loves, and her sense that she is the creator of her fantasy leads her to assume shameful responsibility for being beaten as well" (Cvetkovich 389).

In presenting how victims' minds can condense disparate elements, Allison urges readers to consider how victims' ambivalent associations to their mistreatment can account for their silence and conflicted self-conceptions. In these sadomasochistic fantasies, Horvitz argues, Bone internalizes the conditions shaping her life (5), that is, the relation of the more powerful to the less powerful. Allison also cautions readers against any simplistic interpretations of a survivor's possible complicity. Allison wants to create sympathy for a child victim who is not passive, innocent, or desexualized (Cvetkovich 388).

Fire is the principal symbol used in the text to underscore the dangers, anguish, and hopes for redemption that Bone experiences in a traumatized state. Fire is a multifunctional, condensed image throughout the text, connoting, among other things, destruction and death, redemption and purification, fear of and embrace of annihilation, violence, pain, and eroticism. An intricate symbolic equivalence of pleasure and pain emerges in Bone's masturbatory fantasy "struggling to get free while [a] fire burned hotter and closer," almost destroying her (63). Associated in her mind with physical pleasure and danger, she also wishes for fire to destroy her town and purify her of her shame. "I thought about fire, purifying, raging, sweeping through Greenville and clearing the earth. . . . Fire, I whispered . . . Yes. I rocked and rocked, and orgasmed on my hand to the dream of fire" (253–54). She reads of punishing but redemptive biblical fires in the book of Revelation, wherein she takes "comfort in the hope of the apocalypse, God's retribution on the wicked. I liked Revelation, loved the Whore of Babylon and the promised rivers of blood and fire. It struck me like gospel music, it promised vindication" (152). When Glen brutally rapes her toward the end of the text and comes as close as at any point to killing her, Bone again imagines biblical-style revenge: "'You'll die, you'll die,'

I screamed inside. . . . 'Your bones will melt and your blood will catch fire. I'll rip you open and feed you to the dogs. Like in the Bible, like the way it ought to be, God will give you to me'" (285). Fire also expresses her rage at Glen and the world: "My insides were boiling, and my skin burned. My hatred and rage were so hot I felt like I could have spit fire" (258). When Shannon Pearl is killed by fire in an accident, however, Bone is stunned by the reality of it, which makes her contemplate the frightening and sad aspects of death and question her desire to die when Glen humiliates her. Shannon's death makes her consider her own possible death and fear more that Glen will actually kill her. The mythical image of fire, personalized by her imagination, is a kind of displaced symbol used to resist traumatic effects, but it is not the cleansing dose of reality needed to begin healing, Allison suggests.

As the novel progresses, the stories Bone tells herself and others reflect increased ego integration, a more controlled use of her imagination that to some extent revisits her terrors yet also helps her to reconnect socially. In safer, happier times in the novel Bone is surrounded by Boatwrights, telling her cousins hair-raising stories to entertain and educate them. These self-created horror stories represent a potential creative life that might arise out of trauma and violence—stories about death told to help conquer the fear of it. "My stories were full of boys and girls gruesomely raped and murdered, babies cooked in pots of boiling beans, vampires and soldiers and long razor-sharp knives. Witches cut off the heads of children and grown-ups. . . . I got to be very popular as a baby-sitter; everyone was quiet and well-behaved while I told stories, their eyes fixed on my face in a way that made me feel like one of my own witches casting a spell" (119). Her controlled way of dealing with fear clearly appeals to other children.

In her stories, women break out of gender confinement, ride motorcycles, and set fire to houses. The "mean sister" and "girls who rob banks" games she plays with her cousins help her to construct a provisional identity of toughness to replace the reality of being a helpless girl. The acting out of violence in these games does not resolve her conflicts but reconstructs a sense of self capable of action. Later, while living with Raylene, she imagines scenarios of the future such as heading up a road going north by herself, that is, she can envision independence and moving away from her situation.

Bone begins to form a more stable identity in the steady company of her aunt Raylene. Raylene does not take Anney's place but becomes a powerful surrogate when Anney fails Bone. Raylene helps Bone shape a strong positive sense of self and tries to give Bone a sense of proportion about the complexities of love and adult relationships. Raylene gives her niece tasks she can excel in, praises her and encourages her independence by example and reinforcement. It is Raylene who tries to soften the incredible rage that builds up in Bone and makes her fear that she will be a "terrible person" (298) and makes Bone aware of how she acts with other people, encouraging her to have empathy for others and not to judge by appearances. Raylene's attention and guidance reminds Bone that she is loved. Because she is caring but also self-sufficient, confident and lesbian, Raylene offers an alternative model to the other Boatwright women's subjection. Raylene is symbolic of Allison's own healing, her creation a part of Allison's scriptotherapy, where she imagines a mother figure who provides protection and security, something neither Bone's nor Allison's own mother could do.[11]

In order to overcome the trauma-induced involuntary acting out, repetitions, and internalizations that block her development, Bone must confront a number of realizations about her mother and Glen and come to terms with her losses. Her first significant recognition is that he will not change and that her mother will not leave him. On this basis Bone decides she cannot live with him and not be in danger. This is something her mother does not seem able to face. Bone's decision in a way forces Anney to make a choice between her daughter and Glen. Bone's most important realization—that her mother still cannot leave Glen even after she catches him raping her—helps Bone to de-idealize her mother and hate her mother's failure to protect her. Glen's rape of Bone seems less traumatizing than her mother leaving her, but the rape forces decisions that leave Bone with Raylene and a heart-breaking disillusionment with her mother that is important to her own healing. Only toward the end of the novel does Bone recognize the extent of her mother's betrayal; like many children who are victims of incest, she has protected herself and her family by resisting awareness of this betrayal (Freyd 4). Bone repeatedly relives the memories of her mother leaving her alone at the hospital and showing sympathy for Glen after the rape. Allison presents these as even more traumatic images than those of Glen during the rape, because it is Anney's betrayal that most devastates Bone. It is especially tragic because Anney desires to be a loving, responsible parent but fails because of her own needs. Like many mothers in these situations, she has enabled her daughter's abuse (Meiselman 23–25). "My mama had abandoned me, and that was the only thing that mattered" (302). Raylene continues to remind Bone that her mother loves her and that her actions are complex and shame-filled, something Bone will only be able to comprehend later. When her mother visits, Bone has become emotionally numb, looking at her mother as if "underwater," no longer able to be comforted by her mother's explanations of how the situation transpired because she could not imagine Glen being so brutal. Bone can no longer pretend to comfort her mother. "I had lost my mama. She was a stranger, and I was so old my insides had turned to dust and stone. Every time I closed my eyes, I could see again the blood on Glen's hairline, his face pressed to her belly, feel that black despair whose only relief would be death. I had prayed for death. Maybe it wasn't her fault. It wasn't mine. Maybe it wasn't a matter of anybody's fault" (307). In giving Bone her birth certificate without a stamp of illegitimacy, Anney makes one contribution to the possibility of remaking her identity, although this gesture seems inadequate given the context. Bone can now throw off the stigma of social disapproval. This loss, however, will clearly mark her for life: "I was already who I was going to be" (309). This is an important variation on how Anney was "changed forever" by her first husband, Lyle's, death.

In the last moments of the book, at age twelve, Bone thinks about her future identity and wonders if it will resemble her mother's. "Fourteen and terrified, fifteen and a mother, just past twenty-one when she married Glen. Her life had folded into mine. What would I be like when I was fifteen, twenty, thirty? Would I be as strong as she had been, as hungry for love, as desperate, determined, and ashamed?" (309). Yet the path toward that adulthood will be in the more reliable hands of her aunt Raylene: "I . . . let my head tilt to lean against her [Raylene], trusting her arm and her love. I was who I was going to be, someone like her, like Mama, a Boatwright woman. I wrapped my fingers in Raylene's and watched the night close in around us" (309). Though loss of the mother is absolute, Raylene joins Bone in facing her dark existence, in contrast to Kincaid's and Duras's heroines, who face this alone.

Allison's portrayal of Anney is perhaps the most disturbing for readers. In depicting a mother whose daughter is sexually abused, and in part a version of Allison's own mother, Allison challenges readers to re-assess their preconceptions of motherhood and to consider their own fears and hopes about mothering. This portrait of a loving mother who cannot stop her husband from beating and raping her eldest daughter poses many challenges for the reader. I have never taught a novel that brought a greater response, more feelings of pity, dread, fear and out-right hatred in my student readers. Although there are usually mixed opinions about Anney, depending upon the students' backgrounds and their awareness of the workings of family abuse situations, she still comes under the most vociferous attacks of any character in fiction that I have taught. One could conclude that Allison anticipates powerful re-actions by taking great pains to create sympathy for Anney's life and to establish her as a loving, financially struggling mother, so that when she abandons Bone at the end of the novel, the loss seems even greater because she does seem to love her daughter.

Allison voices strong love and ambivalence for her own now-deceased mother in her autobiography *Two or Three Things I Know for Sure*, which also analyzes the socioeconomic and gender factors that account for her mother's and for Anney's behavior. Important con-tributing factors are the time period (1950s and 1960s), the legacy of Southern poverty, and a masculine-dominated culture limiting these women's choices. Judith Herman also found in her study that incest was more common in families where patriarchy and the sexual division of labor were predominant (Herman and Hirschman 62).

Allison recalls her mother leaving her husband and then having to return simply because she could not make it on her own financially. Many women, however, are still locked in such threatening and dis-possessed situations. One major difference between the actual and fictional mothers is that her own mother did not leave her as Anney does Bone; Ruth Gibson Allison continued to stay with her abusive husband, but made him agree he would not rape Dorothy any more. He stopped, but he still beat her. The ending of *Bastard out of Carolina* could be interpreted as symbolic of a deeply felt sense of the mother's emotional abandonment. One could argue that Dorothy Allison might have felt more betrayed by her mother because she should have known better. However, we are urged to understand that Anney Boatwright and Ruth Allison are thwarted by circumstances and the belief that they should hold their families together no matter the cost. Their fears become misdirected, says Allison. "Look at Anney . . . what she's most afraid of is losing this family she's held together. That's not what she should be afraid of; she loses her family when she loses her daughter. She doesn't know enough to be really afraid of that" (Megan interview 77). Deborah Horvitz observes that Anney pays a tremendous price for lying to herself and "refusing to bear witness to her own story" (52). Thinking of her mother's circumstances, Allison suggests that rushing to judgment is too easy when people live continually in dangerous circumstances: "How do you forgive someone for not saving you on one particular day when she saved you on five others? How do you forgive someone for not saving you when I lied to her and everyone lied to her? Women in impossible situations manage to perform miracles repeatedly" (Sherwin interview).

Not being able to withstand the daily assaults on bodily and emotional integrity is not a moral flaw but a reasonable breaking point psychologically. Readers from safer life situations might have difficulty understanding how few available choices, economic necessity, and a minimal sense of self-worth are primary forces shaping many poor women's lives. "Psychological trauma is an affliction of the powerless" says Judith Herman (*Trauma* 33) and is all too common amongst the poor.[12] Choices are not only limited but at times impossible. When a victim's ethical compass is destroyed as she tries to survive in extreme circumstances, observers tend to reject the possibility of not having a choice because it challenges our conceptions of subjectivity.

I would suggest that an incapacitated mother, one who loves her children and yet can seem to do little to protect them, scares the parent and child in many readers. How could a mother let her child be victimized so? This is a question frequently posed about mothers in these situations by readers who have trouble identifying with Anney. Such questions reveal a fear that we cannot always act in ways that measure up with our best views of ourselves or what we would do in adverse circumstances. What about if the mother in her own way is helpless? Anney herself displays many symptoms of trauma, such as silence, dissociation, and denial. She isolates herself out of shame; her identity and agency have deteriorated in ways similar to Bone under terrorizing circumstances. Bone describes her as if experiencing a kind of paralysis after Glen screams at her: "Mama froze . . . Her face was like a photograph, black-and-white, her eyes enormous dark shadows and her skin bleached in that instant to a paper gloss, her open mouth stunned and gaping" (69). And later, she is always "tired, sad, scared" (207). Anney denies Glen's betrayal, and her failure to recognize the abuse in her own home until it reaches disastrous proportions well illustrates the defense mechanisms that people employ to survive not only adversity but normal relationships as well.

Her portrayal may threaten readers' own capacities for denial or for looking the other way. She is torn between the husband and daughter who she both loves and who are locked in a violent and obsessive relationship of their own. What may appear as Anney's choice of Glen over Bone could be attributed to a sense of her own shame and failure as a mother. Or perhaps it could be an example of how Glen has asserted extreme control of his wife by manipulating her with lies into violating her own principles or attachments to others to the extent that she will tolerate his violence and protect him from her brothers, who are hunting him at the end of the book (Herman 83). Complicating the situation is Anney and Glen's strong sexual and emotional bond; their mutual dependence keeps them locked together. This ending is shocking to our conceptions of motherhood, but Anney's leaving represents how many abused children feel betrayed and abandoned by the one who allows them to be abused.

A mother's denial, an abuser's justifications, an abused child's fear to tell are all familiar elements of the incestuous household. Allison tries not only to unmask the truths that remain hidden in such a situation, but also to bring readers into the difficult territory of each player's role and motivations. She reminds us, "[I]f we begin to agree that some ideas are too dangerous, too bad to invite inside our heads, then we . . . silence everyone who would tell us something that might be painful. . . . Everything I know, everything I put in my fiction, will hurt someone somewhere as surely as it will comfort and enlighten someone else" (172–73). Allison seems to have a higher cause for literature in mind and promotes engagement in a kind of scriptotherapy when she says, "Writing is an act that claims courage and meaning, and turns back denial, breaks open fear, and heals me as it makes possible some measure of healing for all those like me" (181). In *Trash*, Allison says she found comfort in writing stories of her family and childhood:

"Writing it all down was purging. Putting those stories on paper took them out of the nightmare realm and made me almost love myself for being able to finally face them" (9).

As with Duras, Allison shares a special bond with her readers. For her, the writer and reader form a community, and her editor Carole De Santi calls her the "Lourdes of writers" to reflect the healing power of her work on some readers (Allison, "Patron Saint"). Nevertheless, readers who have not personally experienced severe traumas can still be part of a community of individuals who affect one another. Stories such as Allison's can help us realize the social and psychological issues at stake in everyday life and help us bear witness to how extreme experience takes us out of the realms of conventional morality, easy social judgment, and ideals of personal integrity. Her work encourages readers to examine and critique "the dynamics of power structures that allow, perhaps even promote, the continuation of violence" (Horvitz 51).

Situations of trauma elude easy definitions. They force us to view the worst aspects of human behavior and to contemplate a difficult past that is not easily comprehensible intellectually or emotionally. The capacity to know oneself falters in the traumatic situation that must first be survived. Kincaid's Xuela expresses an incapacity to know herself at times: "[I]t was not the only time that I did not admit to myself my own vulnerability" (15). Each of the narrators extends this personal sense of dissociation and bewilderment into a powerful sense of the unfathomability and the inconstancy of life, the helpless plunge into the hole of trauma and how it is survived. Through Xuela, Kincaid ponders how "The mystery of the hole in the ground gives way to the mystery of your fall; just when you get used to falling and falling forever, you stop; and that stopping is yet another mystery, for why did you stop, there is not an answer to that any more than there is an answer to why you fell in the first place. Who you are is a mystery no one can answer, not even you. And why not, why not!" (202). Duras's puzzlement over this same unknowability and bewilderment over a traumatic past became a repetitive theme of her writing. She has revisited the anguished memories of her youth in Indochina multiple times over the course of her career. Allison has similarly tried to understand how she and her mother ended up in the abusive circumstances that would mark their lives forever and has tried to explain this in her characterizations. Each of the authors and protagonists carries many questions about a traumatic past that remains essential yet elusive to them, life changing and mysterious. These trauma texts become narrative/imaginary means by which to articulate a kind of truth about this experience through storytelling that approximates the anguish, uncertainties, and defenses accompanying such experience.

All three writers pursue common themes that are raised and problematized by trauma: life/sexuality and death, living with pain, quest for self, and the possible role of imagination in healing. Their works present a conflation of life and death typical of traumatic circumstances where there can be a sense of death encroaching on life because of fear or emotional withdrawal, and a symbolic or literal fear of the annihilation of self. Also explored are the meaning and consequences of pain. Trauma can close off self-knowledge, but mourning and working through leads to reconcilement with pain that must be acknowledged if healing is to occur. Kincaid has said, "I think life is difficult and that is that. I am not at all—absolutely not at all—interested in the pursuit of happiness. I am interested in pursuing a truth, and the truth often seems to be not happiness, but its opposite" (Kincaid, "Happy Endings" 29). Each text pursues a quest for self that is undertaken despite self-knowledge being impeded by lack of recognition, failed nurturance, and a fragmented sense of self. Because each protagonist must function in isolation, her quest must take the shape of an inward journey, where she creates a safer space for herself in narcissistic contemplation. The authors' use of these first-person narrators makes the characters into writers or creators of some sort, creating correspondences between artistic creation and self-creation. Imagination is presented as part of a process toward healing, or a way of displacing trauma, allowing, for example, Xuela to create her mother's presence in her mind. Imagination is not a panacea but provides representations from which protagonists and readers can contemplate conflicts and imagine a sense of agency and the possibility of reparation. Through narcissistic self-nurturing, transferential relations, and reimagining their lives through fantasy, narration, and storytelling, all of these narrators engage in a process of reconstituting a self diminished by loss.

Each of the authors seeks an attitude-changing if not an emotional relationship to readers. Duras recognized her long-term audience in *The Lover* as witnesses to her previous attempts to explore a painful past, indicating that "reader and text weep and grieve together." Allison knows her writing will both hurt and heal readers, but above all, she wants to change them. Kincaid's purpose is to create empathy and awareness as she demystifies positions of power and victimization. "I am always interested in how the powerful and the powerless relate. . . . I am interested in the defeated and identify with the defeated even though I don't feel defeated myself. . . . People are always saying, 'I am not a victim.' Well, sometimes you are and it is not your fault. Actually, the great thing about being the victim is that you identify with the victim, and that may save you from victimizing. If you can keep in mind who suffers, it might prevent you from causing suffering. I think. I hope" (Ferguson interview 171).

This chapter has dealt with very personal, internalized responses to traumatic conflicts. Chapter 5 turns to texts that emphasize how individual traumatic experience embodies larger issues of social and historical trauma. These works also call for reader empathy, but attempt to place characters and readers together in collective visions of understanding and healing.

FIVE

REMEMBERING HISTORY
THROUGH THE BODY

And there is only my imagination where our history should be. CRISTINA GARCIA

The three texts considered in this chapter—Toni Morrison's *Beloved*, Pat Barker's *Regeneration* trilogy, and Larry Heinemann's *Paco's Story*—explore traumatic historical events (slavery, World War I, and the Vietnam War) and their lingering consequences. All were events of incredible scope and complexity, impossible to define satisfactorily, and involve differing circumstances, populations, ideologies, intentions, and effects. But the similarities we discern by comparing these fictional renderings can offer us valuable insights into understanding the structures and effects of institutionalized oppression.[1] They all raise the question of what history is, who is represented and by whom, recognizing that much of traumatic history, particularly that which affects the socially marginal, has remained repressed, unwritten. Examining the traumatic aspects of underclass exploitation, their works have a disillusioning function of unmasking how social controls and myths are utilized to abet trauma. Each demonstrates how a will to power destroys those *over* whom and *with* whom it seeks dominion. These authors engage their imaginations and fictional techniques in order to fill in gaps left by official histories, pointing to unhealed wounds that linger in or on the body, in sexuality, intrusive memory, and emotional relations. The three texts guide their audiences through an experiential approach to memory and history, both elucidating and confronting us with the interconnections between traumatic historical events, memory, and the body, as well as how we can ascribe meaning to the past.

Each of these writers uses similar narrative approaches to explore traumatic history. Social conflicts are enacted in characters' personal conflicts, where historical trauma is personalized by exploring its effects in bodily violations and wounds, in sexuality, or in the struggle to achieve emotional intimacy. Further, one particular character is singled out to enact and represent social conflicts and traumatic histories. Each text depicts oral testimonials; voices end silences that disguise the heretofore unspeakable and reassert marginal lives by re-creating their racial, class, and gender identities. Testimony is achieved through creating a dialogism of multiple perspectives and a visceral quality to the narratives. The costs of alienation, the "ethics" of life in extremity, and the possibilities for collective healing are also explored. All the texts recognize the sociohistorical connections to individual bodies; the body becomes the testing ground of human endurance, as voiced by one of Barker's characters: "In the end moral and political truths have to be proved *on the body*, because this mass of nerve and muscle and blood is what we are" (*Eye* 112, italics in the original).

The texts in this chapter focus on living memory as an alternative history and means to express consciousness and recover forgotten segments of the past. Traumatic memory is a haunting if disguised presence that is used to structure characters' thoughts and narrative. Traditional history is an intellectualized, written reconstruction of the past, and though these trauma narratives are created out of specific historical awareness (each writer has prepared with significant historical research), they focus on living memory in order to provide missing perspectives of the past, to dispute and even alter distortions of conventional history. Pierre Nora, in "Between Memory and History," distinguishes between memory and history:

> Memory and history, far from being synonymous, appear now to be in fundamental opposition. Memory is life, borne by living societies founded in its name. It remains in permanent evolution, open to the dialectic of remembering and forgetting, unconscious of its successive deformations, vulnerable to manipulation and appropriation, susceptible to being long dormant and periodically revived. History, on the other hand, is the reconstruction, always problematic and in-

complete, of what is no longer. Memory is a perpetually actual phenomenon, a bond tying us to the eternal present; history is a representation of the past. (8)

The last thought on memory is appropriate to the lingering effects of
trauma, where the past is relived in an emotional and physical sense
rather than remembered in a conscious sense. Continuing with Nora's
thoughts:

> Memory, insofar as it is affective and magical, only accommodates
> those facts that suit it; it nourishes recollections that may be out of
> focus or telescopic, global or detached, particular or symbolic—re-
> sponsive to each avenue of conveyance or phenomenal screen, to
> every censorship or projection. History, because it is an intellectual
> and secular production, calls for analysis and criticism. Memory is
> blind to all but the group it binds—which is to say, as Maurice Halb-
> wachs has said, that there are as many memories as there are groups,
> that memory is by nature multiple and yet specific; collective, plu-
> ral, and yet individual. History, on the other hand, belongs to every-
> one and to no one, hence its claim to universal authority. Memory
> takes root in the concrete, in spaces, gestures, images and objects
> [and the body]; history binds itself strictly to temporal continuities,
> to progressions and to relations between things [all of which are un-
> dermined by traumatic experience]. (8–9, my additions in brackets)

The more personalized, memorial history offered by these texts is a
needed supplement because the distortions and drawbacks to recorded
history are manifold. It "can be ordered for transmission only by being
regularized through a 'fatal falsity,' through a dubious omniscience created by official myth, historiographical paradigm, or even fictional exploitation" (Hartman 247).

Memory has become a crucial problem in the past two centuries,
which have witnessed unprecedented genocide, disappearing cultures,
and social, economic, and political changes. Shifts from rural to indus-
trial/urban life have disconnected people from the histories of places,
generations, and vocations. According to Geoffrey Hartman, the mass
media in our age contributes to this crisis of memory with illusory images that create "derealization, or a general weakening of the sense of
reality," and repetitive and distancing forms of public knowledge that

can alienate us from personal space and desensitize our emotions and imaginations ("Public Memory" 240, 243), that is, all that trauma fiction strives to reawaken. Richard Terdiman says memory comes to be perceived in material things, practices, and institutions rather than in perceived consciousness, as it was once passed down in families (29–30). In the twentieth century this desire is reflected in the proliferation of personal histories, archives, and museums that represent a democratizing and decentralizing of how memory is represented in this period. Not only the church, the state, and the wealthy keep records, but individual testimonies have also become important, particularly to group experience and identity and to historians who value knowing the daily lives of ordinary people as part of social history.

Several factors make articulating traumatic memory problematic. The past fades with the passage of time, of course; however, the forces working against such memory are many-faceted, collective, and psychological. The desire to repress knowledge can come from motivations as disparate as personal fear, ideology, or maintaining social order. Traumatic events create emotional paralysis and are repeatedly relived rather than remembered, with the survivors often lacking a language with which to narrativize it in an accessible way. Ghosts in some of these texts represent the dreaded past and provoke anguished memory, survivor guilt, and confrontations with death. Traumatic experience makes us recognize that absorption by the past can be dangerous as well, especially if it is never integrated within memory and consciousness. Still, as Cathy Caruth suggests, this most anguished sense of the past as lived in the body and the indirect telling of it can be the most faithful rendition of traumatic history (*Unclaimed* 26–27).

What is the role of a trauma narrative in constructing or rearticulating a difficult past, then? Literature has often functioned as a carrier of public memory, its language and symbols used to sustain public memory and express social context, indicates Hartman ("Public Memory" 239). Skillful and authentic storytelling enables readers to access older modes of contemplation not present in mass media, and if done well can "assimilate history to prevailing archetypes and paradigms," making the past more accessible to readers (244). For example, trauma is a familiar concept for our age, a way of thinking about the past that responds to a century of horrific events and is also a staple of popular culture (see discussion in chapter 1). Morrison echoes Hartman, believing that "narrative remains the best way to learn anything, whether history or theology, so I continue with narrative form" (Leclair 372). These trauma writers have a keen awareness of historical time but also want to create a sense of living, if not always accessible, memory. They approach storytelling as an act of remembering, creating invented memory through narrative modes that immerse readers in the past through characters' experiences.

In *Writing History, Writing Trauma*, Dominick LaCapra examines the usefulness and truth value of fiction that represents historical and traumatic contexts. His points about determining the value of truth claims have bearing on my textual interpretations in this chapter as I ascertain how these texts present authentic and intimate experience that is missed or glossed by cultural suppressions or conventional historical texts. LaCapra believes literature has value in conveying the emotional experience of a traumatic phenomenon like slavery, for instance. Works of art can also "offer significant insights (or, at times, oversights), suggesting lines of inquiry for the work of historians (for example, with respect to transgenerational processes of 'possession' or haunting)" (15). Important too is whether art makes valid use of historical knowledge and research. It is imperative for LaCapra that fictional narratives not allow too much identification with the protagonist or too much fidelity to trauma or the dead, and that the text presents a working-through process that differentiates readers from text and experience:

> Working through is an articulatory practice: to the extent one works through trauma (as well as transferential relations in general), one is able to distinguish between past and present and to recall in memory that something happened to one (or one's people) back then while realizing that one is living here and now with openings to the future. This does not imply either that there is a pure opposition between past and present or that acting out—whether for the traumatized or for those empathetically relating to them—can be fully transcended toward a state of closure or full ego identity. But it does mean that processes of working through may counteract the force of acting out and the repetition compulsion. These processes of working through, including mourning and modes of critical thought and practice, involve the possibility of making distinctions or develop-

ing articulations that are recognized as problematic but still function as limits and as possibly desirable resistances to undecidability, particularly when the latter is tantamount to confusion and the obliteration or blurring of all distinctions (states that may indeed occur in trauma or in acting out post-traumatic conditions). (22)

Readers of trauma literature can undergo some version of this working-through process if texts can immerse them in a state of

empathic unsettlement . . . [which] involves a kind of virtual experience through which one puts oneself in the other's position while recognizing the difference of that position and hence not taking the other's place. Opening oneself to empathic unsettlement is . . . a desirable affective dimension of inquiry which complements and supplements empirical research and analysis. Empathy is important in attempting to understand traumatic events and victims, and it may (I think, should) have stylistic effects in the way one discusses or addresses certain problems. It places in jeopardy fetishized and totalizing narratives that deny the trauma that called them into existence by prematurely (re)turning to the pleasure principle, harmonizing events, and often recuperating the past in terms of uplifting messages or optimistic, self-serving scenarios. (78)

Trauma texts are a kind of testimonial literary history, a means of recovering cultural memories and traditions of groups often neglected or suppressed by mainstream culture. Testimonial literature ("testimonio") has been particularly effective for politically or socially marginalized people who have not traditionally had access to public discourse. For example, Morrison indicates the goal for herself and other African American writers: "[T]he reclamation of the history of black people in this country is paramount in its importance because while you can't really blame the conqueror for writing history his own way, you can certainly debate it. There's a great deal of obfuscation and distortion and erasure, so that the presence and the heartbeat of black people has been systematically annihilated in many, many ways and the job of recovery is ours" (Davis interview 142). This literature does not just concern individuals but also the individual as representative of a social class or group (95), and as John Beverley insists, "involve[s] an urgency to communicate, a problem of repression, poverty, subalternity . . . struggle for survival, [that is] implicated in the act of narration itself" (94). Dominant culture places less emphasis on individual memory than marginalized groups who have not been fully assimilated or need to preserve their collective cultural memories as a type of historical record, for survival, or to maintain their identities. This notion of testimony is important to Morrison's *Beloved* in its attempts to articulate a continuity between past and present and to fill in gaps in cultural memory through connecting to ancestors or through storytelling forms that involve a difficult relation to memory and reconstruction through many voices. In creating his amnesiac and tormented protagonist in *Paco's Story*, Larry Heinemann testifies in unprecedented ways to the ways many wounded Vietnam veterans carry a horrific past within them. Similarly, Pat Barker's subtly gendered take on the reconstruction of soldiers' war experience within a therapeutic context resists official ideologies about war and masculinity.

Beloved: Witnessing the Unspeakable

Morrison recognizes how the silencing forces of trauma and oppression have shaped and distorted our conceptions of history and human capacity. She challenges these forces by (re)creating experience through testimony, dialogism, and imagination informed by historical record, and by exploring the complex interrelations of collective and personal history.[2] *Beloved* articulates one of the primary aspirations of her work, that is, to recover the silenced voices and experiences of African Americans by re-creating the struggle to witness despite what she regards as a "national amnesia" about the trauma of slavery as well as the largely unacknowledged trauma of racism (Angelo interview 120). Morrison carefully examines traumatic processes of forgetting and revision, reminding us that repression is a social as well as personal response, producing selective memories and cultural legacies. Therefore, we must always look critically at what knowledge is passed down and why. Responding to the omissions of white-dominated history, she tells stories of and by "discredited" people, attempting to reclaim our racial history in order to understand our present situation (Davis interview 142). Recognizing the unique ability of art and imagination to re-create difficult experience, Jill Matus argues that "Morrison draws attention to the special nature of literary testimony, which may have something to do with the fact that literature is able to explore the taboo, the psychic, as well as the historical. It can dwell on the imagined interior world and the formation of subjectivity. It is able to elicit powerful responses and urge ethical considerations" (14). She prepares readers carefully with gradual exposure to traumatic events, doling out clues and bits of information, so at times they are only partially aware, much like her characters. Morrison also recognizes "a necessity for remembering . . . in a manner in which it can be digested . . . my story, my invention, is much, much happier than what really happened" (Darling 5). By confronting her readers with the limitations to memory, its affective connections and survivor dilemmas, Morrison attempts to provide readers a means by which to reconceive history as lived and to elucidate the interconnections between traumatic historical events, memory, and our interpretations of past and present. For Morrison, slavery is an important context for these issues, an "originary moment for Afro-American culture in the 20th century" with far-reaching implications (Smith 353).

Trauma, as Cathy Caruth suggests, becomes a "symptom of history" particularly in enormous and horrific contexts such as the Holocaust and slavery, because "the traumatized person . . . carries an impossible history within them, or they become themselves the symptom of a history that they cannot entirely possess" ("Psychoanalysis" 4). It is not "their" history, because it cannot be remembered as part of the victim's usual experience; it is knowledge that possesses or inhabits the individual rather than being possessed by him or her (4). Consequently, although trauma is often experienced communally, trauma fragments memory and identity, thereby alienating individuals from their own experience and from others. For traumatic memory to lose its power as a fragment and symptom and be integrated into memory, "a process of constructing a narrative, or reconstructing a history and essentially of reexternalizing the event has to be set in motion" (Felman and Laub 69). Trauma narratives attempt this reconstructive process for readers.

In creating *Beloved*, Morrison recognized the difficulty of making catastrophic events accessible to those who have not experienced them. Although she utilizes scholarly, historical, and testimonial documentation, the unique aspect of her project is a focus on individual witnesses, foregrounding their voices and their individualized experience within re-created traumatic contexts in order to bring forth what has lost its immediacy in historical analysis. Morrison wants readers to confront slavery "in the flesh" (qtd. in Darling 5). She has said, "I wanted that haunting not to be really a suggestion of being bedeviled by the past, but to have it be incarnate" (qtd. in Rothstein). *Beloved* evokes the physical and durational qualities of witnesses' experiences, "incarnating" them through a consciousness of trauma that can offer us, as Caruth suggests, alternative histories ("Psychoanalysis II" 423) that break through obstacles to remembering, for instance, silence, simultaneity of knowledge and denial, dissociation, resistance, and repression. The dilemma of traumatic experience has been described as "being caught between the compulsion to complete the process of knowing and the inability or fear of doing so" (Laub and Auerhahn 288). The testimonial aspects of the narrative reveal the tensions and conflicts implicit in retelling and reexperiencing traumatic events, where victims try to maintain a "balance between the emotion recurrently breaking through the 'protective shield' and numbness that protects this shield" (Friedlander 51). Further, if rethinking history through trauma does not bring comprehensive knowledge, it does at least allow "*history* to arise where *immediate understanding* may not" (Caruth, *Unclaimed* 11, italics in original). Morrison's *Beloved* attempts to do this with a narrative that seeks to reveal through the sometimes-unknowing consciousnesses of the characters.

Morrison's innovative narratives utilize dialogical conceptions of witnessing, where many voices, emotions, and experiences intermingle to produce memory. She creates a dialogue between historical accounts and individual testimonies as a narrative strategy to explore the interconnections and differences between collective and personal perspectives. Individual witnesses answer to the collective denial and repression affecting traditional historical accounts. Through their voices she seeks to recover a history previously neglected because of racial and social constraints, perpetrators' denials, and ignorance about traumatic responses. Similarly, multiple testimonies can be correctives to individual repression and denial, or they can reinforce individual perspectives.

Morrison both engages with and responds to the descriptions of slavery in slave narratives, historical accounts, documentation and the testimonies of former slaves collected in the late 1930s by the Works Progress Administration (WPA). Her concerns most reflect slave women's narratives and testimonies, which were relatively rare—only 12 percent of oral testimonies (Blassingame, "Testimony" 83). As in former slave Harriet Jacobs's autobiographical narrative, Morrison focuses on the particular problems of women under slavery: the pains of mother-hood, sexual exploitation, and Jacobs's assertion that "slave women ought not to be judged by the same standard as others," because they had to function under a system where conventional moral standards held no validity (qtd. in Yellin 274).[3] Although she adopts narrative el-ements of nineteenth-century narratives (e.g., first-person testimony, escape and adventure elements, and so forth), Morrison also fills in gaps and challenges some of their content and goals. These narratives were written specifically for a white audience, using structures of sentimen-tal fiction, with the immediate goals of abolishing slavery and estab-lishing a black culture and identity in writing at a time when even thinkers like Kant and Hegel asserted black inferiority based partly on their not having a body of written work (Davis and Gates xxiii, xxvi). Morrison, however, does not need to concern herself with pleasing or placating a white audience as did the slave narrators and the WPA in-terviewees (Olney 154; Woodward 51).

In trying to re-create the periods of slavery and Reconstruction, Morrison borrows from historical accounts but also must imagine her topic. Because slaves were considered property and not individuals, they were documented as such; in fact, few records exist that list the names of individual slaves, particularly those making the Middle Pas-sage, sixteen percent of whom died during the voyage (Wright 43). Con-sequently, Morrison has said what she needs to know is only partially addressed in history books, and the rest must be recalled (through oral legacies) or must be necessarily reconstructed through an "act of imag-ination" (Jones and Vinson interview 176; "Site" 111). Sethe is a fic-tionalization of a real slave woman, Margaret Garner, who attempted to kill her children, stood trial for murdering a daughter, and was a cause célèbre for abolitionists, who viewed her infanticide as proving the dev-astations slavery wreaks on the psyche. Morrison largely reconstructs this woman's character and makes important changes in her story to emphasize how a slave mother can love her children; what claims, if any, she might have to motherhood; and how one frees oneself from ownership. Margaret Garner's story is important historically because it is emblematic of slaves' resistance to dehumanizing oppression.[4]

History must be made to live for us in the present if we are to feel it is ours, argues Walter Benn Michaels (7). Morrison gives readers a stake in history and makes it present through her depictions of ghosts, and I would add, her experiential approach to narrative. Caroline Rody observes that *Beloved* is one of a number of literary works about slavery committed to reconsidering the influence of the past:[5] "Inserting authorial consciousness into the very processes of history that accomplished the racial 'othering' of the self, novels of slavery make their claims to knowledge and power face-to-face with destruction. We might think of such fictions as structures of historiographic desire, attempts to span a vast gap of time, loss, and ignorance to achieve an intimate bond, a bridge of restitution or healing, between the authorial present and the ancestral past" (97). Morrison locates for readers the traumas of slavery as lived on the most intimate terms. Her focus involves what was undeveloped in the early narratives and accounts, such as slavery's effects on the inner lives of survivors and on the lives of mothers and children: "[P]opular taste discouraged the writers [of slave narratives] from dwelling too long or too carefully on the more sordid details of their experience. . . . For me—a writer in the last quarter of the twentieth century, not much more than a hundred years after Emancipation, a writer who is black and a woman—the exercise is very different. My job becomes how to rip that veil drawn over 'proceedings too terrible to relate'" ("Site" 90–91).

Recovery of slavery and postslavery conditions begins with details from previous accounts but then reconstructs more obscure, detailed aspects of traumatic history by exploring characters' struggles with memory, their sensory perceptions, bodily responses, and physical and emotional intimacy within these conditions. In order to reveal the effects of slavery through characters' fragmented consciousness and memories, Morrison had to jettison linear or chronological approaches to narrative. She says, "It's a kind of literary archeology: on the basis of some information and a little bit of guess-work [sic] you journey to a site to see what remains were left behind and to reconstruct the world that these remains imply" ("Site" 92). She also makes use of cultural and familial memories, but her imagination seems most effective in that it can "penetrate areas that seem erased from history," such as interior life (Matus 17).

Morrison wants her contemporary audience to recognize collective loss through a personal and experiential approach as she attempts to recapture the emotional effects of familial separation under slavery. Early

in the novel, Baby Suggs's life and thoughts set the pattern for the ac-
cumulation of horrors constituting slave life. She is allowed to keep
only one of her eight children, her son Halle (Sethe's husband), "[t]o
make up for coupling with a straw boss for four months in exchange for
keeping her third child, a boy, with her—only to have him traded for
lumber in the spring of the next year and to find herself pregnant by the
man who promised not to and did. That child she could not love and the
rest she would not. 'God take what he would,' she said. And He did, and
He did, and He did and then gave her Halle who gave her freedom when
it didn't mean a thing" (23). Here Morrison uses an affective narrative,
indirectly conveying Baby Suggs's feelings in the third person about her
accumulated experiences of sexual exploitation, loss of children, and
the gradual wearing away of her will. Through this individual portrait,
we view some of the worst conditions of slavery: the situations of familial separation, female slaves' sexual exploitation, and the trauma of
being owned.

Each of Morrison's characters has some claim as part of a collective
and yet has their own history. Each of their stories is part of a larger one;
many different experiences create catalysts for memory and hope for
collective survival, but Morrison also suggests that individualized situations resurrect experience more accessibly for readers. Paul D's wanderings and experiences (e.g., prison, escape, fighting for both sides in
the war, meeting Indians) give readers a panorama of the upheavals during and after the Civil War and a male experience of slavery and escape.[6]
Yet we also see the personal effects. Paul D is afraid to love Sethe and
yet is willing to try despite his recognition that his heart has become a
rusted tobacco tin, a "sealed casket of history," where his painful past
is buried (Harding and Martin 163). Lady Jones, although tormented by
the white origins evident in her light skin and yellow hair, devotes her
life to the education of black children so they can have a place in American society. The collectivity and individuality of suffering also issue
from Baby Suggs's spiritual revivals, where she exhorts her many fol-
lowers to cry, love their flesh, and reclaim the self-love that whites had
taken away (88–89). Beloved also embodies both these elements; she is
a needy child who demands her mother but is also one of the millions
of lost and dead. Ultimately, she remains personally inaccessible, given
shape by others' memories and desires.

Morrison's narrative incorporates the gaps, uncertainties, dissociations, and affects that characterize traumatic experience in attempting to re-create the visceral details of living in extraordinary circumstances. Conflicted, unconscious, and uncertain traumatic knowledge takes shape in the narrative through dialogism, fragmentation of memory, repetition (e.g., manifestations of involuntary returns of memory and emotion), images, transference, dissociation, incongruities, and silence. In capturing the struggle with memory in fiction, Morrison's depictions include the obstacles to testimony that Holocaust witnesses encountered and that are not usually present in literary testimony. Like video testimonies, Morrison's narrative includes "the pauses and hesitations in the telling of a story . . . [t]he sense of incoherency of experiences, the associative nature of reconstructing them, the visible groping for terms and language" (Young 161). Morrison avoids standard chronology and linear storytelling, seeking out the paths of elicited survivor memories that are characterized by the struggle to both remember and forget. Silence is an especially important manifestation of repression, secrecy, and loss. The most horrific events must be narrated indirectly, as the characters have an incomplete vocabulary for their suffering. Moreover, because trauma is a fragmenting and alienating experience, Morrison has ensured that it "cannot be looked for and located in a single place" in *Beloved* (Morgenstern 112). What follows here is a discussion of how Morrison uses these narrative elements to convey traumatic history.

Problematics and Figurations of Memory

Memory not only guides the narrative of *Beloved* but enacts an attempted recovery or supplement of forgotten or suppressed aspects of the lived past. Recognizing the difficulties of accessing such experience, Morrison enacts a psychotherapeutic approach, a kind of "working through" process within her narrative, in order to explore for readers memories of horrifying events in *Beloved*. Working through is "a sort of psychical work which allows the subject to accept certain repressed elements and to free himself from the grip of mechanisms of repetition" (Laplanche and Pontalis 488). LaCapra's notions of working through as countering acting out and repetition compulsions is also relevant here, as the protagonist Sethe is forced to confront the past despite a vociferous resistance, a longing to remain immersed in it as she re-creates her bond with her dead child. This fidelity to the dead is a common resistance to working through (LaCapra 22). Morrison also re-creates the complexities of traumatic memory in her creation of Beloved. As a ghost, her daily returns over eighteen years represent Sethe's only partially emerging past, enabling Sethe to acknowledge connection with this lost child and yet avoid events surrounding her death. Eventually, Sethe is made to confront her past when the daughter she killed is seemingly resurrected and when she is made to relive the decisive moment before the murder. Making the presence of the dead palpable establishes the continued impact of the dead on survivors and draws the readers, like the characters, into the reemergence of traumatic memory. Also, in guiding readers through the process of "rememoration," that is, resisted but repeated returns of the past ("it's going to always be there waiting for you," 36), Morrison make us aware that much of what we know and how we know is constructed via a dialogue of knowledge and denial, particularly when it concerns painful episodes.

Beloved's return embodies Sethe's strong link with the past. She returns, perhaps metaphorically to the reader, but literally to the characters, characteristic of the way memories return to trauma victims, in a sudden, vivid, and "literal return of the event against the will of the one it inhabits" (Caruth, "Psychoanalysis" 3). She is envisioned as an involuntary memory because although she provides some measure of emotional fulfillment, she is also unsettling, confronting many of the characters with their pasts and the shame they endure in trying to survive. As Beloved evolves from ghost to flesh, Sethe slowly acknowledges her identity. This painful return to the past identifies Beloved's death as an "event [that] is not assimilated or experienced fully at the time, but only belatedly, in its repeated *possession* of the one who experiences it" (Caruth, "Psychoanalysis" 3). Sethe in fact is possessed by the ghost and then the girl Beloved, refusing to leave her haunted house or try to escape the past: "To be traumatized is precisely to be possessed by an image or event" (3). Once the young woman Beloved returns in the flesh, Sethe does not immediately identify the connection between them. This connection is felt in her body; the pseudo birth-water breakage manifests unconscious memory and Sethe's reemerging symbiotic bond with Beloved. When Sethe accepts that this is her daughter, Beloved becomes the remnants of what has remained unresolved for Sethe.

Another important obstacle to memory and resolution lies in the irreconcilability of the traumatic past with normal existence. Survivors try to avoid encounters with what Lawrence Langer would term tainted, or unheroic memory, which creates a diminished sense of self. Resistance to memory is also important for the day-to-day survival and sanity of Morrison's ex-slave characters. Survivors like Ella and Sethe fight it back every day ("The future was sunset; the past something to leave behind. And if it didn't stay behind, well, you might have to stomp it out," 256). Ella is irrevocably damaged by the sexual abuse of father and son slave owners ("the worst yet"), and although *Beloved* chronicles Sethe's slow process toward confronting past traumas (both her own and her children's), no resolution to her past is possible, because Sethe can never reconcile her loving intentions with her murderous actions. In fact, the text "moves through a series of narrative starts and stops that are complicated by Sethe's desire to forget or 'disremember' the past" (Mobley, "Remembering" 360). Morrison's narrative framework puts the focus on analyzing and exploring the problematics of action in insurmountable circumstances. It demonstrates the warping of values under oppression to the extent that positive action by victims is impossible, and the standards by which these events can be measured and judged have to extend beyond the fact-based logic of historical inquiry or the myths of humanism.

Morrison's slave testimonies, much like Holocaust testimonies, reveal that action is "forged by circumstances" and not moral ideals (Langer 199). The characters are made to struggle, with mixed success, to keep their humanity and sense of right and wrong when faced with contexts designed to deny individuals any moral high ground. For example, a threatened return to slavery places Sethe in a situation where she feels she has to kill her children in order to maintain their human integrity. She tries to prevent them being tainted like herself, that is, considered as a farm animal, dirtied "so bad you couldn't like yourself anymore" (251). Langer says that living in these situations means lying outside moral systems (125). Rather than leading readers to judge, though, Morrison endeavors to immerse us in the individual experience of terror, arbitrary rules, and the psychological or physical breakdown of victims so that we might begin to appreciate their situations. The story is framed such that readers understand Sethe's love, suffering, and good intentions previously to and simultaneously with her deadly actions.

Similarly, the accumulated details of Paul D's history become assaults on his consciousness that threaten to break his will to resist: "A shudder ran through Paul D. A bone-cold spasm that made him clutch his knees. He didn't know if it was bad whiskey, nights in the cellar, pig fever, iron bits, smiling roosters, fired feet, laughing dead men, hissing grass, rain, apple blossoms, neck jewelry, Judy in the slaughterhouse, Halle in the butter, ghost-white stairs, chokecherry trees . . . Paul A's face . . . or the loss of a red, red heart. . . . 'Tell me something, Stamp. How much is a nigger supposed to take?'" (235) In its accumulated historical details of slave life, its figurations of pain, loss, and haunting, this passage well illustrates Morrison's use of what LaCapra terms post-traumatic forms of writing that come out of and express traumatic history (179). This passage could not appear in any historical text, but it in fact well represents what Caruth and LaCapra call the "privileged places" of art and literature "for giving voice to trauma as well as symbolically exploring the role of excess" (*Writing* 190). Here, Paul D remembers his own bodily and psychological humiliations, the destruction of friends, madness, scars, and so forth, that defined the realities of slavery for so many. The narrative attempts to close the gap of safe historical distance, directly engaging the overwhelming (un)reality of traumatic experience by filtering huge events through individual consciousness, desires, and bodily needs.

For Sethe, connection to the painful past is displayed and replayed through the body, even lashed into her flesh. In this way, Morrison demonstrates the intimate, physical way trauma is experienced. Bodily assaults, deprivations, and humiliations are often some of the worst aspects of traumatic experience. The hunger and filthy conditions concentration camp survivors had to endure are often mentioned as most humiliating. Bodily humiliation is especially significant for sexual assault victims. Horrifying physical conditions are also often part of war experience. There is a personal sense of defeat that comes with bodily violations and torments. In slavery Sethe endures whipping, is deprived of the intimate physical bond between herself and her mother, and to her particular outrage, she suffers the humiliation of having her mother's milk sucked out of her breasts by her master's nephews. The scars on Sethe's back from her master's lashing are initially described as a chokecherry tree with trunk, branches, and leaves (16) and then as "the decorative work of an ironsmith too passionate for display" (17). Sethe receives her lashes while nine months pregnant and escapes in this condition. Luckily, others assist her during and after she has her baby on the way to freedom. Remnants of her slave past, the scars also draw others' attention and sympathy. Amy Denver and Baby Suggs help to nurse her wounds, and Paul D "rubbed his cheek on her back and learned that way her sorrow, the roots of it; its wide trunk and intricate branches" (17). Scars represent Sethe's narrow escape from death. A keen reminder of her slave life, the scars are also a metaphor for the push and pull of traumatic memory—knowing and not knowing. She knows it is there, but it is numb and she cannot see it. Her scars are also focal points and obstacles to potentially intimate or sexual relations. Others are attracted and repelled by these scars; at first there is curiosity and sympathy, but then the pain that underlies these scars becomes overwhelming. Paul D tries to comfort Sethe by kissing her scars, in effect saying, *I share these wounds, they are not foreign to me.* Eventually her suffering and its consequences become overwhelming and scare him away, but he returns to her at the end of the novel and is about to give her a nurturing bath as readers are left with the hope for reconnection between the couple.

Responses to Forgetting: Dialogism and Testimony

Morrison articulates many issues surrounding traumatic experience and its transmission through dialogism in *Beloved*. Through the interconnecting and juxtaposed narrative voices existing in past and present textual time, Morrison suggests the struggle between memory and forgetting, between differing viewpoints and responses to oppression, between attempted explanation and the inexplicable, and various possibilities for witnessing. Morrison constructs for readers a process of looking at events from several perspectives that sometimes contradict each other, sometimes interlink or reinforce one another.

Dialogism, the expression of voices and data among which "there is a constant interaction between meanings, all of which have the potential of conditioning others" is often found in the novel genre (Holquist 426). Mikhail Bakhtin's conception of dialogism articulates well Morrison's intermixtures; it is not just argument, transcribed voices, contradictions, or dialectical opposites, but instead it is a dynamic, living process where interactions have a quality of being in process and unfinalizable (Morson and Emerson 49–50). "The word, directed toward its object, enters a dialogically agitated and tension-filled environment of alien words, value judgments and accents, weaves in and out of complex interrelationships, merges with some, recoils from others, intersects with yet a third group" (Bakhtin 276). Bakhtin viewed human identity as engaged in communication with others and conceived of individual and social entities as interconnected (Morson and Emerson 51). Therefore, dialogical voices often counter authoritative, that is, inherited or unquestioned discourse.

This notion of the social context as multivocal and dynamic is used by Morrison to offset dominant discourses that have either erased or misconstrued individuals living in slavery. Morrison illustrates this by opposing Schoolteacher's false history of classifying slaves as animal-like with Sethe's personal narrative of humanity and pain (Henderson 69–72). However, Morrison limits these voices and experiences to particular moments and details. They do not focus on characters' or witnesses' explanations but rather involuntary memories or memories of specific details. Dialogical interrelations can be vitally important to helping individuals emerge from traumatic stasis and repression if their experience is integrated into a narrative memory structure in a relationship with, for example, a therapist or a witness (Herman 183). *Beloved* seems to be addressing the cultural amnesia/trauma around slavery by engaging in a communal "talking cure" (Rody 99). Dialogism can effectively express a multidimensional historiography in trauma texts, emphasizing undecidability but also forcing interaction between differing perspectives (LaCapra 197). Morrison constructs dialogical spaces for characters and living survivors that foster reliving and recalling events, but the subjects of their representations do not necessarily fully understand or resolve their conflicts. Hence, their narratives must also provide multiple sources and dialogic arenas to fill in gaps left by individual witnesses. Dialogism thus has three purposes in *Beloved:* to enable testimony, to juxtapose different perspectives, and to confront the viewer or reader with the complexities of traumatic experience and its interpretation.

In *Beloved,* collective voices and stories are crucial to the recuperation of Sethe's memory. Sethe acknowledges that the past still haunts her and complains about how much horror her memory can hold, often withdrawing from her memories for fear of what might surface (70). She cannot remember her own history as clearly until Paul D fills in missing pieces of their past and she is questioned by the girl who calls herself Beloved. They provoke Sethe's feared and suppressed memories, but with these witnesses, Sethe can, briefly, relive her past and express her outrage within a safe context. To the as yet unidentified Beloved, Sethe recounts her past in earnest as she has not been able with others; clearly, the identity of the interlocutor is an important influence on what can be told or remembered:

> Sethe learned the profound satisfaction Beloved got from storytelling. It amazed Sethe . . . because every mention of her past life hurt. Everything in it was painful or lost. She and Baby Suggs had agreed without saying so that it was unspeakable; to Denver's inquiries Sethe gave short replies or rambling incomplete reveries. Even with Paul D, who had shared some of it and to whom she could talk with at least a measure of calm, the hurt was always there— like a tender place in the corner of her mouth that the bit left.
>
> But, as she began telling about the earrings, she found herself wanting to, liking it. Perhaps it was Beloved's distance from the events itself, or her thirst for hearing it—in any case it was an unexpected pleasure. (58)

Sethe finds her words are healing to someone else. She can speak to Beloved because she already knows unconsciously that this is her daughter, with whom she wants to reenter the past they shared.

Dialogism can also raise questions about the complexities of living within oppressive institutions and responses to historical traumas. The dialogue between Paul D and Sethe (164–65) when he asks her to explain why she killed Beloved presents and critically examines Sethe's complex dilemma (how else could she have saved her children from Schoolteacher?) and others' reactions to it. When Sethe tries to explain and justify Beloved's death, Paul D is appalled by her actions and possessive isolationism with her daughters. To him, she is unable to see her children as separate human beings or her own limitations: "[She] didn't know where the world stopped and she began" (164). Sethe cannot tell the whole story, however, particularly what happened and why, when she killed Beloved, or how the sight of Schoolteacher's hat set off in her a protective impulse toward her children. This attempt to voice a traumatic experience alien to others illustrates how the positions of the interlocutors can limit the dialogic situation—the possibility for communication—and can, in effect, render an individual speechless. Sethe has difficulty reaching her listener, in bridging the gap between his point of view and her own "inner speech" (Morson and Emerson 215) that explains her love and need to act for her children. Her next words to Paul D are defensive and chilling for him: "I stopped him [Schoolteacher]. I took and put my babies where they'd be safe" (164). Their succeeding argument and breakup express a dialogism among possible responses to traumatic events.

> "Your love is too thick," he said . . .
>
> "Too thick? . . . Love is or it ain't. Thin love ain't love at all."
>
> "Yeah. It didn't work, did it? Did it work?" he asked.
>
> "It worked," she said.
>
> "How? Your boys gone you don't know where. One girl dead, the other won't leave the yard. How did it work?"
>
> "They ain't at Sweet Home. Schoolteacher ain't got em."
>
> "Maybe there's worse."
>
> "It ain't my job to know what's worse. It's my job to know what is and to keep them away from what I know is terrible. I did that."
>
> "What you did was wrong, Sethe."
>
> "I should have gone on back there? Taken my babies back there?"
>
> "There could have been a way. Some other way."
>
> "What way?"
>
> "You got two feet, Sethe, not four," he said . . . (164–65)

Although Sethe and Paul D share much, they each have their own baggage, defensiveness, guilt, ways of surviving, and self-definitions that emerge as he questions and she defends her actions. Here Paul D makes an understandable and yet hasty judgment, given her circumstances, which he quickly recognizes and regrets: "How fast he had moved from his shame to hers" (165). He seems to project onto her his own feelings about what he has done to survive and about his sexual involvement with Beloved. Clearly his judgment of Sethe is a self-judgment as well. Further, although in many ways Paul D and Sethe share an understanding of the world, they differ in their sense of identity in relation to others. Paul D needs connection but fears that it will be taken away as well, and has mostly survived by being independent of others. Sethe's identity is absolutely as a mother, in connection to her children, and her obsessive focus on them and her extreme actions are created, and can only be understood, within the context of slavery. As at the murder scene, when dialogue shuts down between Sethe and the community, silence and distance spring up between her and Paul D, indicating that neither has resolved their own relationship to the past. Their mutual absorption with Beloved is further evidence of this irresolution. This type of narrative could contribute to formulating and enacting a conception of history LaCapra proposes that involves "an objective reconstruction of the past and a dialogic exchange with it and other inquirers into it wherein knowledge involves not only the processing of information but also affect, empathy and questions of value" (35).

The Problem of Silence and Figuring Loss

Silence has multivalent meanings when considering trauma and narrating specific elements and processes of that experience. It is a strong "presence" in *Beloved*, connected to repression, isolation, loss, and hidden knowledge; this is a heretofore unspoken history. Silence can represent a traumatic gap, a withholding of words because of terror, guilt, or coercion; it characterizes traumatic memory as wordless, visual, and reenactive rather than cognitive/verbal when facing the unspeakable. Silence at times is textually represented with page or section breaks, but most often in what is not said, what the characters avoid saying or cannot say ("[Sethe] and Baby Suggs had agreed without saying so that it [the past] was unspeakable," 58). For Morrison, silence is insidious and harmful, indicative of impotence and isolation. The focus on personal testimony in *Beloved* counteracts the silences of the dead and the omissions, denials, and distortions of early historical accounts. The dead rise up again through Morrison's reconstructions, but the will to forget and leave the past behind is so strong that at the end of the novel, Beloved again becomes silent to those who remember her; "other than what they themselves were thinking, she hadn't said anything at all" (274). She becomes part of their own grief they want to forget.

Beloved here is a personalized figuration of one of the forgotten "sixty million and more" who died in slavery and to whom the novel is dedicated, bearing witness and testifying for the other "disremembered and unaccounted for" (274). Morrison's creation of Beloved illustrates the difficulty of gaining access to traumatic history, indicating that trauma "both urgently demands historical awareness and yet denies our usual modes of access to it" (Caruth, "Psychoanalysis II" 417). Beloved represents the belatedness and dislocation of traumatic memory, which creates gaps in knowledge. She rarely speaks and is arrested in time, often acting like the infant she was when Sethe last saw her eighteen years before. With few firsthand slave accounts of the Middle Passage available,[7] Morrison is able to suggest a lot about this experience through the eyes of a traumatized child witness whose words create pictures that are impressionistic, regressive, and perhaps pre-Oedipal as Jean Wyatt suggests (481). Her words also resemble traumatic flashbacks, with events and images emerging unembellished, with no context but one of immediate pain. Her words reflect her experience of the slave ship, but they can only suggest, not explain, the larger context of this ship or of slavery. As Sethe is possessed by her own traumatic past, Beloved is also possessed by the images of these events on the ship, a collective African American past. In her, Morrison tries to incarnate the impossible, because she is the traumatized child who *can* speak to those willing to hear her, although many resist remembering her and the horrors of slavery. A viewpoint such as hers contributes to a collective understanding.

Beloved's brief account of her past at Sweet Home and being transported on a slave ship continues the traumatic theme and narrative in extremity with numerous repetitions, silences, or gaps and recurring impressions and images (as opposed to description or evaluation) connected through the character's perceptions and textual proximity, not narrative continuity. She speaks of her experience like a child who does not fully understand everything she sees and yet relates it all through images in the present, in repetitions without full reconstruction: "[H]ow can I say things that are pictures" (210). This resembles how traumatic memory has been characterized as a "series of still snapshots or a silent movie," static and unintegrated into a life story (Herman 175). Of course, Beloved has no life story within which to attach these memories. The constant "presence" of this situation for her, "[a]ll of it is now   it is always now   there will never be a time when I am not crouching and watching others who are crouching too" (210), indicates traumatic memory. That is, it is undiminished by time and further experience, and the pauses and gaps in speech and continuity create an unfinished, repetitious, and cognitively distant trauma narrative, thus distinct from fully realized stories, like the one of Denver's birth told earlier in the text. Her re-creation of the others she sees on the ship—

dead, sick, defecating, making love—gives us a glimpse of their physical agony: "[S]mall rats do not wait for us to sleep . . . if we had more to drink we could make tears" (210). Similarly, she expresses a desire for death and the necessity of dissociation from horror: "[W]e are all trying to leave our bodies behind . . . it is hard to make yourself die forever" (210).

Through the links in Beloved's consciousness, Morrison expresses a distorted and disjunctive sense of time typical of traumatic response, and by association readers are exposed to collective and ancestral trauma. Beloved's presence on the slave ship links her with other generations of slaves, the anonymous travelers of the Middle Passage, but there is also a more deeply personal connection to ancestry—her grandmother (Sethe's mother) came from Africa on such a ship.[8] Morrison interweaves collective relationships and personal need by drawing together the events on the ship with Beloved's desire to recover her mother and her nourishing powers: "a hot thing the little hill of dead people a hot thing the men without skin push them through with poles the woman is there with the face I want the face that is mine . . . when he [a strange man] dies on my face I can see hers" (211–12). Beloved is the abandoned child (and race) whose very being depends on recovering the symbiotic intimacy with her mother who will love, name, and feed her milk ("a hot thing").[9] Traumatized, she can never have a belated, fully cognizant awareness of this past and yet offers powerfully suggestive impressions for readers. Beloved's simple litany of facts and desires sends out historical, collective, and personal reverberations. It is not a history she can possess, but her fragmented account makes collective realities and suffering on slave ships present to readers.

Many of the characters' thoughts and connections to Beloved reveal the close relationship between the living and the dead described by Holocaust and other war survivors, who in their memories cross and recross boundaries between the living and the dead (Felman and Laub 257–58). The proximity of death and life are strong from the beginning of the novel as Beloved's ghost haunts 124. Although she appears to have returned from the dead, her resurrection is still a kind of death in life. Because she is traumatized she is submerged in the past, with the present and future almost nonexistent. The "unspeakable" section reminds the reader that Sethe was about to join Beloved in death, Denver "dies" every night in her dreams, and Beloved has come back to life from being "on the other side." The dead (i.e., Beloved) come to dominate their lives until Sethe is almost starved and Denver finds the courage to leave the house. Nevertheless, with the last word of the novel—"Beloved"—a distanced haunting remains, underscoring the guilt and love that weigh heavily with survivors: "The people who have perished emerge as the real subject of the testimonies, while the circumstances of their death define the unheroic memory that tries to reclaim them, as it does the surviving self diminished by their absence and by its own powerlessness to alter their doom" (Langer 197). The dead are brought back to life through survivors, haunting their memories and achieving life through survivors' unconscious desires for reconnection or resolution. It is not until the symbolic reenactment of the approach of the slave owners occurs that Beloved (i.e., the past) can disappear and Sethe can undo, if only for a moment, her past actions. Afterward, the past still lingers, but on the edge of consciousness.

Finally, although the narrative has positioned Beloved in part as a witness, her words a kind of testimony, doubt is cast about what others are able to remember of her, or more specifically, their own disturbing pasts.

> It was not a story to pass on.
>
> They forgot her [Beloved] like a bad dream. After they made up their tales, shaped and decorated them, those that saw her that day on the porch quickly and deliberately forgot her. It took longer for those who had spoken to her, lived with her, fallen in love with her, to forget, until they realized they couldn't remember or repeat a single thing she said, and began to believe that, other than what they themselves were thinking, she hadn't said anything at all. So, in the end, they forgot her too. Remembering seemed unwise. (274)

Beloved represents what has been lost for each individual who has thought about her, or thought her up. Here the narrative expresses what Felman refers to as a "crisis of truth" (*Testimony* 5–6) concerning traumatic experience; there is always a gap between experience and awareness, an uncertainty as to its truth value, because it cannot be integrated with prior emotional and cognitive experience nor easily reconciled with recuperation, which to an extent necessitates forgetting.

Thus survivors avoid retouching a horrific past: "They can touch it if they like, but don't, because they know things will never be the same if they do" (275). With the last few lines, Morrison reminds us of the complexity of traumatic memories, that despite denials and forgetfulness, they cannot be completely erased: "By and by all trace is gone, and what is forgotten is not only the footprints [Beloved's] but the water too and what it is down there. The rest is weather. Not the breath of the disremembered and unaccounted for, but wind in the eaves, or spring ice thawing too quickly. Just weather. Certainly no clamor for a kiss. Beloved" (275).

Though Naomi Morgenstern has a point when she says *Beloved* is a kind of wish fulfillment on Morrison's part (116–17) because her ending of the novel is certainly more optimistic than Margaret Garner's actual fate, Morrison does not exactly create a happy, unconflicted, or uncontested ending.[10] Morrison emphasizes Sethe's struggle against the odds rather than Garner's actual defeat. *Beloved* chronicles the spirit of endurance, the simultaneous need to remember and forget. Morrison focuses on survival because she is not only dealing with the past, but also with a contemporary audience and culture and how slavery still affects the present. She interrogates how legacies of racism and suppression of voices have become part of our culture. In doing so, her narrative reveals the tenuous nature of survival, the haunting that continues but must be put off to some extent for life to continue in the present. Though we do see some hope for Sethe and Paul D at the end of the novel, the majority of it has recounted their losses and suffering. The last word of the novel is "Beloved." She is the reminder of tragedy, the dead girl, the lost and missing, the one who has torn their lives apart, forced them to confront their pasts and open their hearts. She is a sad, disturbing presence, not sentimentalized, because at times she is destructive, creepy, the victim who returns to be claimed, but eventually must be driven away because such loss cannot be compensated for, only mourned. The other characters' forgetting raises the question of how much one should allow oneself to be affected by the past. Traumatic memory can bring repetition and demoralization. The past should not be repressed or glossed over, but survival and a future life is essential and not always compatible with this kind of memory. "Although she has claim, she is not claimed" (274).

The Battle as "Sexy": Trauma, Repetition, and Sexuality in Barker's War Trilogy

Concerned with the lingering effects of traumatic history, the contemporary British feminist writer Pat Barker examines the complex interconnections of trauma, recovery, war, and sexuality in her World War I trilogy *Regeneration* (1991), *The Eye in the Door* (1993), and *The Ghost Road* (1995). Barker examines how the public face of the war creates private conflict and trauma because there is no way to reconcile the demands of duty with the horrific effects of war on the psyche. The narrative uses an intertextuality of fact and fiction to represent multiple, dialogical points of view through therapeutic dialogues; historical documents (e.g., Billing trial accounts, the "List of 47,000"); the poetry and opinions of historically based characters, such as Siegfried Sassoon and Wilfred Owen; scientists of the time, such as Lewis Yealland; fictionalizations of real case histories; fictionalized characters, such as Billy Prior; diary entries; and first-person narrative memories. Barker includes more intertextual references to historical details, actual people and events than Morrison or Heinemann, interweaving these with her fictionalized characters who embody the lives of more typical, unheralded people of the time, but who also symbolize social relations, conflicts, and changes. These details are intended to augment the truth value of this fiction, acknowledging historical fact while trying to imagine individual suffering and trying to elicit reader empathy and criticism.

Traumatized war veterans are emblematic of the personal and collective losses associated with one of the most devastating twentieth-century wars, bringing with it important shifts in cultural attitudes about war, war trauma, gender, class, and the reliability of authority figures. The story focuses primarily on British soldiers' inner lives and struggles with traumatic memories of their war experience, presented largely in therapy sessions with their military doctors, who prepare them to return to combat. Barker makes extensive use of W. H. R. Rivers's theories of war trauma. Rivers was an actual army doctor, a physiologist, anthropologist, and scholar who used psychoanalysis to treat veterans such as Sassoon, so she casts him as a major character whose perspective helps shape reader awareness of the social forces that hinder healing from historical trauma.[11] Evidence of traumatic effects include soldiers' inability to reconcile or let go of this experience, and their alienation from civilians. Moreover, the compulsion to repeat the war experience, to once again try to either save their men or at least die with them, is evident in the characters' desire to return to war despite their intense psychological conflicts regarding duty vs. self-preservation. Depicting the often unnecessary sacrifices of the soldiers, particularly in the final volume, the trilogy raises questions regarding notions of sacrifice and the legitimacy of authority. Through Prior's insights, Barker warns us that we must recognize and prevent the perpetuation of traumatic circumstances.

Like Morrison, Barker recognizes that the lives of marginal people have been left out of official history. Her subjects are British working-class people, and her work, as John Kirk has noted, endeavors a "reworking of history from below" in how it recovers memory "of neglected experience, forgotten voices, silenced groups" (607, 605). In re-creating the effects of historical circumstances on the lower classes, she also illuminates their role in history and the changing social structure while exploring gender, class, and ideological conflicts. Barker notes that she, and many people, share a common experience of the legacies of historical trauma. She recalls how her badly wounded grandfather and her stepfather experienced the return of repressed World War I memories, even at the ends of their lives (Gross interview). Further, she never knew her father, a pilot who died in World War II. Her mother was devastated by his loss and by the fact that they never married. She saw her daughter, Pat, but had her grandparents raise her. Her readers have reminded Barker that many families share these kinds of memories. Before her war trilogy, Barker's novels concerned the difficult, often violent lives of working-class women, but she links these works and *Regeneration* as works "about trauma and recovery" and sees similarities in the plight of the working-class women she knew and soldiers in war, who face similar issues in coping with their traumas (Perry interview 52).

Barker has said that feminism is not only for women. In applying her feminist eye and gender analysis to traumatized soldiers, "Barker's work suggests that gender stereotypes are ritually dramatized not only in domestic and abuse and prostitution but also in scapegoating and war and that coercive violence is no less political in personal relations than in public ones. At the same time that these gender codes promote aggression against women and other men, they simultaneously deny men the expression of their compassionate and nurturing sides, further dehumanizing them" (Carson 46). Maintaining gender roles becomes national policy in the war situation, Barker points out, citing historical evidence in the Billing trial and other suppressions of gender challenges (suffragettes, pacifists, etc.). We see the costs of rigid gender roles in Rivers's attempts to help his traumatized patients, men who are made helpless and terrified in war, and yet:

> They'd been trained to identify emotional repression as the essence of manliness. . . . The change he [Rivers] demanded of them . . . was not trivial. Fear, tenderness—these emotions were so despised that they could be admitted into consciousness only at the cost of re-defining what it meant to be a man. Not that Rivers's treatment in-volved any encouragement of weakness or effeminacy. His patients might be encouraged to acknowledge their fears, their horror of the war—but they were still expected to do their duty and return to France. It was Rivers's conviction that those who had learned to know themselves, and to accept their emotions, were less likely to break down again. (*Regeneration* 48)

Nevertheless, the culture's values are deeply, psychically absorbed, even by Prior, who in the final volume marches to death with his men, with no illusions about the authorities who have sent them on a suicide mission when the war is virtually over ("I wish I didn't feel they're be-ing sacrificed to the subclauses and the small print. But I think they are" (*Ghost Road* 249). Shortly before his death, Prior recognizes in lan-guage the beliefs that will continue to cause war: the words "us, them, we, they, here, there. These are the words of power, and long after we're gone, they'll lie about in the language, like the unexploded grenades in these fields, and any one of them'll take your hand off" (257). Absorbed by a masculine stoicism, Prior writes to Rivers, "My nerves are in per-fect working order. By which I mean that in my present situation the only sane thing to do is to run away, and I will not do it. Test passed?" (254). "Barker examines how patriarchal constructions of masculinity colonize men's subjectivity in ways that, especially in wartime, prove oppressive, repressive, and wholly brutal in their effects on the male psyche" (Harris 303).

Barker also utilizes Elaine Showalter's *The Female Malady,* which informs Barker's contemporary, gender-based knowledge of trauma and helps Barker elucidate the role of gender myths in creating the internal conflicts that exacerbate trauma. The gruesome realities of war further challenge the mythologies of war glory and the dignity of soldiers. Taking her lead from Showalter, Barker compares soldiers' hysterical symptoms to those of women, recognizing how neurosis could be the result of women's confined lives.[12] According to Rivers, the parental concerns some officers express for their men make their faces resemble "the faces of women who were bringing up large families on very low incomes, women who, in their early thirties, could easily be taken for fifty or more. It was the look of people who are totally responsible for lives they have no power to save" (*Regeneration* 107).

Historical events—in this case, the effects of war—traumatically change both individual and social identity. Barker portrays a culture fundamentally in denial about the consequences of the war effort, using violent suppression, accusation, and surveillance to quash traumatic symptoms or awareness of the senselessness of war. One example of this institutional rigidity is drawn from the actual case of a young man being treated by Dr. Lewis Yealland, whose treatment involved applying electroshock to shell-shock patients. His technique is cruel, as we witness him administer shocks to a man suffering from mutism, not stopping until the man is talking, after hours of often agonizing shocks. Readers observe this through the eyes of Rivers, who is appalled and makes us aware that Yealland's clients still suffer depression, are never asked how they feel, and that the relapse/suicide rates after treatment are never verified (*Regeneration* 224). Yealland reveals his authoritarian ("God-like") manner and expectations of manliness in replying to the patient's inquiry if the treatment will hurt: "I realize you did not intend to ask that question, so I will overlook it" (226). He goes on to recite the principles of treatment: "attention first and foremost; tongue last and least; questions, never" (226). His attitude throughout the session is unsympathetic and adversarial. Later, Rivers has a dream about this encounter he witnessed, which makes him aware that as part of the structures of authority, he has also contributed to the silencing of these men.

The horrors of trench warfare and bombardments change the lives of Barker's veterans, sometimes irreparably, as they experience a variety of symptoms including physical revulsion, terrifying dreams, hallucinations of reappearing dead comrades, and hysterical symptoms. Barker's soldiers suffer from nightmares, amnesia, hysterical/somatic symptoms of mutism, paralysis, and other symptoms of what was viewed at the time as war neurosis. As in Morrison's and Heinemann's works, the visceral and repetitive reliving of trauma is represented in brutal sense memories. For example, one veteran, Burns, starves himself because the smell and taste of food return him to the horror of falling face first in a decomposing corpse during battle. Similarly, Prior's nightmares repeat his holding the disembodied eye of one of his comrades. Significantly, symptoms are different for regular enlisted men and officers. Rivers explains:

> Mutism seems to spring from a conflict between *wanting* to say something, and knowing that if you *do* say it the consequences will be disastrous. So you resolve it by making it physically impossible for yourself to speak. And for the private soldier the consequences of speaking his mind are always going to be far worse than they would be for an officer. What you tend to get in officers is stammering. And it's not just mutism. All the physical symptoms: paralysis, blindness, deafness. They're all common in private soldiers and rare in officers. It's almost as if for the . . . laboring classes illness *has* to be physical. They can't take their condition seriously unless there's a physical symptom. . . . Officers' dreams tend to be more elaborate. (*Regeneration* 96)

Officers' conflicts involve responsibility and guilt over the men they watch over and have left behind, hence both Sassoon and Prior volunteer to return to battle.

Barker's narrative style is not as experimental as those of Morrison or Heinemann. It is largely chronological, with some shifts back to the past; however, Barker also uses a dialogical approach that puts readers in touch with a variety of military and civilian voices and perspectives. She accomplishes this in a number of ways. The stories and thoughts of the two principal characters, Rivers and Prior, run parallel to but are also juxtaposed with one another, as both follow Prior's progress in working through the many traumas in his life. Thereby, Barker can provide readers with theoretical perspectives, a sense of the therapeutic process and the experience of trauma. Other critics have commented on the purposes of Barker's dialogical, multivoiced approach to narrative and how this approach "helps create collective experience . . . and articulates . . . oppressive and exploitative social relations" (Kirk 612–13), and contests or avoids dominant voices and silencing of characters (Carson 45). The numerous therapeutic sessions in the novel are examples of dialogism where Barker explores power relations and psychological depths. The sessions between Rivers and Prior begin as a power struggle because Prior resents Rivers's dominant position, resists, and refuses to reveal himself and appear weak, although this will help him progress. Prior is antagonistic to Rivers and does not understand why he has to reveal his deepest thoughts when Rivers does not. Eventually Prior begins to trust Rivers and engages in the healing process, becoming an insightful observer of Rivers's own traumas, manifested in stammering and deficits in visual memory. Rivers is changed by Prior and Sassoon. Worn down by their pain, he begins to question his own role in returning men to a useless war. Rivers comes to recognize the context-specific nature of these men's traumas: "The vast majority of his patients had no record of any mental trouble. And as soon as you accepted that the man's breakdown was a consequence of his war experience rather than of his own innate weakness, then inevitably the war became the issue" (*Regeneration* 115).

Also, therapeutic dialogues between Rivers and one of his clients, Siegfried Sassoon, explore debates around the fighting of the war, how it is justified and the ethical criticisms of war that begin with Sassoon but are further developed as Rivers begins to shift his position and question his own role in returning emotionally damaged men back to combat. Sassoon, who in reality formally protested the war, provides criticism and exemplifies officers' dilemmas in that he condemns the reckless behavior of authorities who sacrifice soldiers, and yet he is compelled to return to his men in battle.

In the figure of Billy Prior, the other central character aside from Rivers, Barker also brings together various kinds of traumatic experience (e.g., domestic, sexual, war), thereby linking various spheres and groups (prototypical women's and men's traumas in particular). Through Prior, Barker employs contemporary theories that trauma establishes life patterns of dissociative defenses, repetitions, and rage. Early childhood traumas and early sexualization stem from his father's violence toward his mother and sexual abuse by a priest. Consequently, the combat situation arouses sexual and sadistic impulses in him such that sexual arousal becomes conflated with the horrors of battle in Prior's night-

mares. His aggression toward Rivers and his initial resistance to therapy are defensive ploys to avoid returning to the feelings of violation
and helplessness he experienced as a child. Certainly the social context
encouraging war and duty is very strong in Barker's re-creation, so
Prior's childhood abuse is not the only reason for his participating,
but it affects the way he views and fights the war—in that he needs to
feel a sense of power and control—before he successfully completes
therapy.

Barker also places Prior squarely in the middle of class, social, and
sexual conflicts of the time. Through his eyes, readers learn how British attitudes about the war demonstrate the cynical treatment of the
underclass and the hypocrisy about homosexuality in a social system
that segregates the sexes and regularly throws males together in stressful situations from public school to war. Uncharacteristic in that he is
working class and an officer, Prior flaunts traditions through sexual
promiscuity, bisexuality, and using influence at the War Office to help
pacifist friends. His shifting social identity and partial social mobility
create opportunities for connection and self-awareness but also provoke
conflict and alienation from others. He is described uncomfortably by
one bisexual lover of a higher social class as "neither fish nor fowl" in
terms of class and sexuality. Thus this lover, Manning, covers up his
own sexual conflicts with the hope of recovering his more stable prewar
life with wife and children. Prior is frequently at odds with himself. He
is also the product of parents with conflicting values who frequently
abuse one another, psychologically and physically. His mother encouraged upward mobility, while his father was proud of being working
class. Consequently, Prior feels torn between them: "He and she—elemental forces, almost devoid of personal characteristics—clawed each
other in every cell of his body, and would do so until he died" (*Eye* 90).
His self-division reaches crisis proportions as his conflicts over his father, his childhood friend Mac, who is a conscientious objector, and his
own personal investment in the war drive him into a splitting off of part
of his personality into a dissociative fugue state wherein he acts out violently on a colleague and informer who reminds him of his father.[13]
His therapy will lead him out of these blackouts and behavior.

Prior's traumatic war experience and therapy create a context for
reevaluations of his actions and the war. His transgressive thoughts
first appear when he is a shell-shocked patient at Craiglockhart Hospi-

tal under the care of the Freudian psychiatrist Rivers. Here, Prior's traumas are revealed to him in his dreams, which he initially tries to deny but then admits that his "dreams of mutilation and slaughter were accompanied by seminal emissions" (*Eye* 70–71). He reveals later that in his youth he had been sexually molested by a priest. Consequently, his war traumas repetitively return him to this earlier situation of violation and helplessness that sets the pattern for his traumatic response to war and leads to a desire for revenge (war provides a displacement for revenge), which his dream repeats in combining violence with sexual pleasure. However, Prior also displays guilt over these thoughts, and as Judith Herman and other trauma therapists insist, a therapeutic cure of trauma involves acceptance of one's powerlessness in these situations and a knowledge of the traumatic context (Trauma 176). At the end of the trilogy, Prior will have developed substantially and will come to display this kind of knowledge and acceptance.

A sexually active bisexual, Prior longs to break down class and gender barriers through his sexual partners, which range from working-class Sarah, to upper-class officer Manning, to a French farm boy. In the ultimate transgression, Prior seeks out a sexual encounter with one of the women who had suckled him as a child when his mother was ill. "He kissed her mouth, her nose, her hair, and then, lowering his head in pure delight, feeling every taboo in the whole fucking country crash around his ears, he sucked Mrs. Riley's breasts" (*Eye* 118). Through his sexuality and all his diverse sexual encounters, the split-off parts of Prior come together, and this is where his awareness of class, gender relationships, and power takes shape. In this sense Prior's sexual life emulates the social body. His ability to gauge everyone sexually allows him to break down class barriers and pretensions, although he is not above accommodating others' class biases for his own purposes. As the prostitution he once engaged in repeats his sexual exploitation by a priest, his risky sexual behavior as an adult (with taboo partners, in public places) could be seen as a repetition and displacement of the risks of war he is moved to repeat.

The second link in Barker's trilogy, *The Eye in the Door,* examines how the war creates traumatic social change. Through her characters, such as Prior and his girlfriend, munitions worker Sarah Lum, Barker symbolizes the rapid and powerful social changes in Britain as the war touches everyone's lives. For example, the war exerts enormous changes on women's lives; with the men off to war, factory work gives women like Sarah and her friends money and independence. They also embrace greater freedom of movement and less confining clothes. Sexual mores are loosened considerably during the war, particularly between soldiers and civilian women.

Powerful, conservative social figures and structures try to uphold gender codes and other norms in response to these disconcerting social changes, however. *The Eye in the Door* covers some of the trial of Noel Pemberton Billing, a right-wing member of Parliament who went on a crusade to reveal what he viewed as corruption among the British upper classes, particularly sexual and moral corruption (especially homosexuality), which he claimed were either initiated by, or exploited by, their German enemies. Although Billing was acquitted of libel charges against him, the trial was significant because it demonstrated "the ways in which respectable masculine behavior, 'unnatural vice' and anti-alienism were all drawn into the debate about why Britain had failed to secure victory by mid-1918. It confirms the importance of gender roles to fears about the durability of the social order under duress" (Coetzee and Coetzee 181). Billing's worries surfaced in the context of tens of thousands of cases of shell shock, which provided disconcerting evidence that war was "effeminizing" men rather than holding up ideals of masculinity (182).

The Eye in the Door illustrates how the state curtailed individual and occupational liberties during the war effort, willingly throwing over constitutional rights to secure their agenda and weaken their political opponents. In this context, Prior personifies conflicts between the state and the individual and between duty to authority and rebellion. He resents the power of the doctors, the state, and the army and initially both consciously and unconsciously resists recalling his battle experience. Prior hates being out of control; he wants to wield power and yet resents authorities as well. Eventually, through hypnosis and therapy he begins to discuss his nightmares, which contain images of eyes, signifying a gruesome battle experience for Prior (he finds one of his men's disembodied eyes) but also the painted eye in Mac's jail cell, signifying how vigilant social, military, and moral structures try to maintain their authority through surveillance as much of what they believe in is breaking down. The eye is both grotesque evidence of the horror and chaos of war and of the trauma-inducing power of surveillance—from the therapeutic atmosphere of the hospital, to the prisons where conscientious objectors languish, to the civilian volunteers who police sexual behavior. As a military officer, Prior participates in this; authorized to censor his subordinates' mail, he reads one soldier's passionate love letter to his wife, becoming aroused, and feeling it the only sexual thing he has done "that's ever filled me with any shame" (*Ghost Road* 221).

As will also be seen in *Paco's Story*, combat experience creates a profound breach between soldiers and civilians. Civilians are often not capable of providing necessary comforts to soldiers. The relationship between Prior and Sarah illustrates gaps in experience and point of view. Initially Prior takes a predatory approach to her: "He both envied and despised her, and was quite coldly determined to *get* her. They owed him something, all of them, and she should pay" (128). His attitude indicates alienation, yet Barker seeks reconciliation as Sarah experiences her own war trauma. Eventually he realizes she has had her own heartache, losing a fiancé to the war, and comes to know and love her. Even when they become close, he is conflicted about what he should tell her, like many men torn between chivalry and honesty. "Men said they didn't tell their women about France because they didn't want to worry them. But it was more than that. He needed her ignorance to hide in. Yet, at the same time, he wanted to know and be known as deeply as possible. And the two desires were irreconcilable" (*Regeneration* 216).

After therapy, however, reentering the war for the fourth time, Prior's observations are calm, even hyperaware of all the implications of his own and others' behavior on the battlefield. He notes the avoidance and dissociation necessary to survive as he observes the new recruits and his fellow veteran, the poet Wilfred Owen. "I glanced at Owen and he was indifferent. As I was. I don't mean unsympathetic, *necessarily*. (Though it's amazing what you leave behind when the pack's heavy)" (*Ghost Road* 148). And later, "too close to death ourselves to make a fuss. We economize on grief" (241). He becomes aware that his sexual risks (e.g., out-of-doors, with taboo partners) have in part been a reexperiencing of the excitements of the attack in battle ("racing blood, risk, physical exposure, a kind of awful *daring* about it. . . . But I don't feel anything like that now" (172). Similarly, he recalls one of his sexual fantasies, being dressed with a naked lover, as he sees his men naked for a bath (he's dressed; officers bathe separately) and admits this

fantasy makes him feel tenderness as well as arousal: "the sort of tenderness that depends on being more powerful, and that is really, I sup-
pose, just the acceptable face of sadism" (175). He continues thinking
that war is not like sexual games—"here the disproportion of power is
real and the nakedness involuntary"—and feels uncomfortable about
it. Prior realizes there are secondary gains involved even in the midst of
a hideous war. The war allows men to have feelings and even desires
for one another ("Whole bloody western front's a wanker's paradise,"
177). He almost consciously employs defenses to remain a functional
commander ("Refusing to think's the only way I can survive," 193), remaining aware of danger, but detached: "The whole thing was breakdown territory, as defined by Rivers. Confined space, immobility, helplessness, passivity, constant danger that you can do nothing to avert.
But my nerves seem to be all right" (194); "We are Craiglockhart's success stories. *Look at us.* We don't remember, we don't feel, we don't
think—at least not beyond the confines of what's needed to do the job.
By an proper civilized standard (but what does *that* mean *now?*) we are
objects of horror. But our nerves are completely steady. And we are still
alive" (200, italics in original).

In the trilogy, Prior progresses from an intelligent but defensive,
bitter, and resistant analysand to admitting the deep conflicts within
himself and finally to becoming thoughtfully ambivalent, observant,
and caring. With Prior, Barker engages a working through of the process
of psychic trauma and recovery. He confronts and masters his fear
of death, but his hard-won awareness and sensibility, a precious and
unique human consciousness, is, in the end, destroyed in battle.

Dissociation, a classic defense against trauma, is a key theme of
Barker's trilogy. A means of living with painful events, it can lead to a
provisional identity rather than a fully feeling and functioning one.
Barker examines the many possible permutations of dissociation, ranging from the necessary and useful detachment of the professional therapist Henry Head to its utilization by war veterans and civilians to survive war. The detrimental aspects include soldiers risking their lives
because they have become so detached; fugue states brought on by unresolvable conflicted loyalties; splitting between mind and emotions;
the escapism of the public as they focus on more trivial matters while
war rages; and its most destructive manifestation—leading to war—
the objectification of others. Rivers thinks "the same suspension of em-

pathy that was so necessary a part of the physician's task was also, in other contexts, the root of all monstrosity. Not merely the soldier, but the torturer also, practices the same suspension" (*Eye* 164). Prior's dissociations and denials are pathological through most of the progress of the trilogy, a way to maintain self-control, but they also delay therapeutic aid, and his behavior is damaging and out of control in his most dissociated condition. Irreconcilable conflicts about his investment in the war and loyalty to a childhood friend elicit a fugue state, wherein his character splits into two separate entities (multiple personality), one of whom engages in gross acts of betrayal and violence. In this state of mind, he betrays a pacifist friend and physically attacks an informer who is very much like his vulgar and violent father (a similarity he cannot consciously recognize). "Prior had created a state whose freedom from fear and pain was persistent, encapsulated, inaccessible to normal consciousness" (245). Barker examines the many subtle gradations of dissociation that allow necessary functioning abilities and yet can contribute to social and individual repression and violence.

Does Barker's trilogy achieve the empathic unsettlement LaCapra looks for?[14] In terms of characterization, yes, because we are not allowed to sentimentalize either Prior or Rivers. The two undergo a working-through process, but their discoveries do not bring a brighter world; in fact, they are unsettling because of the two men's absorption by destructive systems of which they are aware but can only express minor resistance. These characters do provide a critical perspective for readers, however, pointing out the legacies of violence, its continuance as the culture and even the language contain the seeds of future conflict. As a Freudian adherent, Rivers might have considered war an inevitable expression of human aggressive tendencies, as Freud did. Barker does not portray him this way, however; the novel ends with a gesture toward ending cycles of violence. Rivers's last thoughts in the trilogy are of Njiru, a Melanesian spiritual man he knew, uttering the injunctions of an exorcism in an attempt to throw off the ghosts that threaten the living. Barker's hope is that through an awareness of how social, psychological, and economic forces perpetuate trauma-inducing violence, humanity might one day free itself of the haunting, repetitive aggressions and crushing ideologies that have dominated human history.

Barker values her relationship to readers, hoping to communicate her own and their presently lived connections to the historical past. In the process some of her readers have been grateful because her World War I novels have helped them to "understand their fathers or their grandfathers." One reader told Barker how the war had transformed her grandfather from a humorous, poetry-writing man into a violent one. Such responses are deeply satisfying to Barker: "[J]ust now and again you . . . get a glimpse that sometimes a book has changed somebody's life. Perhaps not changed the life itself, but has changed the way somebody is able to understand their life. And that's a rare moment, but it beats all the good reviews in the world" (Gross interview).

"His Own Wraith": Elusive Redemptions in *Paco's Story*

Like Pat Barker, Larry Heinemann also examines the issues of trauma, recovery, war, and sexuality in his novel about a Vietnam veteran, *Paco's Story* (1986). Representing the personal and psychic costs of war, Barker's and Heinemann's characters are also emblematic of the larger cultural traumas of two devastating and much criticized twentieth-century wars, both infamous for soldiers' inordinate traumatic stress and for provoking important shifts in cultural attitudes about war, war trauma, class, and the reliability of authority figures. Their experiences produce a lost sense of self-identity and reveal the intersections of individual and collective traumas. Moreover, the characters' war experiences bring about profound transformations in their sexual behavior, representing how war both fosters and questions sexual deviance—liberating one protagonist (Prior) from rigid sexual rules and social limitations, but violently cutting the other one (Paco) off from further intimacy and healing.

Both Heinemann and Barker emphasize how fighting men not only suffer from wars that continue for no reasonable cause, but they are also discouraged from psychic recovery because of a predominating masculine ethos and a sense that a reliable, safe community is no longer available. From Heinemann's perspective, veterans' brutalization in war and subsequent public rejection deprived them of a sense of community and trust in authority and caused them to defensively isolate themselves. So many aspects of their situations—the alienating aspects of war, dissociative defenses, and their "therapies," for instance, medications for physical and psychological problems—distance veterans from others. Both authors use their critiques of this ethos to tear the veil of authoritative versions of war history that implement censorship as policy and attempt to maintain the interconnected norms of obedience to authority, hypermasculinity, heterosexuality, and violence in the name of patriotism. They also demonstrate how social norms and policies are destructive to individuals. One of the worst effects of trauma is the sense of alienation and isolation involved. These are socially constructed when trauma victims are rejected, scapegoated, or ostracized because they are painful reminders of violent war, failed leadership, or do not fit into a society that wants to forget, minimize, or repudiate the war.

In his novel *Paco's Story*, Larry Heinemann provides a reexperiencing and reevaluation of a traumatic chapter in U.S. history through an uneasy and very personalized rendering of his isolated Vietnam veteran, Paco. Paco has barely escaped the devastating air strike in which the rest of his company perishes. What he cannot escape is the haunting reminders of his losses and his role in war atrocities. Heinemann demonstrates how historical events and social structures have induced and perpetuated trauma through the exploitation of underclass people, who were overrepresented in the drafting of soldiers (Berg and Rowe 5). His own experience of war and research on other veterans brought him to an awareness of the workings of traumatic stress, which gives him new narrative means to convey such experience. By incorporating the dissociations, incomplete and involuntary memories, humiliations, and affects that characterize traumatic experience, he draws his readers into that experience and provides alternative reexaminations of historical contexts. He portrays a character who has little consciousness or sense of an inner life, who drifts without a sense of having integrated all his life experience. As in other trauma narratives, ghosts symbolize the intrusive and painful persistence of memory and lost loved ones, but in *Paco's Story* they are also the narrators. Finally, Heinemann explores traumatic experience through witnessing, effects on the body, and in contemplating whether such experience can be shared. Heinemann tells the story through these voices because like many PTSD veterans, Paco has been silenced and was deprived of developing a "cohesive and adult sense of self" (Ulman and Brothers 160).

A Vietnam veteran himself, but not the model for Paco,[15] Heinemann faced difficulties in how to transmit traumatic experience, encountering problems with the possibility of creating narrative around events that haunt us yet demand their own repression. In focusing on veterans' suffering from delayed stress in his fiction and essays, Heinemann demonstrates that much has gone unarticulated about the horrific effects of Vietnam on these men and their silencing by an unsympathetic, alienating society. Similarly, Heinemann's narrators allude to how the most violent or salacious war experience was hidden from the public or ignored by cowardly and indifferent journalists. Referring to a particularly raunchy USO-type show, the narrators ask, "Let's tell it true, James, do you expect we'll ever see that scene in a movie?" (13). He feels their war experience has not ended nor been understood by the public and wants to bear witness to events significant both to veterans like himself and to Americans, recognizing that forgetting prevents resolution.

> The role I discovered, writing about an event which is central to my life, is simply to witness—I don't know what else a storyteller can do. The legacy [of Vietnam] for the culture, the bizarre and selfish political stupidities, the arrogance of military careerists . . . the world record tons of bombs dropped, the massacres . . . the whole egregious, nasty business—exerts a push as well as a pull on our collective memory and imagination. We Americans are famous for not picking up after ourselves, but the omission of dealing directly with the aftermath reverberations of the epoch of the Vietnam War is likely to take us to a very strange place, indeed. ("Autobiography" 98)

Heinemann discovered an extensive subculture of "tripwire" veterans in the Northwest whose wounds linger so profoundly years, even decades later, that they still live in battle mode. Heinemann reports one particular veteran's explanation of how he has survived: "[I] discovered—that I couldn't operate around humanity . . . I felt my government shit on me. My family shit on me. The only true, clean thing left was the woods. So I went back to the woods and slowly, slowly mended" (qtd. in "Just Don't Fit" 58). He also found that some of the men most likely to need help were barred from it by spiteful officials.[16] Heinemann's and other veterans' resentment of their exploitation by government and military, along with subsequent trips to Vietnam, have led to a growing identification and connection between American and Vietnamese veterans ("Syndromes" 76).

Although he presents horrific, traumatic material, he allows the readers some distance from the protagonist as well, through narrative voices and humor. He brings the "unspeakable" into narrative by avoiding standard chronology and linear plots, employing oral, storytelling forms and seeking out the paths of elicited survivor memories that are characterized by analysts Dori Laub and Nanette Auerhahn as a struggle to both remember and forget (288). Heinemann's trauma narrative directs an inward, silent process outward to other witnesses (both within and outside the text), provides an experiential approach that illuminates the psychic costs of oppression, elucidates the links between personal and public aspects of traumatic experience, and humanizes overwhelming public events. Heinemann uses shifting points of view, interior monologues and dialogues and addressing his readers directly as "James," a narrative device that he says ensures "the reader is imaginatively involved in the story at basically the same emotional moment that you are telling the story to him or her" (Interview 190). This approach may be an attempt to compensate for the distance felt by veterans and civilians for each other.

His narrative also utilizes a dialogical approach that involves the intermingling of many voices, emotions, and experiences to produce individual and collective memory, and to counteract silence and forgetting. Multiple narrators either set the scene, bear witness for characters silenced by trauma, or give first-person testimony. They tell the story that Paco is unable to tell himself. The witnessing narrators in *Paco's Story*, mostly other war vets, have their own horror stories that establish traumatic experience as historical and collective but offer regrettably few healing connections between themselves and Paco. The army medic who describes finding Paco and his slaughtered company is so horrified by the sight that he never pursues a career in medicine, yet he remains obsessed, still replaying the scene years later at a bar in an alcoholic stupor. Unlike Paco, Ernest Monroe can fully articulate the terror, bitterness, and anger he feels about his World War II experience. He sympathizes with Paco, "recognizes Paco's 1,000-meter stare, that pale and exhausted, graven look from head to toe" (95) and gives him a job. Worn down by others' indifference and ill will, Paco cannot bring himself to confide in Ernest, but wants to talk to another witness, the itinerant Vietnam veteran Jesse, who knows firsthand what Paco had to face. Jesse is also able to share his rage and sense of absurdity about Vietnam and the American attitudes that perpetuated and mythologized it ("I am a fully stamped, qualified *slab* animal—successful species—who made it out of their fucking lab," 155–56).[17] Jesse, however, seems to have survived by isolating himself and avoids both Paco's invitation to stay and his desire to confide in him.

The book presents many missed connections; Paco's condition is affecting, evoking others' personal memories,[18] but not any emotional exchanges, demonstrating how the isolating nature of traumatic experience even puts survivors at cross-purposes. Like Morrison and Barker, though, Heinemann links multiple experiences of trauma in his narrative—here, different war experiences—hoping to suggest a sense that trauma is shared by many, and not to recognize this jeopardizes healing and connection both for these individuals, our culture, and our relation to past history.

Paco's Story also bears witness by making readers experience a confrontation between its protagonist and his guilt over the past, employing ghosts as both catalysts and substance of traumatic memory. Paco tries to live his conscious life in the moment, focusing with enormous concentration on his job as a dishwasher. By employing various psychological defenses against trauma, primarily dissociation and repression, this helps him survive but also wipes out much of his subjectivity. Like many trauma victims, Paco lives out of time, having as yet been unable to create in his mind a clear continuity between past, present, and future, because his past dominates his inner life. It torments his dreams, and at times horrific involuntary memories emerge fully blown in consciousness despite his resistance. He is unable to move beyond the past; it marks his life and makes him different and frightening to others. Paco's guilt over war crimes and surviving his slaughtered Alpha Company comrades is submerged under repression and medications for his physical and psychological injuries, and by his obsessive focus on the details of his work.

The Alpha Company ghosts,[19] the principal narrators, return Paco to the past, at night, when "he is least wary, most receptive and dreamy," (137), trying to provoke Paco into asking the questions that often torment survivors about those left dead: "No, James, Paco has never asked, *Why me!* It is we—the ghosts, the dead—who ask, Why him? So Paco is made to dream and remember" (137, italics in original). Paco's repressed emotions and fears about Vietnam emerge largely in his nightmares, a common manifestation of traumatic memory. The effect of these nightmares on him is evidenced through the diary entries of

Cathy, a young woman fascinated with Paco: "And this guy begins moaning and slamming back and forth on his bed. You know that real thick and solid sound of a mattress. And he's crying—weeping, I mean—Oh no! Don't kill him!" (206). Thus, Heinemann provides an exterior, unsympathetic view of Paco, and then an interior view in the description of his dreams. In one of Paco's dreams, he is lined up with other men "from each platoon . . . chosen by lot, volunteered—to be executed as punishment for some crime never mentioned. Cowardice? Mutiny? A fragging? The men stand bound with leather thongs twisted and looped around their necks and knotted severely around their wrists in back" (141). While some of the men are angry and deny any guilt, executions by injection begin. The expectation or even wish for punishment is expressed in this and other dreams. Bound, the soldiers resemble the teenage Vietcong girl Paco's company has gang-raped and murdered to avenge comrades she killed in war (see below). Further, the denial of guilt expresses the extreme conflicts soldiers had over needless deaths and atrocities perpetrated and condoned in war. Paco's feelings of dehumanization also emerge with these injections as he remembers in the dream that dogs at the pound are eliminated this way.

In his attention to bodily assaults, Heinemann creates visceral portrayals of the characters and the intimate, physical way trauma is experienced. Heinemann says, "I am one of those writers who thinks that 'story' . . . involves the whole body, that perception, point of view, image, literary diction . . . proceed from a visceral and sensual awareness of story" ("Autobiography" 89). Survivors have testified that bodily violations, deprivations, and humiliations are some of the most defeating aspects of traumatic experience. Heinemann's descriptions emphasize grotesque injuries and war conditions, where men are rapidly deprived of limbs and endure oppressive heat, insects, and jungle rot. Paco's painful connection to the past is displayed and replayed through his body, even branded into his flesh. Paco's scars are also described as appearing alive, seeming "to wiggle and curl . . . the same as grubs and night crawlers when you prick them with the barb of a bait hook . . . the way many a frightful thing in this world comes alive in the dimmest, whitest moonlight, the cleanest lamplight" (171). This description suggests that his scars express horrors that remain largely hidden and unspoken. Paco's scars also represent his narrow escape from death in a horrific barrage of air strike bombs and artillery fire. Through modern technology, bodies are "pulverized to ash," and the narrator describes the scene as "everything smelling of ash and marrow and spontaneous combustion; everything—dog tags, slivers of meat, letters from home, scraps of sandbags and rucksacks and MPC scrip, jungle shit and human shit—*everything* hanging out of the woodline looking like so much rust-colored puke" (15–16). Tragically and ironically, the company is wiped out by American "friendly fire," a further reminder of the infantrymen's precarious and exploited position. Heinemann's accumulative style here foregrounds the overwhelming details and excess of traumatic war experience.

Scars become connecting points and obstacles to potentially intimate or sexual relations, drawing others' attention and sympathy until the underlying agony becomes overwhelming for them. Young women find Paco attractive despite the scars covering his entire body. However, in a sexual fantasy that turns grotesque, Cathy imagines Paco taking off his scars and laying them on her: "[A]nd I think I hear *screams,* as if each scar is a scream, and I look up at him again and he's peeling the scars down his arm. . . . Then he's kneeling on my shoulders . . . and he's laying strings of those scars on my face, and I'm beginning to suffocate" (208). She senses that Paco wants to share what has wounded him, literally forcing it in her face, and she is terrified and repelled by the prospect. Like most of the civilians in the novel, she lacks the capacity to understand Paco's torments or the war context; his behavior is strange and frightening, he is a walking reminder of destruction that others want to forget and suppress. Heinemann wants to put his readers in connection with what he realizes is alien to most of us. This passing on of scars expresses a desire for collective acknowledgment and understanding.

Paco has committed many violent, horrific acts with his body in war, so he also seeks salvation through his body. However, although Paco wants to "fuck away all that pain and redeem his body" (173–74),[20] he is deprived of the grace of intimacy. His desire for women, in particular Cathy, is tainted by a memory of his participation in the gang rape and execution of a Vietcong girl. The sounds of Cathy having sex with another man in the next room bring the rape back to Paco's resisting consciousness: "He winces and squirms; his whole body jerks, but he cannot choose but remember" (174). From the detailed description of the rape, Heinemann allows the reader to gauge the lost humanity of men who achieve sexual pleasure from brutalizing another. Paco is fully aware of the effects of their brutality on the girl, and for Paco this is a tainted memory, something irremediable. "Her eyes got bigger than a deer's, and the chunks and slivers of tile got ground into her scalp and face, her breasts and stomach, and Jesus-fucking-Christ, she had her nostrils flared and teeth clenched and eyes squinted, tearing at the sheer humiliating, grinding pain of it" (180). Later he reads Cathy's diary, and in it her sexual fantasy about him also becomes a rape; he cannot escape the hauntings of the past or identification as a rapist in his own or in others' eyes. In connecting these experiences, Heinemann demonstrates Kalí Tal's point that veterans were both victims and victimizers (138) (and who could feel like both), and also how actions can seem unforgivable and cut off further connection with others. As his hopes for recovery on the most basic physical level fail, the possibility of achieving deeper emotional intimacy is even more remote. Complicating this seeming dichotomy of victims and victimizers, trauma studies on veterans have suggested that some of the worst war trauma was experienced by men who either witnessed or participated in atrocities.

Heinemann's depiction of this rape, written in a compelling style that brings the reader into the experience with realistic detail, is designed to have a moral effect on the reader, reminding us of the "banality of rape" in the war context and making readers spectators and "unwilling participants," argues Grant Scott (76). This scene was disturbing to many readers, who complained when an excerpt was printed in *Harper's* magazine (Scott 69). Making the rape analogous to everyday activities and putting readers in the position of the rape victim as well as that of the rapists, Heinemann contextualizes such horrors as the norm, yet makes readers empathize with this girl, and tries to produce in readers a feeling of profound discomfort as Paco agonizes over this experience while also trying to rationalize it on some level.

Aggression is not only sanctioned but provoked by the military in training soldiers, which can be traumatic in that soldiers are expected to lose their civilian personality in adapting to war and then often little has been done to reorient them to civilian life again. They are given a new, warrior identity that makes them unfit to live as a civilian again and for some men prevents them from developing a fully developed adult personality (Ulman and Brothers 155). Military life deliberately frustrates basic needs, such as sexual needs, even degrading sexuality.

"Military life creates an aggressive overload and leads to aggressive frustration," says psychiatrist Emanuel Tanay, who has worked with war veterans (31). Further, the military fosters sadomasochistic relationships between superiors and "inferiors" who accumulate aggression rather than discharging it, predisposing individuals for the "perpetration of atrocities which are guilt provoking" (31). Heinemann and many others have noted that conditions in Vietnam were particularly conducive for atrocities, as soldiers objectified a racially different enemy and encountered perilously uncontrollable circumstances and emotional isolation. Further, the death of fellow soldiers, says therapist Sarah Haley, "led many to the need to avenge the buddy's death through displacement, by repetitive aggression against anyone and anything that represented a reminder of the lost buddy, or who exposed the vulnerability of the surviving soldier" (60).

This training and circumstance become the basis for one of the worst atrocities described in *Paco's Story*—the aforementioned brutal gang rape and murder of the teenaged Vietcong prisoner, punished for shooting two American soldiers. Many members of Paco's company, including Paco, participate in the rape, which is instigated by Gallagher, who also eventually kills her. The commanding officer literally looks the other way, refusing to enforce any rules or inhibitions to this behavior. Afterward, Gallagher seems momentarily relieved by his actions, saying, "That's how you put the cool on gooks" (184). Some of the others, including Paco, however, do not share his sentiments, their consciences are violated and the looks of the medics who arrive make them confront their actions. "We looked at her [dead body] and at ourselves, drawing breath again and again, and knew that this was a moment of evil, that we would never live the same" (184). This is clearly a life-changing experience, a tainted memory.

By prefacing the rape scene with a description of the hopelessly brutal working-class life of Gallagher's family, Heinemann establishes precedent for his savagery. Gallagher already has a deeply ingrained sense of anger toward the world that aggravates his need to avenge the other soldiers' deaths. Heinemann establishes a series of associations and emotional patterns from earlier in Gallagher's life that become part of the impetus for his aggressive violence. Before the rape, Gallagher describes the savage beatings he and his brothers endured from their father, and the anger he expresses about his father's wasted life is provoked by the facial expression of a fellow soldier whose arm has been blown off—an expression as pained and astonished as his father's had been at the end of a hard day at work. In studying veterans with recurring war trauma nightmares, Melvin Lansky encountered men from abusive backgrounds who had volunteered for war for personal reasons, as a way to control the shame and rage they felt because "the [original] sources of their shame and rage are neutralized or rationalized by the wartime situation" (37). Gallagher's portrayal seems to fit this profile, as well as embracing an overly masculinized ideal.

Like Morrison, Heinemann recognizes gender differences in the way trauma is expressed through the body, particularly in women's sexual exploitation. Those victimized are feminized/sexualized from a masculine point of view; for example, a terrible battle is called a "butt fuck." Paco realizes that no male Vietcong would have been subject to rape as the girl was. Moreover, sexual desire is co-opted in the war situation. The Asian women who survive through prostitution are totally objectified by American soldiers like Gallagher, who discusses the merits of "Thai pussy." In depicting this objectification of prostitutes and the rape victim, Heinemann suggests that the soldiers and these women are all exploited members of their respective country's underclass, but that the soldiers do not recognize this at the time. Their training for war has encouraged this objectification and discouraged their more humane characteristics. Looking at the girl's body before the rape, Paco and the narrator can tell she has worked her whole life at sharecropping and yet tries to create a dissociative distance from the men's complicity in brutalizing her. "The dumbest dumbshit on the face of this earth knows that sharecropping sucks; knows you can't spend your life sharing your crop with *yourself,* much less split it between you and the Man. But who knows, maybe Viets enjoyed being gaunt and rickety, rheumy and toothless. Maybe" (179).

Paco's point of view expresses some understanding of the Vietnamese position and yet a sense of superiority too. As Heinemann and other veterans came to feel isolated and alienated in their own country in the years after the war, they surprisingly acquired a strong identification with Vietnamese ex-soldiers and civilians. In the ways that Heinemann frames the confrontations between Americans and Vietnamese in the war, the suffering of those who commit as well as endure atrocities, he suggests an overlooked and untapped linkage between them all. "Could it be that veterans of the war in Vietnam are more intimately connected with the Vietnamese than with our own people and country?" he asks ("Syndromes" 76).

In focusing on the effects of traumatic brutalization, Heinemann's work condemns war as a human-made traumatic situation where social, economic, and political structures target particular groups of people. *Paco's Story* reflects how political imperatives and military structures unnecessarily dehumanized and abused the primarily working-class and minority men drafted into the infantry. Though Heinemann is not specific, Paco's name suggests he could be Latino, implying a marginal identity there as well. Officers and politicians, usually of a higher socioeconomic class, often sacrificed these men to further their careers and expected them to destroy the Vietnamese, including civilians, for no clear reasons. In "Just Don't Fit," Heinemann describes how the structure of the war isolated soldiers, denying them continuity in who they trained or fought with. In this way, they were deprived of the close relationships and supports allowed veterans of World War II, who were allowed time together to work through the aftermath of combat, their guilt over their actions in war, and for surviving their comrades (59). Moreover, World War II veterans were welcomed home and received social and economic benefits (Karner 70).

Paco's isolated life reflects that of many Vietnam veterans suffering from delayed stress. The war and the unsupportive response back home deprived veterans of a sense of community and trust in authority, exacerbating their emotional problems and creating many forms of isolation, as illustrated in Paco's situation. The futility and shame associated with Vietnam cuts him off from veterans of other wars. When Paco's company was decimated, so was the community with which he could share his experience. And, although he is weary of trying to explain what happened to him, Paco is yet unable to connect. Heinemann says, "Paco doesn't talk much because he doesn't have much to say; he hasn't been able to discover the language he needs" (Interview 190). He represses the wounds that remain unbearable and unhealed. Paco's life attests that loneliness, disconnection, silence, and unresolved guilt are the price of mandatory brutality and subsequent denial of communal healing. Like Beloved, he suffers from being unclaimed and unremembered.

There is only one specific reference to his family in the entire novel, when Paco receives medals from a colonel who, clearly moved by the devastation of Paco's body, kisses and whispers to him. During the ceremony, while Paco is still in a hospital bed, he has a fond memory of his father tenderly tucking him in and singing a good-night song. "That was the reason Paco never threw away the medals, or pawned them, as many times as he was tempted and as stone total worthless as the medals were—the Army gave them out like popcorn, you understand, like rain checks at a ball park. It is the kiss he cherishes and the memory of the whispered word" (58–59). As Beloved longed for her lost mother, Paco yearns for his father's affection and love. Though Heinemann is not specific, one can surmise from Paco's isolation and from the stories of other PTSD veterans it is most likely that he has become completely estranged from his family, as many did, because they were still embedded emotionally in the combat situation. They could no longer function in civilian social contexts, feeling estranged, angry, and acting out, sometimes abusively (Karner 74, 76–87). Many men joined the military to "achieve a cultural standard of manhood" that included war duty, being breadwinners, and fatherhood—standards particularly pertinent for the World War II generation (66, 63–64). More importantly, many PTSD veterans went to war to gain a sense of control, to follow in their fathers' footsteps, but also to gain respect or surpass their fathers' war efforts (70). What they discovered was that they had much less control in war, that it made them powerless, impotent (Ulman and Brothers 186–87). Sections of testimonial narratives of PTSD veterans about their family of origin "focused primarily on their youthful quest for adulthood, which seemed to be symbolically located in the father. Everything else faded into the background" (Karner 84). These men, when "they looked to the images of war and its attendant male adulthood, the social definitions of masculinity, soldier, breadwinner, and family man often represented elusive ideals that only contributed to a sense of failure and unattainable manhood" (64). Paco also is unable to achieve any of these roles, even temporary connections. This failure has left a deep cultural trauma and a desire to redress it, even if sometimes through propaganda or fantasy wish fulfillments.[21]

Veterans like Paco faced the impossible situation of being asked to be brutal killers in war and yet be civilized at the same time. The trauma-inducing brutality of war has made these men dissociate from their actions, alienating them from themselves as well as others.

Trauma theories from World War I on indicate that the most significant factor in its development is victims' sense of helplessness in the face of danger. There were many factors in Vietnam that underscored this lack of control: unfamiliar and unfathomable jungle terrain, uncertainty about who the enemy was, incompetent and self-serving commanding officers, lack of a good cause, and others. Soldiers responded with brutal and illegal acts. The toll that fighting and mutual atrocities take on soldiers like Paco is evident in how the soldiers dissociate by medicating themselves with alcohol, marijuana, and other drugs. Paco's deepest trauma comes from a steady erosion of his humanity demonstrated in coldly setting booby traps, the rape, and the ghastly killing of a Vietcong man. Paco's guilt over these acts is immediately suppressed because they are condoned in the war context, but we see the price that he pays almost immediately. After arguably Paco's worst act, plunging a knife in the heart of a Vietcong soldier as he is begging for his life, "the fierce glare of [Paco's] 1,000-meter stare seemed permanent . . . his whole body skittish—Paco always able to recall the tears in the guy's eyes while he whispered clearly and plainly 'I will never see forever.' That night he drank every canteen in sight and smoked dope until he was high out of his mind" (196). Thus begin the defensive dissociations that keep him alive, but also cut him off from his feelings and from human connection.

Rather than leading readers to pass judgment, Heinemann immerses us in the individual experience of terror, arbitrary rules, misdirected acts and the psychic or physical breakdown of those involved so that we might begin to appreciate their situations. He engages us to consider how human costs to oppressive systems linger on unresolved for decades. There is a terrible irony in that so many men in the twentieth century have endured but have not been able to share war experience. For some Vietnam veterans, the failure of the war and public insensitivity or hostility to soldiers' experiences have created a seemingly insurmountable isolation. Not only civilian fears but the nature of war and notions of masculine bravery (World War I and II veterans were not encouraged to speak of their war experience either) are all contributors to this isolation. Heinemann illustrates this well as the many veterans from different wars in the novel never coalesce into a community.

Heinemann has lived this legacy personally, identifying his own brother as one of many men "ruined by the war—something happened to him overseas that he simply could not overcome" ("Autobiography" 87). We must be aware of what humans are driven to and what they are capable of, letting that knowledge guide and not paralyze us. He suggests that for some survivors the taint and disconnection may be insurmountable, but his drive to tell this story indicates a faith that others might be saved if we come to realize that these legacies invade our social and psychological existence and should concern us all. Heinemann, like Morrison and Barker, insists these wounds will not be alleviated until we cease to suppress, rationalize, and mythologize our past.

There is no working through for Heinemann's protagonist. We leave him still wounded, moving on to the next town. As readers, we are left with a sense of waste, loss, emptiness, and both the possibility and failure of human connection that could bring Paco back from his ghostlike existence. A kind of working through occurs for readers in the accumulated critical perspectives and the experiences that help us to understand the forces shaping Paco's, and other men's, desolation. A senseless war; the exploited become the exploiters; the myths and lies that surround notions of duty, winning, and obedience to authority: Heinemann wants us to share his outrage at all the waste resulting from ideological power grabs and irresponsible government policies. We can pity Paco, but we cannot sentimentalize him or view him as heroic. He is a pained, flawed figure, perhaps forever tainted by the brutality that was taught and expected of him in war. He lives this desolation everyday, so readers are not asked to judge or condemn. He and those like him long for a hearing and consolation, but we are left with the unsettling question of whether these will ever be offered, or accepted.

Heinemann joins Morrison and Barker in creating testimonial narratives, where individual recollections merge and multiply such that they come to represent or speak on behalf of larger social groups (Beverley 95). Responding to the unembellished immediacy of testimony exemplified by numerous survivors of traumatic events (e.g., the Holocaust, wars, incest, rape), their works, though literary, attempt to recreate this experience with the uncertain reconstructions and emotional reenactments that characterize oral or first-person testimonies. All three authors critique the rationalizations, obfuscations, universalizing and apolitical mythologizing that Lawrence Langer and Kalí Tal object to in many literary narratives about trauma (Langer 58; Tal 6, 9). Rather, Morrison, Barker, and Heinemann explore the ambivalences, disconnections, and political implications of real traumatic experience. Present in their works is an awareness of how such experience resists narrativization, chronologizing, and moralizing. They adopt narrative approximations of testimony because they recognize the more immediate and emotional impact it carries. In doing so, they hope that these trauma narratives, like testimony, play an important role in a public mourning process where narrativizing of complex and difficult experience is necessary because of the victims' limitations in speaking and collective repression. What Tal calls the "literatures of trauma" re-create that experience to "make it real both to victims and to the community"; storytelling becomes a personal and collective "reconstitutive" act (21).

These narratives also engage a working-through process whereby they make available and comprehensible what has been suppressed and repressed, urging us not to forget or ignore the past. Morrison identifies *Beloved* as a needed memorial: "There is no place you or I can go, to think about or not think about, to summon the presences of, or recollect the absences of slaves; nothing that reminds us of the ones who made the journey and of those who did not make it. There is no suitable memorial or plaque or wreath or wall or park or skyscraper lobby. There's no 300-foot tower. . . . There is not even a tree scored, an initial that I can visit, or you can visit. . . . And because such a place doesn't exist (that I know of), the book had to" ("A Bench" 4). Readers are urged to take on responsibility for these testimonies, to take an active role as empathic listeners who are needed to encourage and to help transmit information that can be shocking and incomprehensible. As witnesses, however, readers must put aside their myths about the world and humanity, says Langer, and must attend carefully the psychological effects on witnesses reflected in emotional and cognitive disconnections, permanent wounds, and shattering of normal beliefs (21, 159–60). *Beloved*, the *Regeneration* trilogy, and *Paco's Story* are examples of authentic trauma narratives that work against the social, political, and cultural contexts that shape and reinforce abuse and forgetting; they clarify our relationship to the past and provide antidotes to false innocence, distortions, and repression.

Cultures all over the world have dissociated from horrors they have wrought, and in doing so have created unresolved, continuing legacies of pain. Slavery is still a painful experience, even to read in fiction over one hundred years later. All of the texts in this chapter (as many trauma texts have, especially those about war) use ghosts to represent the return of the dead or the memory of them. These ghosts are portrayed as aggressive, persistent hauntings of those lost in the past. Ghosts can be narrators or provoke traumatic memory, as in *Beloved* and *Paco's Story*. Ghosts also emphasize the presence of the dead in the lives of survivors, as with Beloved in 124. Characters' dissociative responses can give them a deathlike quality that removes them from others. Paco is described "as if he's a ghost" (206), and having "met his wraith" (208). The dead appear to Sassoon in *Regeneration*, and like Paco's ghostly comrades, cannot understand why he survives and they do not. For all three writers, ghosts also symbolize survivors' guilt. Prior, in *The Ghost Road* refers to a kind of enslavement of the living to the dead: "Cowed subjection to the ghosts of friends who died. . . . Ghosts everywhere. Even the living were only ghosts in the making" that keep him, Sassoon, and others returning to the fighting (46). Sethe and Paco are similarly enslaved to those they have left behind. *Paco's Story* leaves its protagonist in stasis and loss, continuing to live with the dead. Both Morrison's *Beloved* and Barker's final volume, *The Ghost Road*, end with the hope that once the significance of the dead is recognized, they must also be made to leave the living. Yet both writers suggest that leaving the past is a painful struggle; although Beloved seems to disappear, there lingers a "clamor for a kiss" disguised in the weather, and Barker invokes an exorcism as metaphor for this struggle. All three texts discussed in this chapter express the wish for reconciliation with, and then moving beyond, the difficult past.

CONCLUSION

What is the value of studying trauma and its expressions in art, theory, and scholarship? As my inquiries about trauma progressed during the course of my research, I knew that doing justice to this topic would involve consulting a variety of different disciplinary sources. This increased the challenge of completing my study, but also convinced me that combining knowledge from a variety of disciplines reveals the errors, defenses, and ideologies that rule many of our assumptions, which in turn prevent broader conceptualizations that might bring more collective consensus and action. These issues are especially appropriate to trauma studies, because trauma has often challenged the assumptions of both the public and professionals and its treatment has been plagued by misunderstanding. A case in point for changing conceptualizations is how different populations of trauma victims were separated out until recently (e.g., traumas from war, rape, incest, and disasters). Since the inception of the diagnosis posttraumatic stress disorder in 1980, those who study and treat trauma have begun to focus on the similar effects of trauma on diverse populations and examine the kinds of social forces and restrictions that create it. This has helped practitioners disseminate knowledge and assess stressors, social and environmental support, and personality factors and thereby improve treatment. For my own study, it would have been impossible to fully assimilate the accuracy and ethical value of the trauma fiction had I not explored the psychological, historical, and cultural research that helped me to understand the many ways trauma can be manifested and expressed. This research was also invaluable in learning how trauma, and the literary writers from many cultural backgrounds, challenge power relations, subjectivity and institutions as they have been formulated in Western culture. The fact that trauma, especially in colonial and postcolonial contexts, is often created out of cultural conflicts and attempts to efface certain cultures (and by extension the identities of individuals therein) makes it especially important to understand the nature of these conflicts and the mistakes of the past, in the interests of coexistence as the world continues to become more globalized.

What does the study of trauma teach us about ourselves? Trauma leads us to examine the human consequences of sociohistorical phenomena and the interconnections between public and private, the political and the psychological. The array of literary, theoretical, historical, and cultural texts referred to in this study have provided ample evidence and argument that trauma is frequently caused by human-made injustice, oppression, and exploitation. Trauma also has meaning in that it is indicative of basic life issues such as the relation between life and death; the meaning and quality of existence; physical and psychological survival; how people understand and cope with loss and self-diminishment; and the nature of bonds and disconnections among people. Because all these issues have bearing when we consider traumatic responses, it becomes a phenomenon that touches many more people than the most severely traumatized. Examining psychic wounds, how they are expressed and survived, reveals the relation of the cultural to the psychological, the formation or disintegration of subjectivity, the nature of boundaries and excess, as well as making us face the unthinkable that happens in our midst.

In this study I have tried to demonstrate how trauma fiction serves several valuable functions. It is an important way of witnessing or testifying for the history and experience of historically marginalized people. Further, it chronicles lives under duress that need the powers of literary imagination, character development, and symbolic experimentation to be more fully realized for readers. These literary and imaginative approaches provide a necessary supplement to historical and psychological studies. Though these trauma writers have clearly consulted other kinds of trauma studies and research, their contribution is not only making terrifying, alien experience more understandable and accessible, but they also bring a kind of sociocultural critical analysis that helps readers formulate how public policy and ideology are lived in private lives. Bringing these elements together has long been the province of the novel (although other art forms can address trauma effectively as well). Bakhtin's notions of the novel and the expansive dialogism of social, artistic, and subjective elements that constitute it seem to guide these trauma narrative forms used to re-create and reassess the past. Many trauma writers (such as Morrison, Duras, Barker, Heinemann) have used dialogism to convey multiple viewpoints and multifaceted human interconnections and to avoid a single dominant formulation. Certainty, authoritarianism, easy prescriptions, or what Bakhtin would term any sort of authoritative discourse are discredited by all these writers because such views have often wrought the conditions producing trauma.

My intensive focus on the bonds between mothers and children is meant to demonstrate several important connections in the workings and contexts of trauma. First, cultural institutions and identity are inculcated and shaped in this nurturing context, demonstrating the relationships between the public and the private. Also, mothers and children are most frequently vulnerable to situations of oppression, deprivation, and exploitation. Further, mothers are uniquely positioned as powerful nurturers and socializers even if they often have no social power. They are frequently the locus for determining whether legacies of trauma will be resisted or perpetuated. If the stance of the nurturer runs counter to oppression, her awareness provides the means by which readers can see how personal trauma emerges from social problems, as with Duras's portrayal of her mother. Though resistance by the single mother is often defeated, collective efforts are more likely to bring her, or her children, out of isolation and foster healing, many of these works suggest (see *Beloved*, *Bastard out of Carolina*, and *Breath, Eyes, Memory*). Communal healing is also necessary for soldiers and societies as well, Heinemann and Barker indicate.

Theorists like Dominick LaCapra and Kirby Farrell discuss the important cultural, mediatory, critical, and possible mourning functions of fictional trauma. Farrell proposes that the public embraces popular culture expressions of trauma as a safe context from which to explore difficult issues and our own fears. LaCapra wonders if fiction or other art examining trauma can provide us with a "discursive analogue of mourning" in a "[m]odern [secular] society . . . characterized by a dearth of social processes, including ritual processes, which assist individuals during major transitions in life such as marriage, birth or death" (213). LaCapra and Farrell could be right, considering how many readers find these writings therapeutic and the fact that studies of cultural aspects of psychological response indicate that survival and healing depend on whether a society provides supports, meaningful modes of action, and rituals to provide structures for behaviors and emotions (de Vries 401–5). Also crucial for LaCapra: does trauma fiction provide a critical function as well as an empathic one, allowing us not only human understanding but also a critical evaluative process that encourages resistance and change in the future? I would argue that the texts presented here fulfill this (see chapter 5).

My interpretations, more than in other studies, have focused on the visceral qualities of this fiction. These qualities not only make the prose memorable to readers but also immerse them in the bodily lives of the characters, helping to create a situation of intimacy between text and reader. Living history and trauma in the body not only demonstrates some of the most painful aspects of enduring and surviving traumatic situations, but also gives readers a sense of the violations experienced by individuals as larger forces intrude on them. Thus, trauma narratives illustrate in powerful ways the relations between the powerful and the powerless, the fact of living in these circumstances on a daily basis.

Another important aspect of this living experience of trauma that I foreground is how it is imagined and symbolized through the characters. Ultimately, experiences of trauma involve a confrontation with death. Sometimes it is an imminent danger, as in a war or a concentration camp, but it can also involve situations of subjective death: loss of a loved one, numbing, or having one's identity disregarded or effaced. Sometimes there is an allegiance to the dead as a result of guilt, remorse, or longing to keep the memory of them alive, but this also keeps one immersed in traumatic stasis. Attempts at self-creation, establishing some provisional identity through symbolization and fantasy, are symbolic forms of resisting one's annihilation as a subject. Strategies of control, even if illusionary, serve the same purpose. The key link between literature and trauma is explained by this confrontation with death as a universal/essential element of human experience that cannot be fully confronted but can be symbolized. Our first confrontations with it in early life, says Robert Lifton, are "death equivalents: separation, fear of disintegration, [etc.] . . . And in the end, imagery, symbolization, and meaning are in a life/death model or paradigm" (Caruth, *Trauma* 134). Lifton believes that a constitutive factor of human life is "the struggle for vitality and, ultimately, for symbolic immortality" (134). He adds that we aspire to meaning, which must be expressed in image and form; this kind of expression "is central to human experience" (133). The nature of symbolization indicates a subject's relation to objects, and the ability to create metaphors reflects an individual's differentiation and good ego development. Symbolic equations or a failure to create metaphors implies emotional stasis, which often characterizes traumatic experience in these texts. The expressions of human survival and recovery range from the most severe and repetitive (the beggar, Pecola, Paco), to the self-sustaining illusion (Xuela), to stories creating connections and comfort (Bone), to engagements in mourning (Sethe, Beloved, Duras's girl).

Having spent much of his life examining the devastating personal consequences of events such as Hiroshima, the Holocaust, and Vietnam, Lifton sees a shift away from traumatizing conditions founded on the need for the kind of absolute control that fueled nationalism and wars up through the Cold War. Now, he sees a more hopeful shift toward worldwide movements of democratization and a view of the self as "Protean," or vital and fluid, and not based on absolutes (*Protean Self* 1–2, 220–21). Lifton's notion of this malleable self is the brighter version of human adaptability, the darker version of which is the provisional self adopted in traumatic situations where no choice is possible. Trauma fiction testifies to the value of knowledge and resistance, even if is not always successful. We can hope that Lifton's optimistic view— that history has finally responded to a basic human energy that resists manipulation and domination—is becoming a reality; however, these narratives remind us that the past lingers in so many ingrained ways that shifting away from it is necessarily a collective and arduous task.

Finally, how they address their readers is of primary importance to all these trauma writers, who attempt to make readers familiar with material that can often be alienating to them. These authors engage in reconstructions that float between despair and hope, taking readers to the brink, sometimes leaving them with a sense of what has been lost (Duras, Heinemann, Barker), and others providing hope for the future in the face of loss (Morrison, Danticat, Allison). By guiding readers through the intimacies of suffering and survival, these writers attempt to engage readers' empathy and critical faculties, and to build, through fiction, their capacity to contemplate complex human dilemmas and to enrich their own humanity in the process.

NOTES

ONE Representing Trauma: Issues, Contexts, Narrative Tools

1. For discussions of this sense of a crisis of memory, see Richard Terdiman's *Present Past*, Pierre Nora's "Between Memory and History," and Geoffrey Hartman's "Public Memory and Modern Experience."

2. A wide group of scholars and writers in recent decades have reevaluated memory and identity in terms of traumatic reactions to various forms of oppression. Some important early influences in theorizing trauma and its effects include Frantz Fanon, Ashis Nandy, and Albert Memmi, who discuss the psychological effects of oppression and subjugation. More recently, Cathy Caruth, Geoffrey Hartman, Dominick LaCapra, Saul Friedlander, Judith Herman, Lawrence Langer, Kalí Tal, Shoshana Felman, and Dori Laub have examined the psychological and narrative manifestations of trauma, locating these manifestations in a variety of narrative contexts: Holocaust testimonies and fiction, Freud's works, German historical interests, and poetry by survivors, including Paul Celan and W. D. Ehrhart. Fiction embracing all these issues and utilizing elements of trauma narratives includes works by Jerzy Kosinski, Toni Morrison, Marguerite Duras, Bessie Head (*A Question of Power*), Larry Heinemann, Pat Barker, Margaret Atwood (*Cat's Eye*), Dorothy Allison, Sapphire (*Push*), Jamaica Kincaid, and Edwidge Danticat.

3. See, for example, Langer's *Holocaust Testimonies*, Hartman's anthology *Holocaust Remembrance*, Felman and Laub's *Testimony*, Tal's *Worlds of Hurt*, and Claude Lanzmann's film *Shoah*.

4. Trauma narratives are a unique genre in the sense that they reveal insights similar to those of contemporary theoretical and cultural approaches to trauma. In addition, they create and combine narrative techniques that represent traumatic conflicts. Previous critical work has outlined the relationship between trauma and literary narrative and formal elements indicative of trauma. Geoffrey

Hartman describes how figurative language explores the gaps between experience and understanding common to trauma, how trauma studies address public concerns and common adaptive life processes, as well as issues of "reality, bodily integrity and identity" ("Traumatic" 547). Deborah Carlin articulates well how trauma narratives bear "the burden of representation, the dilemma of how to inscribe fragmentation, the discontinuity of memory, and the rupture of linear, narrative consciousness within a text that must achieve some kind of coherence in order to be persuasive, engender empathy, and effect belief" (478). In her evaluations of artistic representations of the Holocaust experience, Felman explains how artists can create forms that incorporate the disjunctures, symptoms, and radical perversions of normality in traumatic situations, particularly in her analysis of Paul Celan's poem "Death Fugue" (29–30). Laurence J. Kirmayer suggests the influence of dissociation on narrative as both revealing and concealing traumatic ruptures (181).

5. *Book Review Digest* lists dozens of titles in this period dealing with trauma in fiction, mystery, suspense, and even children's literary genres.

6. Popular culture is a mixed bag in the way it regards and depicts trauma. Some works clearly exploit fear and horror or offer stereotyped portrayals of crazed war veterans, while others give more careful consideration to its effects on individuals. Peter Weir's 1995 film *Fearless* stands out as an effective portrayal of trauma and recovery of air crash survivors. Also, the depiction of detective Bud White in *L. A. Confidential* (1997) presents a compelling example of childhood trauma (he witnesses his father murder his mother) repeated in adulthood in violence toward abusers and protectiveness toward women. Roger Schlobin sees a displacement of the realities of trauma onto objects of evil in mass culture horror films and fiction. For example, these genres employ oppressive and inescapable environments, victims' immobilization, helplessness, and violations that are frequently associated with the worst trauma-inducing circumstances (32, 36). Horror films may appeal to individuals' sense of wanting to be the perpetrator, to have power and license without punishment, in contrast to their own lack of power (43).

Working within the horror genre, Stephen King has recreated domestic abuse situations and portrayals of traumatized women with some degree of accuracy and sympathy in *Rose Madder* and *Delores Claiborne*. He demonstrates traumatic reactions through victims' thoughts and symptoms, including hypervigilance, dissociation through drug abuse, and repressed memories. The often broadly drawn, good or evil character portraits (abusers are inhuman, evil monsters) and the heavy emphasis on tension, horror, and plot resolution, however, take us away from the true conflicts and effects of abuse situations.

Novelist Pat Conroy explores traumatizing events and familial abuse in all of his novels. By his own admission, most have autobiographical components: his abusive and violent military father, his beautiful but sociopathically manipulative mother, the insanity and suicides of his siblings. These are serious issues to Conroy and have clearly shaped him as a person and as a writer. Two of his novels, *The Prince of Tides* and *Beach Music*, slowly unravel traumatic contexts in the interrelationships within the families and small towns he describes. Rather than fully exploring its causes and effects, trauma unfortunately at times becomes a plot payoff. In creating epic dimensions to his stories, traumas not only include familial abuse but at times outlandish scenarios. In *The Prince of Tides* the mother, sister, and one son are all raped by escaped convicts, who the remaining son finally dispatches by unleashing the family's pet tiger on them. Conroy is most successful when he demonstrates how trauma lingers on, shaping the characters' lives and forming the defensive survival tactics (bitterness, sense of humor, control, etc.) that characterize and compromise their adult relationships. This is a small sample of the many ways popular culture acknowledges trauma. As artists attempt to appeal to large audiences, one recognizes noticeable pressure toward sensationalized representations over more authentic ones.

7. *Cat's Eye* (1988) by Margaret Atwood represents the lingering effects of childhood trauma on the protagonist and narrator, Elaine. Ultimately, the conflict within Elaine between repression and reemergence of traumatic memories becomes the focus of the novel. This struggle is played out in her adult relationships, in her unconscious feelings, and in her art. Traumatic experience has helped shape Elaine's artistic vision and forms of expression. Her powerful visual sense has emerged from the defensive strategies she used as a girl to elude her abusive playmates. Atwood illustrates dimensions of trauma in a less extreme context than some of the other texts discussed here, but very importantly demonstrates how trauma is part of more normative situations.

8. Although the numbers have seen some improvement in recent years, worldwide, women and girls suffer disproportionately from poverty, violence, sexual assault, neglect, and illiteracy. See statistics on Web sites of UNICEF, the United Nations, and the U.S. Department of Justice (1994) (Web addresses listed in Works Cited).

9. "[Trauma] can represent not only a paranoid posture, with exaggerated defenses always anxiously in need of renewal, but also a defining stimulus for healthy engagement with identity themes and the future. In a paradoxical way the idea of trauma can function as an organizing or focusing tool for a creature [i.e., humans] that must constantly balance conflicting needs for stability and change, defense and creativity" (Farrell 19).

10. Significant examples of this are the "unspoken" subconscious monological and dialogical thoughts of Sethe, Denver, and Beloved articulated in the "unspeakable thoughts" section of *Beloved* (200–217), wherein the emotions of past and present merge and where traumatic obsessions and guilt and joy at reunion converge to bring the reader a fuller sense of the thoughts and feelings attributed to these characters, as well as the immediacy of the emotions that have lingered near the surface and have finally erupted.

11. Whether an individual will develop severe traumatic symptoms depends on a number of factors including age, personality traits, previous psychiatric disabilities, genetic predisposition, and available social supports. Symptom patterns are related to the individual's personal history and his or her "adaptive style," for example, how the individual has previously learned to interact with others or to cope with stress (Andreasen 1519). Those more likely to acquire posttraumatic stress disorder are single, divorced, widowed, or of low socioeconomic status. Most trauma cases are acute, not lasting more than six months, but chronic abuse, continued over time, inflicts debilitating long-term psychological damage,

particularly to children (Herman 117). Social class and education can also affect recovery outcome; better-educated individuals seem to adjust more easily (Green et al. 59–62). Abuse can further lower the perhaps already fragile self-esteem of a person of low socioeconomic status. An individual with high status in a community, however, may be motivated to recover quickly or to hide their situation from public view (McCann and Pearlman, *Psychological Trauma* 116).

12. Evidence of this as a common disorder was found in a survey of 1,245 American adolescents where 23 percent were victims of physical or sexual assault; of those, 20 percent developed PTSD (Van der Kolk and McFarlane 5). Children are especially at risk, either as victims or witnesses of domestic violence and murders. Nearly 40 percent of murders are the result of domestic violence; in Los Angeles 10 to 20 percent of homicides are witnessed by children (Everstine and Everstine 115).

13. Many inner-city children are exposed to violence and abuse regularly. A constant sense of threat and fear pervades neighborhoods where violence is frequent, unpredictable, and random (Bell and Jenkins 177). Children can be seriously damaged by witnessing or undergoing violence in social or familial environments, which can cause traumatic stress symptoms in children and dysfunctional behavior such as poor achievement in school, substance abuse, or acting out (Healy 114; Bell and Jenkins 175, 181).

14. A study by John P. Wilson, W. Ken Smith, and Suzanne K. Johnson comparing PTSD incurred from different types of events found that Vietnam veterans experienced the most severe depression and PTSD symptoms. Rape victims experienced the next highest levels (167). The study looked at elements such as degree of life threat, duration of trauma, potential for reoccurrence, degree of moral conflict in the situation and role of the person, and the proportion of the community affected by trauma (149–51). Victims are stigmatized by having experienced such life-threatening events and feel further stigmatized by talking about it; yet not speaking about it indicates defensive avoidance and can increase the probability of depression (169). In the 1970s political activism led many Vietnam and rape survivors to reevaluate and reject the social mores that put them in jeopardy. Men questioned their participation in a military hierarchy or system of domination (Tal 142–44). Women began to question their subordinate sexual role, discovering that typically feminine behavior can make them vulnerable to rape and other abuse (Herman 199).

15. Postwar studies of Vietnam veterans contributed significantly to knowledge of the workings of traumatic stress. They found that different kinds of war stress predicted the presence and severity of PTSD symptoms. Most researchers agree that combat experience is the primary contributing factor in evaluating the effects of war, but other aspects of war stress are also important, for example, atrocities, exposure to abusive violence, and the physical environment (Laufer et al. 81). Those who did not seek help about their war experience often acted it out in disastrous relationships or in self-destructive or self-numbing behavior. Subsequently, the Veterans Administration set up outreach centers; as of 1985 there were seven hundred such facilities (Heinemann, "Just Don't Fit" 62).

16. Some studies indicate that childhood sexual abuse happens to 10 to 30 percent of American girls (Waites 2; Herman and Harvey 4). A conservative estimate

of rape victims, an underreported crime, put their numbers above those of war veterans even in 1980, and the problem may be even larger than suspected (Kilpatrick et al. 116). Studies of psychiatric in-patients in the 1980s revealed that one-half of the women sampled had histories of sexual or physical abuse or both. It was also discovered that women were much more likely to be victims of such abuse than men and that many suffered long-term abuse, some throughout their lives (Waites 9).

17. See Erikson, Healy, Herman, Waites, Tal, Green et al., and Wilson et al. in *Trauma and Its Wake*, ed. Charles Figley.

18. Countertransference is defined as "the analyst's emotional involvement in the therapeutic interaction," which can have a therapeutic or counterproductive effect for the analyst or the client (Reber 170).

19. The recent controversies surrounding false memories, Cathy Caruth observes, make us encounter "the difficulty that many people have in believing memories that seem to them to be false simply because they do not appear in easily recognizable forms." Hence, she asserts, "the urgency of creating new ways of listening and recognizing the truth of memories that would, under traditional criteria, be considered to be false" (*Trauma* viii).

20. "One could not have predicted . . . the virtual explosion of critical interest in survivor discourse and in narratives of recovery precipitated not only by Herman and Caruth, but by theorists like Dori Laub, Shoshana Felman, Dominick LaCapra, Jennifer Freyd, Anne Hunsaker Hawkins, and Thomas Couser, to name only a few. Over the last decade, scriptotherapy has infiltrated the imagination of therapists, literary critics, mental health workers, and narratologists alike" (Henke xiii).

21. The critical, educational, and relative popular acceptance of many of these writers, preeminently Morrison, Duras, and Allison (whose works have been made into mainstream films), indicates a degree of public acceptance of these topics.

22. Greenberg and Mitchell list Winnicott's formulations of a child's developmental needs: "The child has built-in needs for: a holding environment; mirroring; the actualization of his omnipotence; the opportunity of object-usage; the toleration of the ambiguities of his transitional experience; the opportunity to console. The child's early objects are prepatterned according to the templates provided by the child's own developmental needs" (223).

TWO Subjugation, Nurturance, and Legacies of Trauma

1. For more detailed discussions by postcolonial critics read Frantz Fanon, Ashis Nandy, Albert Memmi, Octave Mannoni, Homi Bhabha, Stuart Hall, and Geraldine Moane. For specific discussions of trauma and oppression, also see Brown, Erikson, Herman, and Tal.

2. The traumatic effects of such devaluation on Pecola are discussed more fully in chapter 3.

3. Toni Morrison is but one of many African American writers who have responded to cultural impositions, acknowledging they have been internalized defensively at times for survival, but also sometimes for expediency. She explores the process of this absorption; whereas, before her Ralph Ellison's *Invisible Man*

explored the possibilities of awareness and resistance as his protagonist tries to overcome the "internalized oppression in which blacks surrendered their identity to the master culture of whites to win economic and social benefits" (Sandhu 46). Ellison's work focused on an emblematic character's growing consciousness of the forces working on black people in an existentialist mode, while Morrison's emphasis lies in the psychological consequences of cultural coercion and the need for collective healing.

4. Morrison's and Duras's examinations of the psychological damage created in oppressive social contexts runs consonant with trends of colonial and post-colonial fiction, particularly South African fiction, representing one of the last and arguably worst cases of colonial oppression. Stephen Clingman notes that madness is a common theme in colonial literature and that madness is situated in South African literature as a "product of social relations," deeply embedded in history and in shifting human relations (234). First, in Peter Abraham's *The Path of Thunder* (1948) madness and death are the prices of apartheid, which denies the bonds between black and white, even while the living proof of relations, the "coloureds," is evident. Also, in Doris Lessing's *The Grass is Singing* (1950) madness represents the colonizers' sense of alienation and fear in a foreign land. Unhinged by the perceived threat of their loss of control (i.e., the liberation of blacks), they base their rule on mastery and control out of which they create "fixities of identity and social hierarchy"; "colonial consciousness feels an overwhelming need to tame the foreign environment" (244, 249). Clingman's assessment of South African novels of the twentieth century attests to the connection between systems of domination and the psychopathological reactions (though varied) of all concerned; madness is the result of "unwarranted assertions of power . . . [and] unwarranted subservience to it" (246). In response to this literature, literary critics began to show how psychological theory can help to elucidate not merely the artistic depiction of colonized subjects but also the narrative techniques used in politically conscious fiction. Patrick Colm Hogan, for example, has used Lacan's notions of the socially imposed ego to explore the relations between cultural domination and madness in Bessie Head's *A Question of Power*.

5. For theoretical discussions, see Jessica Benjamin's *The Bonds of Love*, Christine Everingham's *Motherhood and Modernity*, and Nancy Chodorow's *Reproduction of Mothering*.

6. See Everingham 6, Benhabib 84–87, Calhoun 14–20, and G. Lloyd's "The Man of Reason."

7. See Memmi; White; Markus, Mullally and Kitayama; Barrett and McIntosh; and Everingham, among others.

8. Cross-cultural studies of mothering present the diverse ways in which cultures organize their societies to raise children and meet basic needs. Nancy Scheper-Hughes's study of mothers in a Brazilian shantytown "demonstrates the impact of the material environment on ideas relating to caregiving behavior" and undermines the biological and attachments models of mothering (qtd. in Everingham 12). Attachments between mother and child do not necessarily form in situations of extreme poverty, Scheper-Hughes found. "The weaker, more passive babies are not highly regarded and are selectively neglected by their poverty-stricken mothers. The community of mothers have developed an ideology that helps to le-

gitimate this neglect, through envisaging life as a power struggle between strong and weak. Passive, non-demanding infants are believed to lack a drive towards life, so that it is thought best that the weaker babies die young, 'without a prolonged and wasted struggle'" (12–13). Such studies "highlight the socially constructed nature of caregiving" and demonstrate that mothering practices "are contingent and therefore receptive to social change," Everingham argues (13). From an idealized perspective of motherhood we might judge these mothers as uncaring, but as Morrison's and Duras's de-idealized portrayals remind us, the exigencies of survival and destitution do not allow for the luxury of constant nurturing possible in better circumstances.

9. A mother's powerlessness can make her turn on her children or exert power to feel her own agency, as Morrison's portrayal of an abusive mother in *Tar Baby* demonstrates. On the surface Margaret Street would seem to have all the privileges of the world—a rich husband, beauty, a child she loves. We learn, however, that she traumatized her son with physical abuse when he was a small child and as an adult he rarely sees her. Her circumstances are revealed to be less than ideal once the surface of her life is penetrated. Her wealthy husband, Valerian, is much older than she, a tyrant and a recluse. She has escaped the poverty of her family with her beauty queen looks, but her life has been largely shaped by the plans and choices of others, particularly her husband's. Unfortunately, into her mothering—the one area where she is given some autonomy—she brings frustrations and desires to act out what seems to be a well-repressed aggression that expresses her impotence in the world. Valerian pays little attention to raising their son and is only marginally aware of the boy's traumatic symptoms. Margaret loves her son and regrets her cruel behavior as a young mother, expressing the wish that others would have guided or confronted her.

10. Though slowly improving, conditions of women worldwide as reported by the United Nations and UNICEF agencies still reveal that women and children suffer disproportionately from poverty, hunger, illiteracy, homelessness, abuse, and lack of social and economic influence. Statistics are available from the Web sites of the U.S. Government Census, UNICEF, the United Nations, the National Organization for Women (NOW), and the United States Department of Health and Human Services (Web addresses listed in Works Cited).

11. Holden-Kirwan notes that "in killing her own children Sethe insists upon her subjectivity" (424). However, as Elliot observes, subjectivity cannot be formed in slavery (185).

12. Bhabha interprets the murder of Sethe's child as a repetition of the profusion of black infant deaths in the years 1882–95 (*Location* 11).

13. Her father drove a cab and her mother worked in a textile factory to raise money to bring Edwidge to the U.S. when she was twelve (Wucker 41).

14. Translates as "bogeyman," connoting a haunting, terrorizing presence.

15. This mother plays a central or important role in Duras's novels *The Sea Wall, The Lover, The North China Lover, The Vice-Consul*, and in her dramas *L'Eden Cinéma*, and *Whole Days in the Trees*. Many of the other mothers Duras portrays are uninvolved or passive (as the woman in *Moderato Cantibile* or Lol in *The Ravishing of Lol V. Stein*) or are traumatized children themselves (as Lol in *L'Amour*, the beggar in both *The Vice-Consul* and *The Sea Wall*) and are ineffec-

tual or unintentionally murderous mothers. See discussion of the beggar in chapter 3.

THREE The Traumatized Child as Outcast in Duras and Morrison

1. For example, Ashis Nandy drew attention to the way the relationship between the colonizer and the colonized was constructed as one of "civilizing" parent/"primitive" child (34), just as Frantz Fanon demonstrated the way that racist attitudes could be internalized and could transcend any obvious issue of skin color (*Black Skin* 162), and as Albert Memmi examined the self-loathing emerging from conditions of oppression—"injustice, insults, humiliation and insecurity" (*Colonizer* 16, 19–20). Similarly, Holocaust scholar Lawrence Langer and therapist Dori Laub note that survivor memories of the concentration camps are so powerful and immediate decades later that they destroy the individual's sense of agency and often preclude retreat to a safer present. Psychologist Yael Danieli also found that Holocaust survivors transfer their own traumatic reactions, such as silence, fear, and avoidance, onto other family members.

2. Carol Hofmann says of Anne Marie Stretter that she "absorbs, deflects, and focuses the energy and needs of others" (135) and that she "absorbs others' pain, facilitates understanding and . . . becomes the process of forgetting itself" (136).

3. Before Fanon, W. E. B. Dubois spoke of a double consciousness affecting African American identities and participation in American society in *The Souls of Blackfolk* (1903). He contended that denigrating perspectives held by a predominantly white U.S. culture created a divided and devalued sense of self in African Americans.

4. The title "Woman of the Ganges" gives us an intertextual link between the beggar and Lol, because the beggar often swam in the Ganges and the woman in *L'Amour* seems clearly to be Lol from textual details including her wanderings, location, and her relationship to the two male characters.

5. There is a similar linkage in her screenplay *Hiroshima Mon Amour*, where a French woman's traumatic loss of her German soldier lover during World War II can only be revealed within her relationship to a Japanese lover from Hiroshima years later.

6. As illustrated in debates over skin color from Malcolm X to the films of Spike Lee (most particularly *Schooldaze* and *Jungle Fever*) as well as in the recent book about continued conflicts over perceptions of skin color in the African American community, *The Color Complex.*

7. Panivong Norindr also notes that Kristeva engages in a kind of interpretation that "evacuates history and ignores the important ways the colonial situation and the specificity of historical context figure in her [Duras's] work" (53). See also Cerasi and Holmlund, both of whom discuss the implicitly political, historical, and socially conscious nature of much of Duras's work.

FOUR "A Loved Version of Your Life": Healing and the Provisional Self

1. My inspirations for my thoughts on narcissism came out of the 1999 NEH Summer Seminar on Object Relations Theory, in particular, formulations on nar-

cissism by Melanie Klein and Joan Riviere. Klein emphasizes the importance of how the individual internalizes the environment in infancy by introjecting objects—that is, people, traits, things—into the self, thereby beginning the processes of socialization and identity formation. Both theorists suggest that self-love is built upon object relations in two important ways: (1) that the infant begins to know the world and feel comfortable in it by molding it to its own fantasies (Hinshelwood 355), and (2) that narcissism is built on the introjection of others (their traits, etc.) into the self (Riviere 138). Considering trauma narratives, these concepts led me to think of regressions under trauma and to reconsider how characters form a sense of self in traumatic situations, sometimes without guiding object relations. These characters either invent a self-love to compensate for lack of nurturance or build on residues of nurturance still left to them.

2. Domestic abuse has been described by survivors as a totalitarian situation, analogous to colonization. "Survivors describe a characteristic pattern of totalitarian control, enforced by means of violence and death threats, capricious enforcement of petty rules, intermittent rewards, and destruction of all competing relationships through isolation, secrecy, and betrayal. Even more than adults, children who develop in this climate of domination develop pathological attachments to those who abuse and neglect them, attachments that they will strive to maintain even at the sacrifice of their own welfare, their own reality, or their lives" (Herman 98).

3. Leigh Gilmore thinks this text is one more variation on Kincaid's frequent representation of daughters able to individuate only through separation from the mother; in this case, the mother is obliterated (115). This process of separation and individuation is traumatic, however (103).

4. See Kincaid's *A Small Place, Lucy,* and *Annie John* and discussions of Kincaid's views in Covi, Byerman, Niesen de Abruna, and Simmons.

5. Kincaid has maintained her persistent sense of injustice about women being sacrificed, because her own mother made her quit school despite the fact she was a brilliant student to support her family (Gilmore 116–17). Niesen de Abruna also discusses how Kincaid connected her mother with cultural imperialism and felt as though her mother was living in history and could not really nurture one of her own (181).

6. She will repeat such self-assertive substitutions, recapturing her identity with every loss or conflict as in this dream fantasy: "I walked through my inheritance, an island of villages and rivers and mountains and people who began and ended with murder and theft and not very much love. I claimed it in a dream. Exhausted from the agony of expelling from my body a child I could not love and so did not want, I dreamed of all the things that were mine" (*Autobiography* 89).

7. Keith Byerman articulates these views thus: "Independence produced no real changes in the dominant order. The silencing of the people has continued, even though the leaders are now from among them. Wealth and power are in the hands of a very few, all of whom, in Kincaid's view, are corrupt and indifferent to the welfare of the people" (93).

8. Kincaid's rendition of Xuela's traumatic memory and sense of the proximate void bears similar images and processes. See especially the fantasy section

(96–100) and Xuela's memories at the end of the novel (205–28), which resemble memories described by Holocaust survivor Heda Kovaly in *The Victors and the Vanquished:*

> My memories are not simple recollections. They are a return to the bottom of an abyss; I have to gather up the shattered bones that have lain still for so long, climb back over the crags, and tumble in once more. Only this time I have to do it deliberately, in slow motion, noticing and examining each wound, each bruise on the way, most of all the ones of which I was least conscious in my first headlong fall. But I know I have to do it. My future stands aside, waiting until I find meaning in all that has been. I feel as if I had to overcome some almost physical obstacle, and feel drained, breathless from the effort. (qtd. in Langer 127)

9. In discussing the presentation of Claude Lanzmann's *Shoah*, a documentary film about Holocaust memories, Shoshana Felman notes the importance of experiencing or narrating traumatic experience from both inside and outside the event as inherent to the split positioning of trauma victims who on some level find their experience either unbelievable or overwhelmingly painful, but also helpful to "break the frame" enclosing traumatic experience from understanding. See especially pp. 227–53 of *Testimony*.

10. Dorothy Allison describes how she escaped involvement in the extremities of heterosexual love that were so detrimental to the women she knew, perhaps because of her abuse and because she will eventually realize she is a lesbian:

> Love was something I would not have to worry about—the whole mystery of love, heartbreak songs, and family legends. Women who pined, men who went mad, people who forgot who they were and shamed themselves with need, wanting only to be loved by the one they loved. Love was a mystery. Love was a calamity. Love was a curse that had somehow skipped me, which was no doubt why I was so good at multiple-choice tests and memorizing poetry. Sex was the country I had been dragged into as an unwilling girl—sex, and the madness of the body. For all that it could terrify and confuse me, sex was something I had assimilated. Sex was a game or a weapon or an addiction. Sex was familiar. But love—love was another country. (*Two or Three Things* 55)

11. Many victims of incest wish for or establish relationships with surrogate mothers, feeling their own were unable to unwilling to help them (Herman and Hirschman 103–4).

12. Meiselman reports that the increase in divorces and stepfathers over the last fifty years has heightened risk of intrafamilial sexual abuse of girls (16–17).

FIVE Remembering History through the Body

1. The traumatic events of the Holocaust and the testimony and literature that have followed have greatly informed these contemporary trauma narratives, my readings of them, and how we might consider the difficulties of defining, recovering, and transmitting memory. The Holocaust, with its tremendous individual and community losses, became a focal point for investigating traumatic history

and forgetting. Its aftermath has raised important questions about how to retrieve horrific, and therefore repressed events, and the unbelievability and incomprehensibility of traumatic experience.

The alien nature of this experience has provoked new approaches to history, testimony, and ways of representation to help interpret and reconfigure traces of evidence and memory. Similar inquiries have followed concerning other ethnic, colonized, and vulnerable groups, and many of the texts here pursue these issues. See Langer, Tal, Young, and Vickroy's "*Beloved* and *Shoah.*"

2. Helen Lock places Morrison in a larger literary movement, establishing that "many recent African-American written narratives have sought to propose an alternative approach to the past, by foregrounding the functioning of oral memory both thematically and structurally: not to recall a fixed original or a singular truth, but to reconstruct and regenerate (inter)subjectively many kinds of truth. This approach ultimately enables participation in, as well as preservation of, the past, and provides the potential for its transformation and the exorcism of its pain" (111).

3. Gurleen Grewal discusses the impact of slave narratives on *Beloved* in her book *Circles of Sorrow, Lines of Struggle; The Novels of Toni Morrison*, 99–103.

4. See Barbara Christian's discussion on being owned and the relation between freedom and ownership that is central to American culture and to Morrison's portrayal of Sethe, which she alters from Margaret Garner's story, freeing her so that she can confront her actions and pursue the moral dilemmas slavery forces on slave mothers (39, 41). Garner herself was never freed, and according to conflicting accounts, either jumped off a boat with her baby while being sent back to slavery, or else died of typhoid fever. See discussions in Wolff (427–34) and Rushdy (574).

5. Other recent fictional works on slavery include Margaret Walker's *Jubilee* (1966), Ernest Gaines's *The Autobiography of Miss Jane Pittman* (1971), Gayl Jones's *Corregidora* (1975), Alex Haley's *Roots* (1976), Ishmael Reed's *Flight to Canada* (1976), Barbara Chase-Riboud's *Sally Hemings* (1979), Octavia Butler's *Kindred* (1979), David Bradley's *The Chaneysville Incident* (1981), Sherley Anne Williams's *Dessa Rose* (1986), Charles Johnson's *Middle Passage* (1990), Jewelle Gomez's *The Gilda Stories* (1991), J. California Cooper's *Family* (1991), Maryse Conde's *Tituba: Black Witch of Salem* (1992), Caryl Phillips's *Cambridge* (1992), and Alice Randall's controversial tale *The Wind Done Gone* (2001).

6. "During, before and after the War he had seen Negroes so stunned, or hungry, or tired or bereft it was a wonder they recalled or said anything. Who, like him, had hidden in caves and fought owls for food; who, like him, stole from pigs; who, like him, slept in trees in the day and walked by night; who, like him, had buried themselves in slop and jumped in wells to avoid regulators, raiders, paterollers, veterans, hill men, posses and merrymakers. . . . [A Negro man he met said he once] saw a witless coloredwoman jailed and hanged for stealing ducks she believed were her own babies" (66).

7. *Beloved* echoes the horrors reflected in Olaudah Equiano's account of his own passage from Africa—the crowding, filth, stench, and dehumanization (33–36).

8. Iyunolu Osagie posits that textual evidence offers many possibilities and doubts as to Beloved's identity. Her portrayal supports, at least partially, that she could be the Devil child of African fable, an extension of Sethe's desires, a ghost returned, or another young woman who is isolated and abused by white men as Ella was.

9. Marianne Hirsch was the first to make the important connection between milk—"a hot thing"—and the strong links between mothers and daughters in this text. She also identifies this as blood (105).

10. Mary Puniccia Carden argues that *Beloved* has two endings that makes us hold competing notions of history together: 1) the hopeful one, where Sethe may have a future with Paul D, and 2) a less optimistic and unknown one, as Beloved can really find no resolution to her losses and faces an uncertain future with her unborn child (423).

11. See Anne Whitehead's discussion of the influence of Rivers's theories on Barker in "Open to Suggestion" (679–81).

12. Rivers believed

that it was prolonged strain, immobility and helplessness that did the damage, and not the sudden shocks or bizarre horrors that the patients themselves were inclined to point to as the explanation for their condition. That would help to account for the greater prevalence of anxiety neuroses and hysterical disorders in women in peacetime, since their relatively more confined lives gave them fewer opportunities of reacting to stress in active and constructive ways. Any explanation of war neurosis must account for the fact that this apparently intensely masculine life of war and danger and hardship produced in men the same disorders that women suffered from in peace. (*Regeneration* 222)

13. A fugue state is a severe dissociative disability where a person suddenly leaves home, assumes a new identity, has no recollection of his or her earlier life, and has rigorously repressed events occurring in the fugue state. It is also called dissociative psychogenic fugue (Reber 301).

14. Martin Loschnigg questions whether Barker's overreliance on past literary accounts of war (e.g., Sassoon's and Owen's) might cause her to perpetuate myths about World War I and its veterans. Noting that her narrative style seeks coherency rather than discontinuities typical of trauma, and reinforcing a mythology about shell-shock victims as feminized, he questions how effectively she fulfills her responsibility of being true to the past (227). I would argue that she sees her primary responsibility as helping contemporary readers to understand the past. By using trauma paradigms from past and present and by linking male and female trauma experience, she helps her readers to better access soldiers' experience and to recognize trauma as collective.

15. Heinemann has said of his tour:

The first time I went to Vietnam was as a draftee, and I submitted to conscription with what can only be described as soul-deadening dread. I was twenty-three years old, and did not want to be there. We were treated like meat and were expected to behave like meat. I did not like it there and took *that* out on the Vietnamese. I never shot anyone who didn't deserve to be shot (of that I am sure; I've sat up many a long night to reason *that* out). I did my tour as best I could, never mind that the war overwhelmed me. We rode roughshod over the countryside, delighting in the destruction we caused. I came home absolutely determined to forget that place and put the war behind me, never mind that *that* was not possible and did not happen. ("Syndromes" 72, italics in original)

Heinemann also benefited from the fact that he had good superior officers who did not allow atrocities in their unit.

16. "[T]he thousands of GIs with "bad-paper" discharges—more often than not shoved at them out of sheer spite for their "attitude"—are barred by law from obtaining treatment of any kind from the Veterans Administration, even if they suffer service-connected health problems: wounds received in active combat, Agent Orange exposure, delayed stress, and the like" ("Just Don't Fit" 62).

17. The words from an actual veteran that Heinemann gives to his character ("Just Don't Fit").

18. Such as the elderly African American woman who remembers her own devastated son coming home from Korea "who was ever after morose and skittish . . . who had ever since lapsed into a deep and permanent melancholy" (42).

19. Much Vietnam war fiction and poetry includes ghosts, the dead who are still very much part of the lives of survivors, says Tal, adding Holocaust survivor Terrence Des Pres's assertion that "It is not an exaggeration, nor merely a metaphor, to say that the survivor's identity includes the dead" (qtd. in Tal 87).

20. Heinemann emphasizes sexual healing upon veterans' return home: "And make no mistake: if you have any healthy impulses left at all, you want to find a woman and take her to bed. . . . You want to feel good in your body and re-establish those powerful human feelings" ("Just Don't Fit" 60).

21. From politicians to horror films, attempts have been made to reclaim masculine power by re-representing Vietnam veterans, engaging in the POW/MIA obsession, often taking the form of bizarre mythologizing such as the *Rambo* series of films. See discussions in Tal, Jeffords, and Howell.

WORKS CITED

Agger, Inger, and Soren Buus Jensen. "Testimony as Ritual and Evidence in Psycho-therapy for Political Refugees." *Journal of Traumatic Stress* 3.1 (1990): 116.

Allen, Douglas. "Social Constructions of Self: Some Asian, Marxist and Feminist Critiques of Dominant Western Views of Self." *Culture and Self: Philosophical and Religious Perspectives, East and West.* Ed. Douglas Allen. New York: Westview, 1997. 3–26.

Allison, Dorothy. *Bastard out of Carolina.* New York: Penguin, 1992.

———. "Believing in Literature." *Skin: Talking about Sex, Class and Literature.* Ithaca, NY: Firebrand, 1994.

———. Interview by Carolyn E. Megan. *Kenyon Review* 16 (fall 1994): 71–83.

———. "Patron Saint of Battered Women Writes, Forgives." Interview by Elisabeth Sherwin. UC Davis Web site, http://www.dcn.davis.ca.us/~gizmo/1998/dorothy.html, accessed June 11, 2000.

———. *Trash.* Ithaca, NY: Firebrand, 1988.

———. *Two or Three Things I Know for Sure.* New York: Plume-Penguin, 1996.

Andreasen, Nancy C. "Posttraumatic Stress Disorder." *Comprehensive Textbook of Psychiatry III.* Ed. Harold I. Kaplan, Alfred M. Freedman, and Benjamin J. Sadock, Vol. 2., 3rd ed. Baltimore: Williams and Wilkins, 1980.

Anzaldua, Gloria. *Borderlands.* San Francisco: Spinsters, 1987.

Armel, Aliette. *Marguerite Duras et l'autobiographie.* Paris: Le Castor Astral, 1990.

Atwood, Margaret. *Cat's Eye.* New York: Doubleday, 1988.

Avni, Ora. "Narrative Subject, Historic Subject: *Shoah* and *La Place de l'Etoile.*" *Poetics Today* 12.33 (1991): 495–516.

Awkward, Michael. "'The Evil of Fulfillment': Scapegoating and Narration in *The Bluest Eye.*" Gates and Appiah 175–209.

Bakhtin, Mikhail. *The Dialogic Imagination: Four Essays by Mikhail Bakhtin.* Trans. Caryl Emerson and Michael Holquist. Austin: U of Texas P, 1981.

Barker, Pat. *The Eye in the Door.* New York: Penguin, 1993.

———. *The Ghost Road.* New York: Penguin, 1995.

———. Interview by Terry Gross. *Fresh Air.* July 13, 1999.

———. Interview by Donna Perry. *Backtalk: Women Writers Speak Out.* New Brunswick, NJ: Rutgers UP, 1993. 43–61.

———. *Regeneration.* New York: Penguin, 1991.

Barrett, Michèle, and Mary McIntosh. *The Anti-Social Family.* London: Verso, 1982.

Bassin, Donna, Margaret Honey, and Meryle Mahrer Kaplan, eds. *Representations of Motherhood.* New Haven: Yale UP, 1994.

Bell, Carl C., and Esther J. Jenkins. "Traumatic Stress and Children." *Journal of Health Care for the Poor and Underserved* 2.1 (1991): 175–85.

Benhabib, Seyla. "The Generalized and the Concrete Other." Benhabib and Cornell 77–95.

Benhabib, Seyla, and Drucilla Cornell, eds. *Feminism as Critique: On the Politics of Gender.* Minneapolis: U of Minnesota P, 1987.

Benjamin, Jessica. *The Bonds of Love: Psychoanalysis, Feminism, and the Problem of Domination.* New York: Pantheon, 1988.

———. "The End of Internalization: Adorno's Social Psychology." *Telos* 32 (1977): 42–64.

———. "The Omnipotent Mother: A Psychoanalytic Study of Fantasy and Reality." Bassin et al. 129–46.

Berg, Rick, and John Carlos Rowe. "Introduction: The Vietnam War and American Memory." Rowe and Berg 1–17.

Beverley, John. "The Margin at the Center: On *Testimonio* (Testimonial Narrative)." Smith and Watson 91–111.

Bhabha, Homi K. "Difference, Discrimination, and the Discourse of Colonialism." *The Politics of Theory.* Ed. Francis Barker, et al. *Proceedings, Essex Sociology of Literature Conference.* Colchester, Eng.: U of Essex, 1983. 194–211.

———. *The Location of Culture.* New York: Routledge, 1994.

———. "Remembering Fanon: Self, Psyche and the Colonial Condition." Williams and Chrisman 112–23.

Blassingame, John W. *The Slave Community: Plantation Life in the Antebellum South.* New York: Oxford UP, 1972.

———. "Using the Testimony of Ex-Slaves: Approaches and Problems." Davis and Gates 78–98.

Borgomano, Madeleine. "L'histoire de la mendiante indienne." *Poetique* 48 (1981): 479–94.

Bouson, J. Brooks. *Quiet as It's Kept: Shame, Trauma and Race in the Novels of Toni Morrison.* Albany: State U of New York P, 2000.

Brazelton, T. Berry, B. Koslowski, and Mary Main. "The Origins of Reciprocity: The Early Mother-Infant Interaction." Lewis and Rosenblum 49–76.

Brenkman, John. *Culture and Domination.* Ithaca, NY: Cornell UP, 1987.

Brown, Laura S. "Not Outside the Range: One Feminist Perspective on Psychic Trauma." *American Imago* 48.1 (1991): 119–34.

Burgess, A. W., and L. L. Holmstrom. "Rape Trauma Syndrome." *American Journal of Psychiatry* 131 (1974): 981–86.

Byerman, Keith E. "Anger in *A Small Place:* Jamaica Kincaid's Cultural Critique of Antigua." *College Literature* 22.1 (Feb. 1995): 91–102.

Calhoun, Craig, ed. *Social Theory and the Politics of Identity.* Oxford, UK: Blackwell, 1994. 9–36.

Carden, Mary Paniccia. "Models of Memory and Romance: The Dual Endings of Toni Morrison's *Beloved.*" *Twentieth Century Literature* 45.4 (winter 1999): 401–27.

Carson, Sharon. "Pat Barker." *British Writers Supplement IV.* Ed. George Stade and Carol Howard. New York: Scribner's, 1997. 45–63.

Caruth, Cathy. "Introduction: Psychoanalysis, Culture, and Trauma." Spec. issue of *American Imago* 48.1 (1991): 1–12.

———. "Introduction: Psychoanalysis, Culture, and Trauma II." Spec. issue of *American Imago* 48.4 (1991): 417–23.

———. *Trauma: Explorations in Memory.* Baltimore: Johns Hopkins UP, 1995.

———. *Unclaimed Experience: Trauma, Narrative, and History.* Baltimore: Johns Hopkins UP, 1996.

Cascardi, Anthony J. *The Subject of Modernity.* New York: Cambridge UP, 1992.

Cerasi, Claire. *Marguerite Duras, de Lahore à Auschwitz.* Paris: Champion, 1993.

Charles, Carolle. "Gender and Politics in Contemporary Haiti: The Duvalierist State, Transnationalism, and the Emergence of a New Feminism (1980–1990)." *Feminist Studies* 21.1 (spring 1995): 135–64.

Cheek, Jonathan M., and Robert Hogan. "Self-Concepts, Self-Presentations, and Moral Judgments." *Psychological Perspectives of the Self.* Ed. Jerry Suls. Vol. 2. Hillsdale, NJ: Erlbaum, 1983. 249–73.

Chester, Suzanne. "Writing the Subject: Exoticism/Eroticism in Marguerite Duras's *The Lover* and *The Sea Wall.*" Smith and Watson 436–53.

Chodorow, Nancy. *The Reproduction of Mothering: Psychoanalysis and the Sociology of Gender.* Berkeley: U of California P, 1978.

Chodorow, Nancy, and Susan Contratto. "The Fantasy of the Perfect Mother." *Rethinking the Family: Some Feminist Questions.* Ed. Barrie Thorne and Marilyn Yalom. Boston: Northeastern UP, 1992. 191–214.

Christian, Barbara. "Beloved, She's Ours." *Narrative* 5.1 (Jan. 1997): 36–49.

Clingman, Stephen. "Beyond the Limit: The Social Relations of Madness in South African Fiction." *The Bounds of Race: Perspectives on Hegemony and Resistance.* Ed. Dominick LaCapra. Ithaca, NY: Cornell UP, 1991. 231–54.

Coetzee, Marilyn Shevin, and Frans Coetzee. *World War I and European Society: A Sourcebook.* Lexington, MA: Heath, 1995.

Collins, Patricia Hill. "Shifting the Center: Race, Class, and Feminist Theorizing about Motherhood." Bassin et al. 56–74.

Conroy, Pat. *Beach Music.* New York: Bantam, 1996.

———. *The Prince of Tides.* New York: Bantam, 1987.

Covi, Giovanna. "Jamaica Kincaid's Primatic Self and the Decolonialisation of Language and Thought." *Framing the Word: Gender and Genre in Caribbean Women's Writing.* Ed. Joan Anim-Addo. London: Whiting, 1996. 37–67.

Criso, Rachael. *"Elle est une autre:* The Duplicity of Self in *L'Amant." In Language and in Love Marguerite Duras: The Unspeakable; Essays for Marguerite Duras.* Ed. Mechthild Cranston. Potomac, MD: Scripta Humanistica, 1992. 37–51.

Cutter, Martha J. "The Story Must Go On and On: The Fantastic, Narration, and Intertextuality in Toni Morrison's *Beloved* and *Jazz." African American Review* 34.1 (spring 2000): 61–75.

Cvetkovich, Ann. "Sexual Trauma/Queer Memory." *GLQ: A Journal of Lesbian and Gay Studies* 2.4 (1995): 351–77.

Danieli, Yael. "The Treatment and Prevention of Long-term Effects and Intergenerational Transmission of Victimization: A Lesson from Holocaust Survivors and Their Children." Figley 295–313.

Danticat, Edwidge. *Breath, Eyes, Memory.* New York: Soho, 1994.

———. "A Conversation with Edwidge Danticat." Interview by Eleanor Wachtel. *Brick* 65–66 (fall 2000): 106–19.

———. "The Voice of the Storytellers." Interview by Zoe Anglesey. *Multicultural Review* 7:3 (Sept. 1998): 36–39.

Darling, Marsha. "In the Realm of Responsibility: A Conversation with Toni Morrison." *Women's Review of Books* (Mar. 1988): 5–6.

Davies, Carole Boyce. "Mother Right/Write Revisited: *Beloved* and *Dessa Rose* and the Construction of Motherhood in Black Women's Fiction," *Narrating Mothers: Theorizing Maternal Subjectivities.* Ed. Brenda O. Daly and Maureen T. Reddy. Knoxville: U of Tennessee, 1991. 44–57.

Davis, Charles T., and Henry Louis Gates Jr., eds. *The Slave's Narrative.* Oxford: Oxford UP, 1985.

Davis, Cynthia A. "Self, Society, and Myth in Toni Morrison's Fiction." *Contemporary Literature* 33.3 (1982): 323–42.

Delbo, Charlotte. *Auschwitz and After.* Trans. Rosette C. Lamont. New Haven: Yale UP, 1995.

———. *Days and Memory.* Trans. Rosette Lamont. Marlboro, VT: Marlboro, 1990.

DeBattista, Maria. "The Clandestine Fictions of Marguerite Duras." *Breaking the Sequence: Women's Experimental Fiction.* Ed. Ellen G. Friedman and Miriam Fuchs. Princeton: Princeton UP, 1989. 284–97.

Dinnerstein, Dorothy. *The Mermaid and the Minotaur: Sexual Arrangements and Human Malaise.* New York: Harper, 1976.

DuBois, W. E. B. *The Souls of Blackfolk.* New York: Fawcett, 1968.

Duras, Marguerite. *L'Eden Cinéma.* Paris: Actes Sud-Papiers, 1988.

———. *The Lover.* Trans. Barbara Bray. New York: Pantheon, 1985.

———. "Mothers." *Marguerite Duras.* San Francisco: City Lights, 1987.

———. *The North China Lover.* Trans. Leigh Hafrey. New York: New Press, 1992.

———. *Practicalities: Marguerite Duras Speaks to Jérôme Beaujour.* Trans. Barbara Bray. New York: Grove Weidenfeld, 1987.

———. *The Ravishing of Lol V. Stein.* Trans. Richard Seaver. New York: Grove, 1966.

———. *The Sea Wall.* Trans. Herma Briffault. New York: Harper, 1986.

———. *The Vice-Consul.* Trans. Eileen Ellenbogen. New York: Pantheon, 1968.

Duras, Marguerite, and Michelle Porte. *Les Lieux de Marguerite Duras.* Paris: Éditions de Minuit, 1977.

"Edwidge Danticat." *Contemporary Authors Online.* July 19, 1999. http://www.galenet.com/servlet/GLD/hit...taType&n=10&1=d&NA=danticat%2C+Edwidge.

Elliott, Mary Jane Suero. "Postcolonial Experience in a Domestic Context: Commodified Subjectivity in Toni Morrison's *Beloved.*" *MELUS* (fall-winter 2000): 181–202.

Equiano, Olaudah. "The Interesting Narrative of the Life of Olaudah Equiano." *The Classic Slave Narratives.* Ed. Henry Louis Gates Jr. New York: New American Library, 1987. 1–182.

Erikson, Kai. "Notes on Trauma and Community." *American Imago* 48.4 (1991): 455–71.

Everingham, Christine. *Motherhood and Modernity: An Investigation into the Rational Dimension of Mothering.* Buckingham, Eng.: Open UP, 1994.

Everstine, Diana Sullivan, and Louis Everstine. *The Trauma Response: Treatment for Emotional Injury.* New York: Norton, 1993.

Fanon, Frantz. *Black Skin, White Masks.* Trans. Charles Lam Markmann. New York: Grove, 1967.

———. *The Wretched of the Earth.* Trans. Constance Farrington. Harmondsworth, UK: Penguin, 1967.

Farrell, Kirby. *Post-Traumatic Culture: Injury and Interpretation in the Nineties.* Baltimore: Johns Hopkins UP, 1998.

Felman, Shoshana. "Film as Witness: Claude Lanzmann's *Shoah.*" Hartman, *Holocaust* 90–103.

Felman, Shoshana, and Dori Laub. *Testimony: Crises of Witnessing in Literature, Psychoanalysis, and History.* New York: Routledge, 1991.

Figley, Charles, ed. *Trauma and Its Wake. Brunner/Mazel Psychosocial Stress* No. 4, New York: Brunner Mazel, 1985.

Fivush, Robyn, and Janine Buckner. "The Self as Socially Constructed: A Commentary." Neisser and Jopling 176–81.

Fox-Genovese, Elizabeth. *Within the Plantation Household: Black and White Women of the Old South.* Chapel Hill: U of North Carolina P, 1988.

Fraser, Nancy. "What's Critical about Critical Theory." Benhabib and Cornell 31–56.

Freyd, Jennifer J. *Betrayal Trauma: The Logic of Forgetting Child Abuse.* Cambridge: Harvard UP, 1996.

Friedlander, Saul. "Trauma, Transference, and 'Working Through' in Writing the History of the *Shoah.*" *History and Memory* 4 (1992): 39–59.

Gaines, Atwood D. "Trauma: Cross-Cultural Issues." *Advanced Psychosomatic Medicine* 16: 1–16.

Garland, Caroline, ed. *Understanding Trauma: A Psychoanalytical Approach.* London: Duckworth, 1999.

Gary, Lawrence E. "Poverty, Stress, and Mental Health." *Ethnicity and Health, Ethnicity and Public Policy Series.* Vol. 7. Ed. Winston A. Van Horne. The University of Wisconsin System Institute on Race and Ethnicity. Madison, WI: Board of Regents University of Wisconsin System, 1988.

Gates, Henry Louis, and K. A. Appiah, eds. *Toni Morrison: Critical Perspectives Past and Present.* New York: Amistad, 1993.

Gibson, Donald B. "Text and Countertext in Toni Morrison's *The Bluest Eye.*" *LIT: Literature Interpretation Theory* 1 (1989): 19–32.

Gilmore, Leigh. *The Limits of Autobiography: Trauma and Testimony.* Ithaca, NY: Cornell UP, 2001.

Grant, Jacques. "Entretien avec Marguerite Duras." *Cinema 75* 200, 102–16.

Green, Bonnie L., John P. Wilson, and Jacob D. Lindy. "Conceptualizing Post-traumatic Stress Disorder: A Psychosocial Framework." Figley 53–69.

Greenberg, Jay R., and Stephen A. Mitchell. *Object Relations in Psychoanalytic Theory.* Cambridge, MA: Harvard UP, 1983.

Grewal, Gurleen. *Circles of Sorrow, Lines of Struggle: The Novels of Toni Morrison.* Baton Rouge: Louisiana State UP, 1998.

———. "Poetics of Loss and Recovery in Joy Kogawa's *Obasan* and Toni Morrison's *Beloved.*" *Memory and Cultural Politics.* Ed. Amritjit Singh. Boston: Northeastern UP, 1996. 140–74.

Grubrich-Simitis, Ilse. "From Concretism to Metaphor: Thoughts on Some Theoretical and Technical Aspects of the Psychoanalytic Work with Children of Holocaust Survivors." *The Psycho-analytic Study of the Child.* Vol. 39. New Haven: Yale UP, 1984. 301–19.

Gwin, Minrose. "Nonfelicitous Space and Survivor Discourse." *Haunted Bodies: Gender and Southern Texts.* Ed. Anne Goodwyn Jones and Susan V. Donaldson. Charlottesville: UP of Virginia, 1997. 416–40.

Hall, Stuart. "Cultural Identity and Diaspora." Williams and Chrisman 392–403.

Harding, Wendy, and Jacky Martin. *A World of Difference: An Inter-Cultural Study of Toni Morrison's Novels.* Westport, CT: Greenwood, 1994.

Hargreaves, Alex G. *The Colonial Experience in French Fiction: A Study of Pierre Loti, Ernest Psichari, and Pierre Mille.* London: MacMillan, 1981.

Harris, Greg. "Compulsory Masculinity, Britain, and the Great War: The Literary-Historical Work of Pat Barker." *Critique* 39.4 (summer 1998): 290–304.

Hartman, Geoffrey H. "On Traumatic Knowledge and Literary Studies." *New Literary History* 26 (1995): 537–63.

———. "Public Memory and Modern Experience." *Yale Journal of Criticism* 6.2 (1992): 239–47.

———, ed. *Holocaust Remembrance: The Shapes of Memory.* Oxford: Blackwell, 1994.

Healy, David. *Images of Trauma: From Hysteria to Posttraumatic Stress Disorder.* London: Faber, 1993.

Heffernan, Teresa. "*Beloved* and the Problem of Mourning." *Studies in the Novel* 30.4 (winter 1998): 558–73.

Heinemann, Larry. "Autobiography." *Contemporary Authors Autobiography Series.* Ed. Joyce Nakamura. 21 (1995): 75–99.

———. Interview. *Contemporary Authors: New Revision Series.* Ed. James G. Lesniak, 31 (1990): 188–92.

————. "Just Don't Fit: Stalking the Elusive 'Tripwire' Veteran." *Harpers* April 1985: 55–63.

————. *Paco's Story.* New York: Penguin, 1986.

————. "Syndromes," *Harpers* July 1991: 68–76.

Henderson, Mae G. "Toni Morrison's *Beloved:* Re-Membering the Body as Historical Text." *Comparative American Identitites: Race, Sex, and Nationality in the Modern Text.* Ed. Hortense J. Spillers. New York: Routledge, 1991. 62–86.

Henke, Suzette A. *Shattered Subjects: Trauma and Testimony in Women's Life-Writing.* New York: St. Martin's, 1998.

Herman, Judith Lewis. *Trauma and Recovery.* New York: Basic, 1992.

Herman, Judith Lewis, and Mary R. Harvey. "The False Memory Debate: Social Science or Social Backlash?" *Harvard Mental Health Letter* 9 (1990): 4–6.

Herman, Judith Lewis, and Lisa Hirschman. *Father-Daughter Incest.* Cambridge: Harvard UP, 1981.

Hewitt, Leah Dianne. *Autobiographical Tightropes: Simone de Beauvoir, Nathalie Sarraute, Marguerite Duras, Monique Wittig, and Maryse Condé.* Lincoln: U of Nebraska P, 1990.

Hill, Leslie. "Marguerite Duras and the Limits of Fiction." *Paragraph* 12.1 (1989): 1–22.

Hinshelwood, R. D. *A Dictionary of Kleinian Thought.* London: Free Association, 1989.

Hirsch, Marianne. "Maternity and Rememory: Toni Morrison's *Beloved.*" Bassin et al. 92–110.

Hofmann, Carol. *Forgetting and Marguerite Duras.* Niwot: UP of Colorado, 1991.

Hogan, Patrick Colm. "Bessie Head's *A Question of Power:* A Lacanian Psychosis." *Mosaic* 27.2 (1994): 95–112.

Holden-Kirwan, Jennifer L. "Looking into the Self That Is No Self: An Examination of Subjectivity in '*Beloved.*'" *African American Review* 32.3 (fall 1998): 415–26.

Holmlund, C. A. "Displacing the Limits of Difference." *Quarterly Review of Film and Video* 13.1/3 (1991): 1–22.

Holtzman, Deanna, and Nancy Kulish. *Nevermore: The Hymen and the Loss of Virginity.* Northvale, NJ: Aronson, 1997.

Horowitz, Mardi J. *Essential Papers on Posttraumatic Stress Disorder.* New York: New York UP, 1999.

Horowitz, Sara. "Voices from the Killing Ground." Hartman, *Holocaust* 42–58.

Horvitz, Deborah M. *Literary Trauma: Sadism, Memory, and Sexual Violence in American Women's Fiction.* Albany: State U of New York P, 2000.

Howell, Amanda. "Lost Boys and Angry Ghouls: Vietnam's Undead." *Bodies of Writing, Bodies of Performance.* Ed. Thomas Foster, Carol Siegel, and Ellen E. Berry. New York: New York UP, 1996. 297–334.

Ingham, Graham. "Mental Work in a Trauma Patient." Garland 96–107.

Iser, Wolfgang. "The Reading Process: A Phenomenological Approach." Tompkins 50–69.

Janoff-Bulman, Ronnie. *Shattered Assumptions: Towards a New Psychology of Trauma.* New York: Free Press, 1992.

Jeffords, Susan. "Tattoos, Scars, Diaries, and Writing Masculinity." Rowe and Berg 208–25.

Johnston, Derek. "Les revenants de Marguerite Duras." *Journal of Durassian Studies* 3 (1992): 13–26.

Jones, Carolyn M. "Traces and Cracks: Identity and Narrative in Toni Morrison's *Jazz.*" *African American Review* 21.3 (1997): 481–95.

Juneja, Om P. "Colonial Consciousness and Identity Crisis: The Case of Black American, Indian and African Novelists." Srivastava 1–4.

Karner, Tracy. "Fathers, Sons, and Vietnam: Masculinity and Betrayal in the Life Narratives of Vietnam Veterans with Post Traumatic Stress Disorder." *American Studies* 37 (spring 1996): 63–94.

Keizer, Arlene R. "*Beloved:* Ideologies in Conflict, Improvised Subjects." *African American Review* 33.1 (spring 1999): 105–23.

Khayati, Abdellatif. "Representation, Race and the 'Language' of the Ineffable in Toni Morrison's Narrative." *African American Review* 33.2 (summer 1999): 313–24.

Kilpatrick, Dean G., Lois J. Veronen, and Connie L. Best. "Factors Predicting Psychological Distress among Rape Victims." Figley 113–41.

Kincaid, Jamaica. *At the Bottom of the River.* New York: Farrar, 1983.

———. *The Autobiography of My Mother.* New York: Farrar, 1996.

———. Interview by Moira Ferguson. *The Kenyon Review.* 16:1 (winter 1994): 163–88.

———. Interview by Allan Vorda. *Face to Face: Interviews with Contemporary Writers.* Ed. Allan Vorda. Houston, TX: Rice UP, 1993.

———. "Jamaica Kincaid Hates Happy Endings." Interview by Marilyn Snell. *Mother Jones.* Sept.–Oct. 1997, 28–32.

———. *Lucy.* New York: Farrar, 1990.

———. *My Brother.* New York: Farrar, 1997.

———. *A Small Place.* New York: Farrar, 1988.

Kirk, John. "Recovered Perspectives: Gender, Class, and Memory in Pat Barker's Writing." *Contemporary Literature* 40 (winter 1990): 603–26.

Kirmayer, Laurence J. "Landscapes of Memory: Trauma, Narrative, and Dissociation." *Tense Past: Cultural Essays in Trauma and Memory.* Ed. Paul Antze and Michael Lambek. New York: Routledge, 1996. 173–98.

Kitayama, Shinobu, and Hazel Rose Markus, eds. *Emotion and Culture: Empirical Studies of Mutual Influence.* Washington, DC: APA, 1994.

Klein, Melanie. "A Contribution to the Psychogenesis of Manic-Depressive States." Mitchell 116–45.

———. "The Importance of Symbol Formation in the Development of the Ego." Mitchell 95–111.

Kogan, Ilany. *The Cry of Mute Children: A Psychoanalytic Perspective of the Second Generation of the Holocaust.* London: Free Association, 1995.

Kosinski, Jerzy. *The Painted Bird.* New York: Bantam, 1965.

Kristeva, Julia. "The Pain of Sorrow in the Modern World: The Works of Marguerite Duras." *PMLA* 102.2 (1987): 138–52.

Lacan, Jacques, "The Agency of the Letter in the Unconscious or Reason Since

Freud," *Ecrits: A Selection.* Trans. Alan Sheridan. New York: Norton, 1977. 146–78.

LaCapra, Dominick, ed. *The Bounds of Race: Perspectives on Hegemony and Resistance.* Ithaca, NY: Cornell UP, 1991.

———. Lecture. Cornell University School of Criticism and Theory. June 1999.

———. *Writing History, Writing Trauma.* Baltimore: Johns Hopkins UP, 2001.

Laguerre, Michel S. *The Military and Society in Haiti.* Knoxville: U of Tennessee P, 1993.

Laing, R. D. *The Politics of the Family, and Other Essays.* New York: Vintage, 1972.

Langer, Lawrence. *Admitting the Holocaust: Collected Essays.* New York: Oxford UP, 1995.

———. *Holocaust Testimonies: The Ruins of Memory.* New Haven: Yale UP, 1991.

———. "Remembering Survival." Hartman, *Holocaust* 70–80.

Lansky, Melvin R., and Carol R. Bley. *Posttraumatic Nightmares: Psychodynamic Explorations.* Hillsdale, NJ: Analytic, 1995.

Lanzmann, Claude. "The Obscenity of Understanding: An Evening with Claude Lanzmann." *American Imago* 48.4 (1991): 473–96.

———. "Seminar with Claude Lanzmann." *Yale French Studies* 79 (1991): 82–99.

———. *Shoah: An Oral History of the Holocaust: The Complete Text of the Film.* New York: Pantheon, 1985.

Laplanche, Jean, and J. B. Pontalis. *The Language of Psycho-analysis.* Trans. Donald Nicholson-Smith. New York: Norton, 1974.

Laub, Dori. "The Empty Circle: Children of Survivors and the Limits of Reconstruction." *Journal of the American Psychoanalytic Association (JAPA)* 46.2 (1998): 507–29.

Laub, Dori, and Nanette C. Auerhahn. "Knowing and Not Knowing Massive Psychic Trauma: Forms of Traumatic Memory." *International Journal of Psychoanalysis* 74.2 (1993): 287–302.

Laufer, Robert S., Ellen Frey-Wouters, and Mark S. Gallop. "Traumatic Stressors in the Vietnam War and Post-traumatic Stress Disorder." Figley 73–89.

Leclair, Thomas. "'The Language Must Not Sweat': A Conversation with Toni Morrison." Gates and Appiah 369–77.

Leed, Eric J. *No Man's Land: Combat and Identity in World War I.* Cambridge: Cambridge UP, 1979.

Levis, Donald J. "The Recovery of Traumatic Memories: The Etiological Source of Psychopathology." *Mental Imagery.* Ed. Robert G. Kunzendorf. New York: Plenum, 1991. 233–40.

———. "The Traumatic Memory Debate: A Failure in Scientific Communication and Cooperation." *Applied and Preventive Psychology* 8.1 (1999): 71–76.

Lewis, Michael, and Leonard A. Rosenblum, eds. *The Effect of the Infant on Its Caregiver.* New York: Wiley, 1974.

Leys, Ruth, "Traumatic Cures: Shell Shock, Janet, and the Question of Memory," *Critical Inquiry* 4.20 (1994): 623–62.

Lifton, Robert Jay. Interview. *American Imago* 48.1 (1991): 153–75.

———. Interview by Cathy Caruth. Caruth, *Trauma* 127–47.

———. *The Protean Self: Human Resilience in An Age of Fragmentation*. New York: Basic, 1993.

Lindy, Jacob D., Mary Grace, and Bonnie Green. "Building a Conceptual Bridge between Civilian Trauma and War Trauma." *Post-traumatic Stress Disorder: Psychological and Biological Sequelae*. Ed. Bessel A. Van der Kolk. Washington, DC: American Psychiatric Press, 1984. 44–57.

Lloyd, G. *The Man of Reason: "Male" and "Female" in Western Philosophy*. London: Methuen, 1984.

Lock, Helen. "'Building up from Fragments': The Oral Memory Process in Some Recent African-American Written Narratives." *College Literature* 22 (Oct. 1995): 109–20.

Loschnigg, Martin. "'. . . the novelist's responsibility to the past': History, Myth and the Narratives of Crisis in Pat Barker's *Regeneration* Trilogy (1991–1995)." *Zeitschrift fur Anglistik un Amerikanistik* 47.3 (1999): 214–28.

Mannoni, Octave. *Prospero and Caliban*. Ann Arbor: U of Michigan P, 1990.

Markus, Hazel Rose, and Shinobu Kitayama. "The Cultural Construction of Self and Emotion: Implications for Social Behavior." Kitayama and Markus 89–130.

Markus, Hazel Rose, Patricia R. Mullally, and Shinobu Kitayama. "Selfways: Diversity in Modes of Cultural Participation." Neisser and Jopling 13–61.

Matus, Jill. *Toni Morrison*. Contemporary World Writers. Manchester, UK: Manchester UP, 1998.

McCann, I. L., and L. A. Pearlman. *Psychological Trauma and the Adult Survivor: Theory, Therapy, and Transformation*. New York: Brunner/Mazel, 1990.

———. "Vicarious Traumatization." *Essential Papers on Posttraumatic Stress Disorder*. New York: New York UP, 1999. 498–517.

McDougall, Joyce. "Sexual Identity, Trauma, and Creativity." *Psychoanalytic Inquiry* 11.4 (1991): 559–81.

Meiselman, Karin C. *Resolving the Trauma of Incest: Reintegration Therapy with Survivors*. San Francisco: Jossey, 1990.

Memmi, Albert. *The Colonizer and the Colonized*. Boston: Beacon, 1991.

———. *Dominated Man*. Boston: Beacon, 1968.

Michaels, Walter Benn. "'You who was never there': Slavery and the New Historicism, Deconstruction and the Holocaust." *Narrative* 4.1 (1996): 1–16.

Miller, Alice. *The Drama of the Gifted Child*. New York: Basic, 1981.

Mitchell, Juliette. "Trauma, Recognition, and the Place of Language." *Diacritics* 28.4 (winter 1998): 121–33.

———, ed. *The Selected Melanie Klein*. New York: Free Press, 1986.

Moane, Geraldine. *Gender and Colonialism: A Psychological Analysis of Oppression and Liberation*. London: Macmillan, 1999.

Mobley, Marilyn Sanders. "A Different Remembering: Memory, History, and Meaning in *Beloved*." Gates and Appiah 356–65.

———. "Narrative Dilemma: Jadine as Cultural Orphan in *Tar Baby*." Gates and Appiah 284–92.

Morgan, Janice. "Fiction and Autobiography/Language and Silence: *L'Amant* by Duras." *French Review* 63.2 (1989): 271–79.

Morgenstern, Naomi. "Mother's Milk and Sister's Blood: Trauma and the Neoslave Narrative." *Differences: A Journal of Feminist Cultural Studies* 8.2 (1996): 101–26.

Morrison, Toni. *Beloved.* New York: Knopf, 1987.

———. "A Bench by the Road." *The World* 3.1 (1989): 4–5, 37–41.

———. *The Bluest Eye.* New York: Washington Square, 1970.

———. Interview by Christina Davis. *Présence Africaine: Revue Culturelle du Monde Noir* 145 (1988): 141–50.

———. Interview by Bessie W. Jones and Audrey Vinson. *Conservations with Toni Morrison.* Ed. Danielle Taylor-Guthrie. Jackson: UP of Mississippi, 1994, 171–87.

———. Interview by Claudia Tate. *Black Women Writers at Work.* New York: Continuum, 1983. 117–31.

———. *Jazz.* New York: Knopf, 1992.

———. "Memory, Creation and Writing." *Thought* 59.235 (1984): 385–90.

———. "The Pain of Being Black." Interview by Bonnie Angelo. *Time* May 22, 1989: 120–22.

———. "Profile of a Writer: Toni Morrison." Interview by Melvin Bragg. *South Bank Show.* London Weekend Television, 1987.

———. Public Lectures on *The Bluest Eye* and *Sula.* Syracuse University, Syracuse, NY. Oct. 5 and 19, 1988.

———. "The Site of Memory." *Inventing the Truth: The Art and Craft of Memoir.* Ed. William Zinsser. New York: Houghton, 1995. 85–102.

———. *Song of Solomon.* New York: New American Library, 1977.

———. *Sula.* New York: New American Library, 1973.

———. *Tar Baby.* New York: New American Library, 1981.

———. "Unspeakable Things Unspoken: The Afro-American Presence in American Literature." *Michigan Quarterly Review* 28.1 (1989): 1–34.

Morson, Gary Saul, and Caryl Emerson. *Mikhail Bakhtin: Creation of a Prosaics.* Stanford, CA: Stanford UP, 1990.

Murphy, Carol J. "Duras's *L'Amant:* Memories from an Absent Photo." *Remains to Be Seen: Essays on Marguerite Duras.* Ed. Sanford Ames. New York: Lang, 1988. 171–81.

Nandy, Ashis. *The Intimate Enemy: Loss and Recovery of Self under Colonialism.* Delhi: Oxford UP, 1983.

National Organization for Women (NOW), http://now.org/issues/violence/stats.html, accessed March 6, 2000.

Neisser, Ulric, and David A. Jopling, eds. *The Conceptual Self in Context: Culture, Experience, Self-Understanding.* Cambridge: Cambridge UP, 1997.

Niesen de Abruna, Laura. "Jamaica Kincaid's Writing and the Maternal-Colonial Matrix." *Caribbean Women Writers: Fiction in English.* Ed. Mary Condé and Thorunn Lonsdale. New York: St. Martin's, 1999. 172–82.

Nora, Pierre. "Between Memory and History: *Les lieux de mémoire.*" *Representations.* 26 (spring 1989): 7–25.

Norindr, Panivong. "Errances and Memories in Marguerite Duras's Colonial Cities," *Differences* 5.5 (1993): 52–79.

N'Zengou-Tayo, Marie-Jose. "Fanm Se Poto Mitan: Haitian Woman, the Pillar of Society." *Feminist Review* (summer 1998): 118–42.

Olney, James. "I Was Born: Slave Narratives, Their Status as Autobiography and as Literature." Davis and Gates 148–75.

O'Reilly, Andrea. "In Search of My Mother's Garden, I Found My Own: Mother-Love, Healing, and Identity in Toni Morrison's *Jazz*." *African American Review* 30.3 (1996): 367–79.

Osagie, Iyunolu. "Is Morrison also among the Prophets?: 'Psychoanalytic' Strategies in *Beloved*." *African American Review*. 28.3 (fall 1994): 423–40.

Patterson, Orlando. *Slavery and Social Death: A Comparative Study*. Cambridge: Harvard UP, 1982.

Pelin, Serap Pahinodlu. "The Question of Virginity Testing in Turkey." *Bioethics* 13.3/4 (July 1999): 256–61.

Pierrot, Jean. *Marguerite Duras*. Mayenne: Corti, 1986.

Plottel, Jeanine Parisier. "Memory, Fiction and History." *L'Esprit Createur* 31.1 (1990): 47–55.

Prior, Stephen. *Object Relations in Severe Trauma: Psychotherapy of the Sexually Abused Child*. Northvale, NJ: Aronson, 1996.

Pynoos, Robert S., and Spencer Eth. "Developmental Perspective on Psychic Trauma in Childhood." Figley 36–48.

Reber, Arthur S. *The Penguin Dictionary of Psychology*. 2nd ed. New York: Penguin, 1995.

Rich, Adrienne Cecile. *Of Woman Born: Motherhood as Experience and Institution*. New York: Norton, 1986.

Riviere, Joan. "A Contribution to the Analysis of the Negative Therapeutic Reaction." *The Inner World and Joan Riviere: Collected Papers 1920–1958*. London: Karnac, 1991. 134–53.

Rody, Caroline. "Toni Morrison's *Beloved:* History, 'Rememory,' and a Clamor for a Kiss." *American Literary History* 7 (1995): 92–119.

Rosenfeld, Herbert. "On the Psychopathology of Narcissism." *International Journal of Psychoanalysis* 45 (1964): 332–37. Hinshelwood 357.

Roskies, David G. "The Library of Jewish Catastrophe." Hartman, *Holocaust* 33–41.

Rothstein, Mervyn. "Toni Morrison, in Her New Novel, Defends Women." *New York Times* Aug. 26, 1987: C17.

Rowe, John Carlos, and Rick Berg, eds. *The Vietnam War and American Culture*. New York: Columbia UP, 1991.

Rubenstein, Roberta. "Pariahs and Community/Toni Morrison." *Boundaries of the Self: Gender, Culture, Fiction*. Urbana: U of Illinois P, 1987. 125–63.

———. "Singing the Blues/Reclaiming Jazz: Toni Morrison and Cultural Mourning." *Mosaic* 31.2 (June 1998): 147–63.

Ruddick, Sara. "Maternal Thinking." *Feminist Studies* 6.2 (1980): 342–67.

Rushdy, Ashraf H. A. "Daughters Signifyin(g) History: The Example of Toni Morrison's *Beloved*." *American Literature* 64 (1992): 567–97.

Said, Edward. "Representing the Colonized: Anthropology's Interlocutors." *Critical Inquiry* 15 (winter 1989): 207.

Sandhu, Ramandeep S. "Motifs of Internalized Oppression in Ralph Ellison's *Invisible Man*." Srivastava 46–55.

Santner, Eric L. "History beyond the Pleasure Principle: Some Thoughts on the

Representation of Trauma." *Probing the Limits of Representation: Nazism and the "Final Solution."* Ed. Saul Friedlander. Cambridge: Harvard UP, 1992. 143–54.

———. *Stranded Objects: Mourning, Memory, and Film in Postwar Germany.* Ithaca, NY: Cornell UP, 1990.

Schapiro, Barbara. "The Bonds of Love and the Boundaries of Self in Toni Morrison's *Beloved.*" *Contemporary Literature* 32.2 (1991): 194–210.

Schlobin, Roger. "Children of a Darker God: A Taxonomy of Deep Horror Fiction and Film in Their Mass Popularity." *Journal of the Fantastic in the Arts.* 1.1 (1988): 25–50.

Scott, Grant. "*Paco's Story* and the Ethics of Violence." *Critique* 36.1 (fall 1994): 69–80.

Segal, Hanna. "Notes on Symbol Formation." *The Work of Hanna Segal: A Kleinian Approach to Clinical Practice.* New York: Aronson, 1981. 49–65.

———. "On Symbolism." *International Journal of Psychoanalysis* 59.2–3 (1978): 315–19.

Sherrard, Cherene. "The 'Colonizing' Mother Figure in Paule Marshall's *Brown Girl, Brownstones* and Jamaica Kincaid's *The Autobiography of My Mother.*" *MaComere* 2 (1999): 125–33.

Showalter, Elaine. *The Female Malady: Women, Madness, and English Culture, 1830–1980.* New York: Pantheon, 1985.

Simmons, Diane. "Coming of Age in the Snare of History: Jamaica Kincaid's *The Autobiography of My Mother.*" *The Girl: Constructions of the Girl in Contemporary Fiction by Women.* Ed. Ruth O. Saxton. New York: St. Martin's, 1998. 107–18.

Smith, Sidonie, and Julia Watson, eds. *De/Colonizing the Subject: The Politics of Gender in Women's Autobiography.* Minneapolis: U of Minnesota P, 1992.

Smith, Valerie. "Circling the Subject: History and Narrative in *Beloved.*" Gates and Appiah 342–55.

Sommer, Doris. "Resisting the Heat: Menchu, Morrison, and Incompetent Readers." *Cultures of United States Imperialism.* Ed. Amy Kaplan and Donald E. Pease. Durham: Duke UP, 1993. 407–32.

Spiegelman, Art. *Maus: A Survivor's Tale.* New York: Pantheon, 1986.

———. *Maus II: A Survivor's Tale: And Here My Troubles Began.* New York: Pantheon, 1991.

Spivak, Gayatri Chakravorty. "Can the Subaltern Speak?" Williams and Chrisman 66–111.

Srivastava, Ramesh K., ed. *Colonial Consciousness in Black American, African, and Indian Fiction in English.* Jalandhar, India: ABS, 1991.

Stern, Daniel. "The Early Development of Schemas of Self, of Other, and of Various Experiences of 'Self with Other.'" *Reflections on Self Psychology.* Ed. Joseph D. Lichtenberg and Samuel Kaplan. Hillsdale, NJ: Analytic Press, 1983. 69–81.

Stone, Martin. "Shellshock and the Psychologists." *The Anatomy of Madness: Essays in the History of Psychiatry.* Vol. II. Ed. W. F. Bynum, Roy Porter, and Michael Shepherd. London: Tavistock, 1985.

Tal, Kalí. *Worlds of Hurt: Reading the Literatures of Trauma.* Cambridge UP, 1996.

Tanay, Emanuel. "The Vietnam Veteran—Victim of War." *PTSD and the War Veteran Patient.* NY: Brunner/Mazel, 1985.

Terdiman, Richard. *Present Past: Modernity and the Memory Crisis.* Ithaca, NY: Cornell UP, 1993.

Tompkins, Jane P. *Reader-Response Criticism: From Formalism to Post-Structuralism.* Baltimore: Johns Hopkins UP, 1980.

Trevarthen, Colwyn. "The Foundations of Intersubjectivity: Development of Interpersonal and Cooperative Understanding in Infants." *The Social Foundation of Language and Thought.* Ed. David R. Olson. New York: Norton, 1980. 316–42.

Ulman, Richard, and Doris Brothers. *The Shattered Self: A Psychoanalytic Study of Trauma.* Hillsdale, NJ: Analytic Press, 1988.

United Nations Children's Fund (UNICEF). http://www.unicef.org/statis.

United States. Department of Health and Human Services. "HHS Reports Child Abuse Statistics." http:/www.acf.dhhs.gov/news/press/2001/abuse.htm.

Van Boheemen-Saaf, Christine. *Joyce, Derrida, Lacan and the Trauma of History.* Cambridge: Cambridge UP, 1999.

Van der Kolk, B. A., and C. R. Ducey. "The Psychological Processing of Traumatic Experience: Rorschach Patterns in PTSD." *Journal of Traumatic Stress,* 2 (1989): 259–74.

Van der Kolk, Bessel, and Alexander C. McFarlane. "The Black Hole of Trauma." Van der Kolk, McFarlane, and Weisaeth 3–23.

Van der Kolk, Bessel, and Onno Van der Hart. "The Intrusive Past: The Flexibility of Memory and the Engraving of Trauma." *American Imago* 48.4 (1991): 425–54.

Van der Kolk, Bessel, Alexander C. McFarlane, and Lars Weisaeth, eds. *Traumatic Stress: The Effects of Overwhelming Experience on Mind, Body, and Society.* New York: Guilford, 1996.

Vickroy, Laurie. "*Beloved* and *Shoah:* Witnessing the Unspeakable." *The Comparatist* 22 (May 1998): 123–44.

———. "Filling the Void: Transference, Love, Being and Writing in Duras's *L'Amant.*" *Marguerite Duras Lives On.* Ed. Janine Ricouart. New York: UP of America, 1998. 123–36.

———. "The Force Outside/The Force Inside: Mother-Love and Regenerative Spaces in *Sula* and *Beloved.*" *Obsidian* 8.2 (1993): 28–45.

———. "The Politics of Abuse: The Traumatized Child in Toni Morrison and Marguerite Duras." *Mosaic* 29.2 (1996): 91–109.

Vircondelet, Alain. *Duras: Biographie.* Paris: Éditions F. Bourin, 1991.

Vries, Marten W. de. "Trauma in Cultural Perspective." Van der Kolk, McFarlane, and Weisaeth 398–413.

Walkerdine, Valerie, and Helen Lucey. *Democracy in the Kitchen: Regulating Mothers and Socialising Daughters.* London: Virago, 1989.

Waites, Elizabeth A. *Trauma and Survival: Post-Traumatic and Dissociative Disorders in Women.* New York: Norton, 1993.

Wesley, Charles H. *The Quest for Equality: From Civil War to Civil Rights.* New York: Publisher's Co., 1968.

White, Geoffrey M. "Affecting Culture: Emotion and Morality in Everyday Life." Kitayama and Markus 219–39.

White, Hayden. "New Historicism: A Comment." *The New Historicism.* Ed. H. Aram Veeser. New York: Routledge, 1989. 293–302.

Whitehead, Anne. "Open to Suggestion: Hypnosis and History in Pat Barker's *Regeneration.*" *Modern Fiction Studies.* 44.3 (fall 1998): 674–94.

Williams, Patrick, and Laura Chrisman, eds. *Colonial Discourse and Post-Colonial Theory.* New York: Columbia UP, 1994.

Willis, Sharon. *Marguerite Duras: Writing on the Body.* Urbana: U of Illinois P, 1987.

Wilson, John P., W. Ken Smith, and Suzanne K. Johnson. "A Comparative Analysis of PTSD among Various Survivor Groups." Figley 142–72.

Winnicott, D. W. *Playing and Reality.* Harmondsworth, UK: Penguin, 1974.

———. *Psycho-analytic Explorations.* Ed. Claire Winnicott, Ray Shepherd, Madeleine Davis. Cambridge: Harvard UP, 1989.

Woodward, C. Vann. "History from Slave Sources." Davis and Gates 48–59.

Woolf, Cynthia Griffin. "'Margaret Garner': A Cincinnati Story." *Massachusetts Review* 32 (fall 1991): 417–40.

Woolf, Virginia. *Mrs. Dalloway.* New York: Harcourt, 1925.

Wright, Donald R. *African Americans in the Colonial Era.* Arlington Heights, IL: Harlan Davidson, 1990.

Wucker, Michele. "Edwidge Danticat: A Voice for the Voiceless." *Americas* 52: 3 (May 2000): 40–46.

Wyatt, Jean, "Giving Body to the Word: The Maternal Symbolic in Toni Morrison's *Beloved,*" *PMLA* 108.3 (1993): 474–88.

Yamamoto, Joe, J. Arturo Silva, Michelle Ferrari, and Kazutaka Nukariya. "Culture and Psychopathology." *Transcultural Child Development: Psychological Assessment and Treatment.* Ed. Gloria Johnson Powell and Joe Yamamoto. New York: Wiley, 1997, 34–57.

Yellin, Jean Fagan. "Texts and Contexts of Harriet Jacobs' *Incidents in the Life of a Slave Girl: Written by Herself.*" Davis and Gates 262–82.

Young, Allan. "Suffering and the Origins of Traumatic Memory." *Daedalus* 125.1 (1996): 245–59.

INDEX